TILE

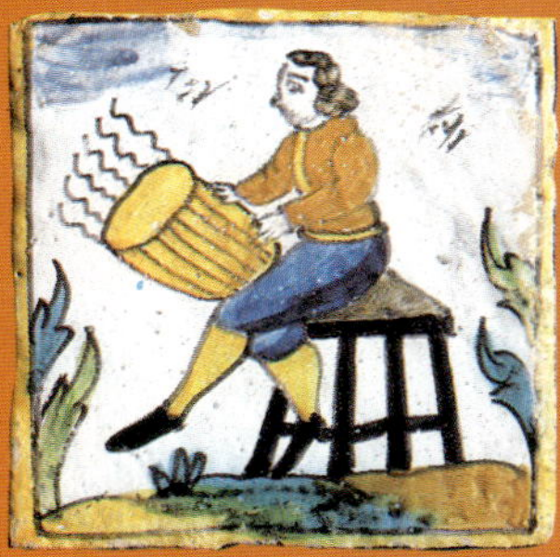

ART

A HISTORY OF DECORATIVE CERAMIC TILES

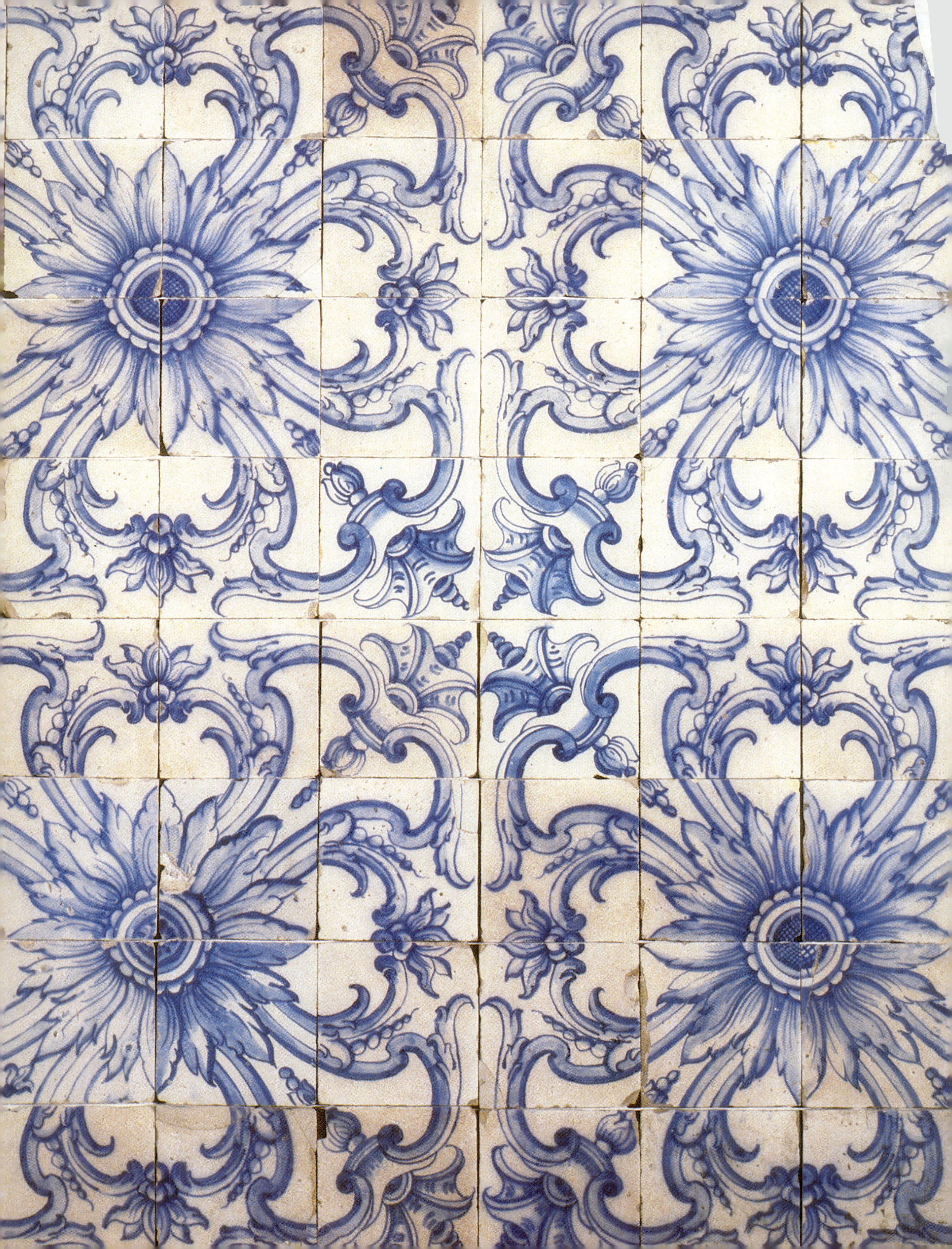

TILE

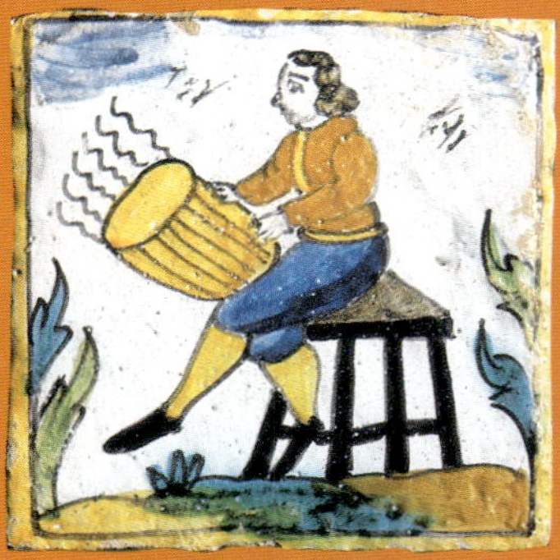

ART

A HISTORY OF DECORATIVE CERAMIC TILES

NOËL RILEY

MAGNA BOOKS

A QUINTET BOOK

This edition published 1992 by
MAGNA BOOKS
Magna Road
Wigston
Leicester, LE8 2XH

ISBN 1-85348-401-6

This book was designed and produced by
Quintet Publishing Limited
6 Blundell Street
London N7 9BH

Art Director: Peter Bridgewater
Designer: Alan Marshall
Editors: Patricia Bayer, Judith Simons
Picture Researcher: Anne-Marie Ehrlich
Illustrator: Lorraine Harrison

Typeset in Great Britain by
Central Southern Typesetters, Eastbourne
Manufactured in Hong Kong by
Regent Publishing Services Limited
Printed in Hong Kong

ACKNOWLEDGEMENTS

The author would like to record her gratitude to Paul Atterbury, Mary Furnell, Jonathan Horne, Clare Prichard, Caroline Russett, Hans Van Lemmen, Lucilla Watson and Peter Williams for their help and information; to her husband Peter Owen and daughters Alice, Polly and Beatrice for their artistic and clerical assistance, and not forgetting Mabel, the office cat.

PICTURE CREDITS

Anglo-Portuguese Foundation, Museu da Cidade, Lisbon, (Photo: Lucinda Symons): **pp 52/53, 80/81, 86/87** *t*, **87** *r*, **88, 88/89, 89, 118/119** Arcaid/Lucinda Lambton: **pp 100, 100/101.** Ark Antiques, New Haven: **pp 109** *t*, **111** *c b*. Arxiu Mas: **pp 6, 7, 82/83.** John Bethell Photography: **pp 24, 25, 28, 36** *l*, **37** *r*, **46** *l*, **50, 52** *l*, **68, 84, 85, 86/87** *b*, **94/95, 107** *t*. British Museum: **pp 32/33, 33, 34/35** *b*, **36/37, 38, 40, 40/41.** Crafts Council: **pp 93, 117** *t*. © Allen Eyles: **p 114** *tr*. Gem Antiques, New York: **pp 108, 109** *b*, **110, 111** *t*, **119.** Barbara Heller (Photo: E Knobloch): **p 27.** Angelo Hornak: **pp 48/49, 49, 104, 105.** Jonathan Horne Antiques (Photo: Eileen Tweedy): **65, 78** *b*, **79** *t*, **92** *b*, **124.** London Transport: **pp 112/113, 117** *b*. National Museum, Stockholm: **p 92** *t*. Pilkington's: **p 116/117.** Noël Riley: **pp 60** *tl*, **99** *c b*, **107** *b*. Royal Doulton: **pp 102/103, 106/107.** Royal Makkum Factory: **pp 10/11, 12, 12/13, 14/15, 16, 54/55.** Scala: **pp 34/35** *t*. Sotheby's: **pp 18/19, 19, 20/21, 22, 23, 26** *bl br*, **29, 31** *r*, **122** *t*, **123.** © Wim Swaan: **pp 8, 9, 26** *t*, **30** *l*, **30/31, 44/45, 45, 91.** Hans Van Lemmen: **pp 7, 11, 13, 17, 43** *r*, **46** *r*, **47, 48** *b*, **51, 55, 57, 58, 59, 60, 61, 62, 63, 64, 69, 71, 74, 75, 76, 77, 78** *t*, **79** *b*, **81, 82** *l*, **83** *r*, **95, 96, 97, 98, 99** *t*, **101** *r*, **113** *r*, **114** *tl b*, **115, 120, 121, 122** *b*, **125.** Werner Forman Archive: **pp 20** (Mrs Bashir Mohamed Collection, London); **pp 39; 42/43** (National Museum of Archaeology, Madrid). World's End Tiles: **p 116** *b*.

Key: *l*=left; *r*=right; *t*=top; *c*=centre; *b*=bottom.

CONTENTS

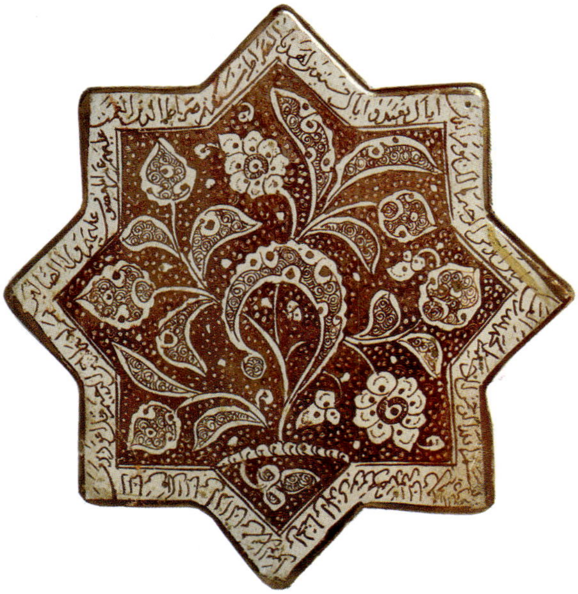

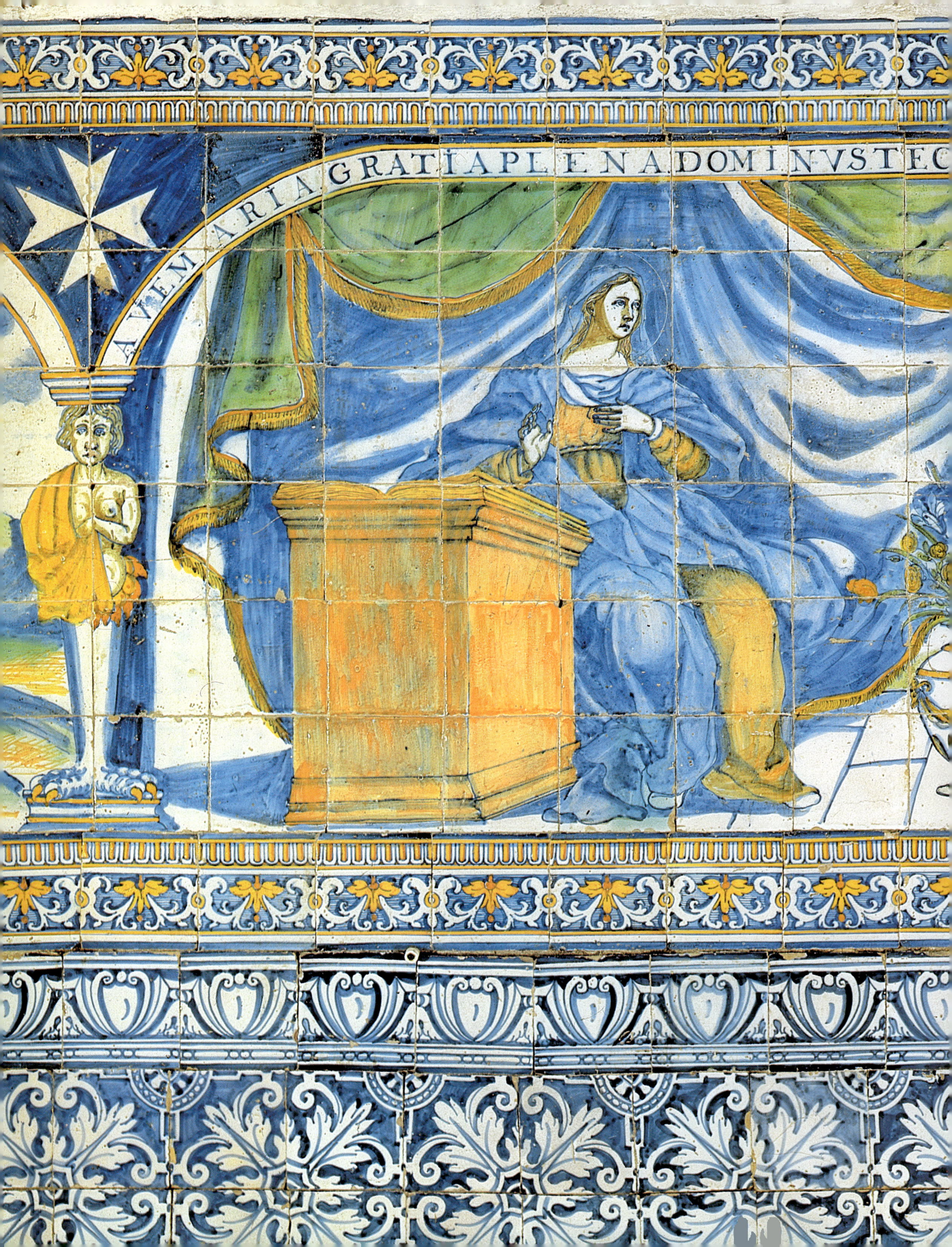
AVE MARIA GRATIA PLENA DOMINUS TEC

CHAPTER ONE

INTRODUCTION

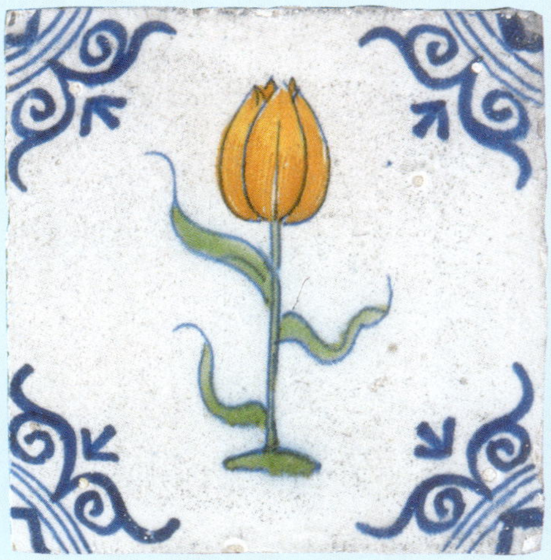

A TILE IS *a many-splendoured object, its practical and decorative uses myriad and wide-ranging. This book encompasses the extensive history of decorative tiling and is intended primarily as a guide to the hugely rich — and ever-growing — field of tile collecting. To this end, mosaics, fireplace bricks, roof coverings and other such tiles are not dealt with: few can be regarded as antique collectors' items, although many are indeed decorative elements.*

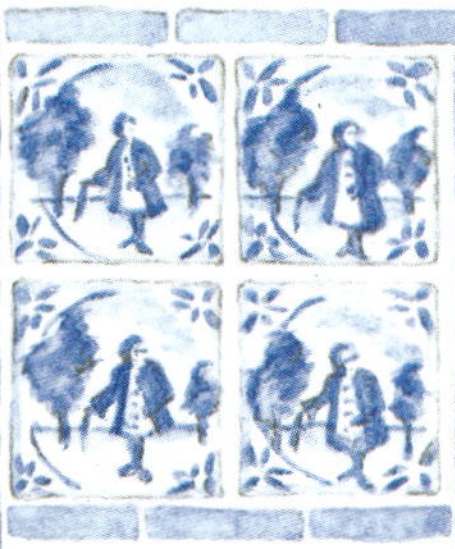

OVERLEAF (BACKGROUND) *A tiled panel illustrating the Annunciation from Our Lady of El Prado, Talavera.*

OVERLEAF (INSET) *Dutch tile depicting a tulip with ox-head corner motifs, early 17th century.*

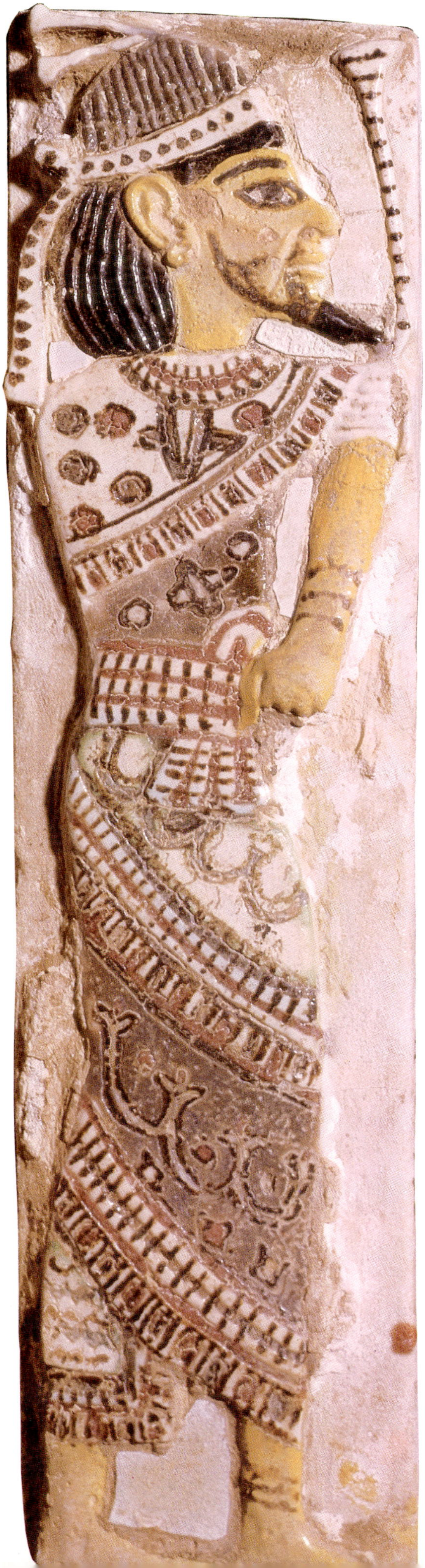

SURPRISINGLY, some aspects of the history of decorative tiles seem to have been largely ignored by scholarly writers. Others are well catered for, and if this book tempts the reader to burrow further into such studies, it will have partly succeeded in its aim. But reading is no substitute for looking, and another of the book's objectives is to draw attention to the visual riches of tiles. For they appear everywhere: in mosques and churches, in schools and shops, in civic buildings from town halls to lavatories, and in all kinds of houses, from the grandest palace to the humblest cottage. Even if we do not collect tiles, we cannot ignore such a vast and colourful heritage.

The history of tiles stretches back to the dawn of civilization itself. As early as the 4th millennium BC the Egyptians were decorating their houses with blue-glazed bricks, and the technique of making tiles inlaid with different coloured clays was developed by the 14th century BC. Tiles with designs scratched into the clay under the glaze appeared a little later.

In Mesopotamia too, glazed bricks were used from an early period, most spectacularly on the Tower of Babel and the Ishtar Gate in the holy city of Babylon, built during the reign of Nebuchadnezzar II (604–562 BC). Awesome lions, bulls and dragons were depicted in huge compositions in which the primary colours of the 10-ft (3-m) high animals contrast strongly with the deep glazed blue of the background. Over 10,000 of these glazed bricks from the Ishtar Gate are now in the Pergamum Museum in East Berlin.

The Assyrians, whose culture was similar to that of the Babylonians, also used glazed bricks in their buildings, notably in the Palace of Nimroud (9th century BC). During the Han dynasty (206 BC–221 AD) in China, relief-decorated pottery tablets were placed in tombs, and in later periods coloured tiles were laid on the roofs of buildings.

But it was in Mesopotamia and Persia that the art of tile-making reached its first peaks of excellence, and it was from these regions that it eventually spread through the Western world.

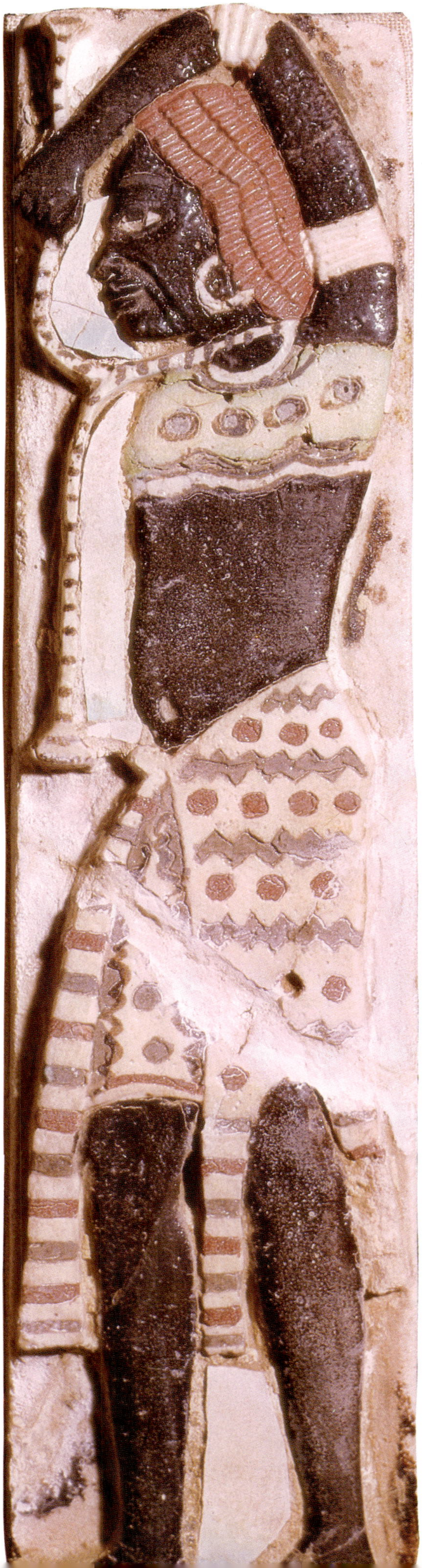

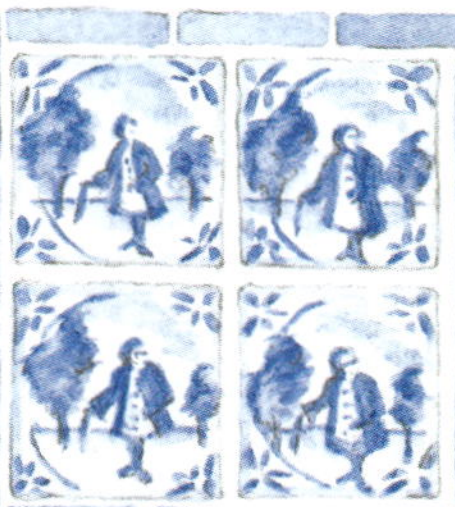

LEFT AND FAR LEFT
Egyptian glazed tiles from the main doorway of the palace of the mortuary temple of Rameses III.

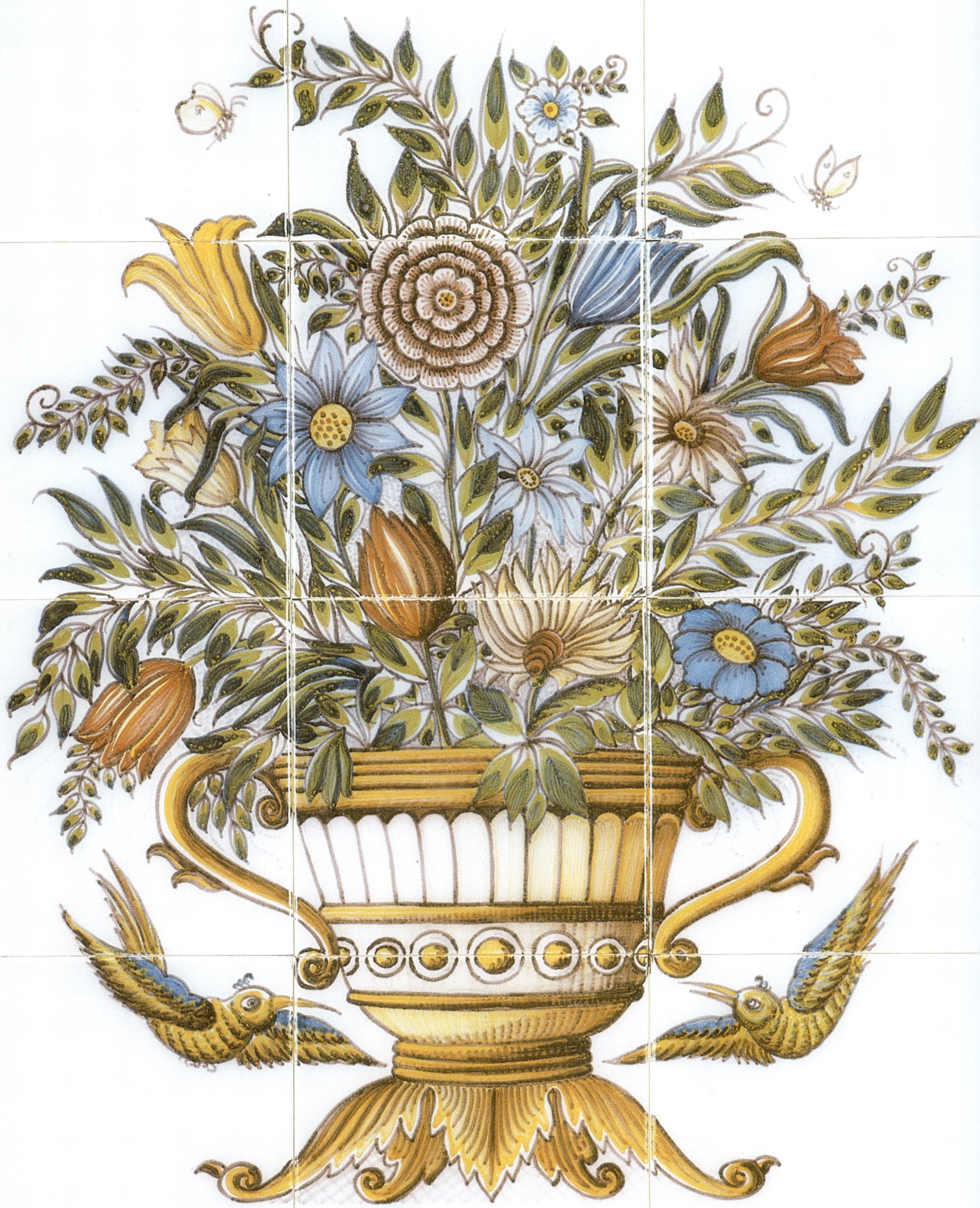

CHAPTER TWO

THE MAKING OF TILES

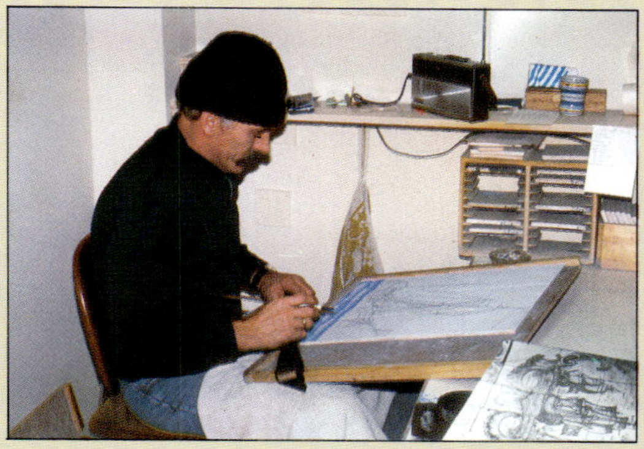

WHILE MANY of the techniques used for making and decorating tiles are described subsequently in the appropriate chapters, knowledge of the underlying principles of tile-making is necessary for an understanding of the finer details.

Different types of clay were available in different parts of the world, even in different areas of the same country, and many of them had properties — such as plasticity, hardness and lightness — which made them suitable for tiles of one form or another. Often, however, the right body for a particular purpose had to be reached by blending clays together and by adding other materials: the search for an ideal clay body was a never-ending one.

OVERLEAF (BACKGROUND) *A modern reproduction, by the Royal Makkum Factory, of a traditional flower-vase panel.*

OVERLEAF (INSET) *A Dutch tile-painter at work on a modern Delftware panel.*

RIGHT *A modern electric kiln after biscuit firing.*

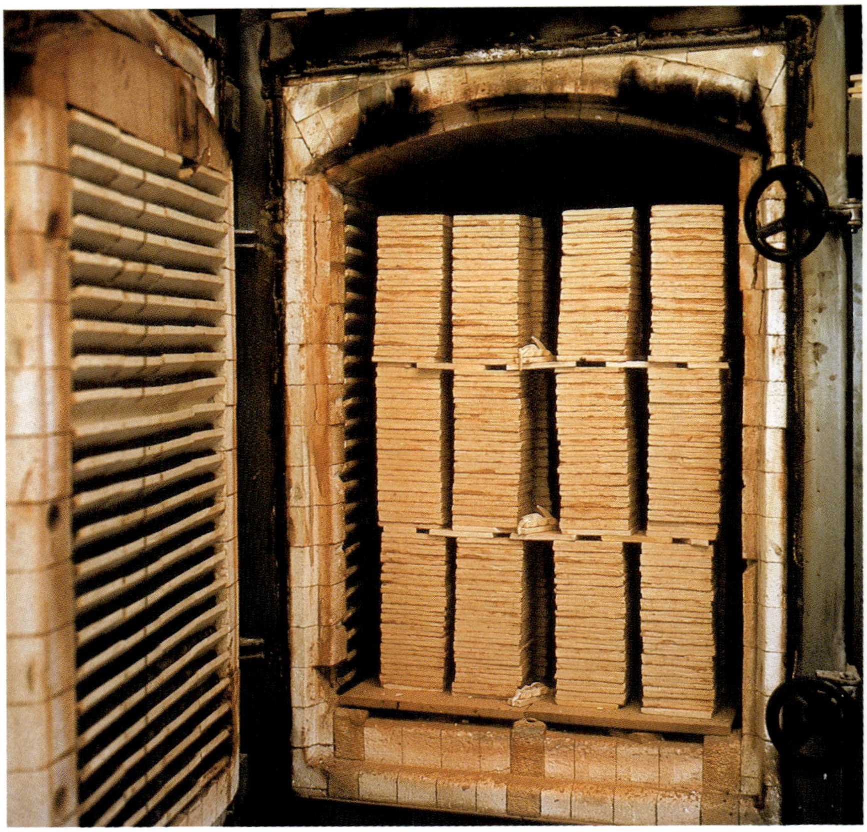

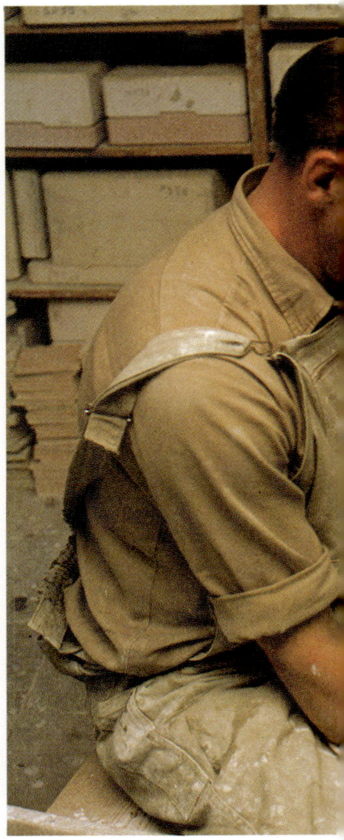

CHALKY clays were considered best for tin-glazed earthenwares, mainly because the lime content gave the clay an especially high rate of shrinkage as it cooled after firing, and prevented the surface glaze from crazing, or cracking. It also gave the fired clay body a desirable whiteness. Chalky clays were often blended with red clays where tin-glazed tiles were made, and, depending on the mixture used, the body clays varied greatly in colour from dark red to near-white.

Silver sand, or grog (ground-up fired clay), could be used to make the clay more 'open', while calcined flint was employed to harden it. Salt was occasionally used to make the clay more fusible and to enhance the shrinkage.

Unsuitable clays could result in problems such as a tendency to chip, crazing of the glaze or warping of the tile itself. The difficulties of firing two kinds of clay together — as in medieval inlaid tiles — are easy to appreciate.

The thickness of the clay bodies of tiles varied enormously. Floor tiles, obviously, tended to be thicker and of a harder clay than wall tiles, and this is still the case today. Stove tiles, for the sake of heat retention, were the thickest of all: some of the early European stove tiles decorated in relief were as much as 3 in (7.5 cm) thick. Medieval floor tiles were usually 1 in (2.54 cm) or more in thickness and, generally speaking, later examples tended to be slightly thinner than earlier. Victorian encaustic tiles may be up to 1 in (2.54 cm) in thickness. The same is true of Dutch and English tin-glazed wall tiles: 17th-century examples tend to be thicker (about ½ in (1.27 cm)) than those of the 18th century, which average ¼ in (0.6 cm), while 19th-century tiles are chunkier than 20th, which are the thinnest of all.

Having selected his clay or blended a suitable mixture for the tiles he was producing, the potter then formed his tile shapes, either by slicing them from a block of clay or by shaping them in a frame or former. Relief decoration might be applied, usually with a wooden stamp, at this stage.

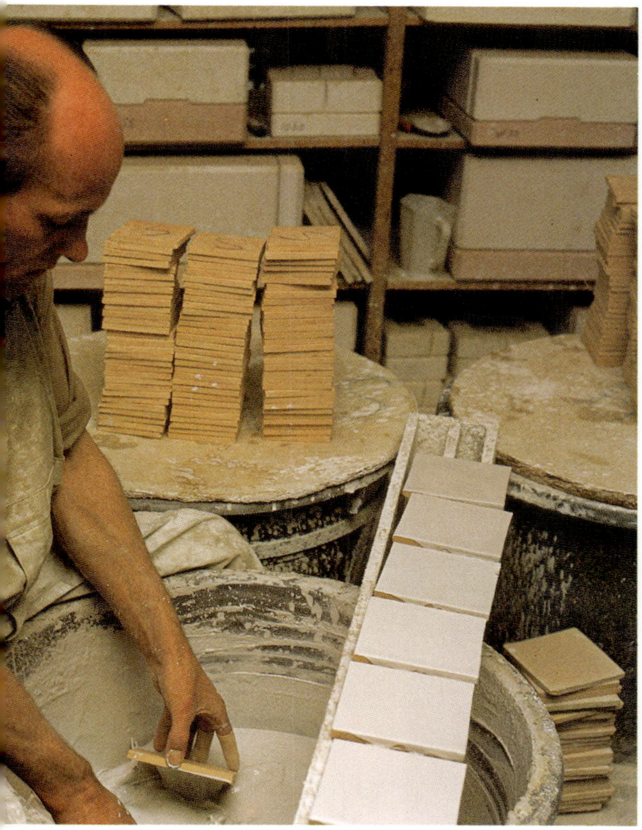

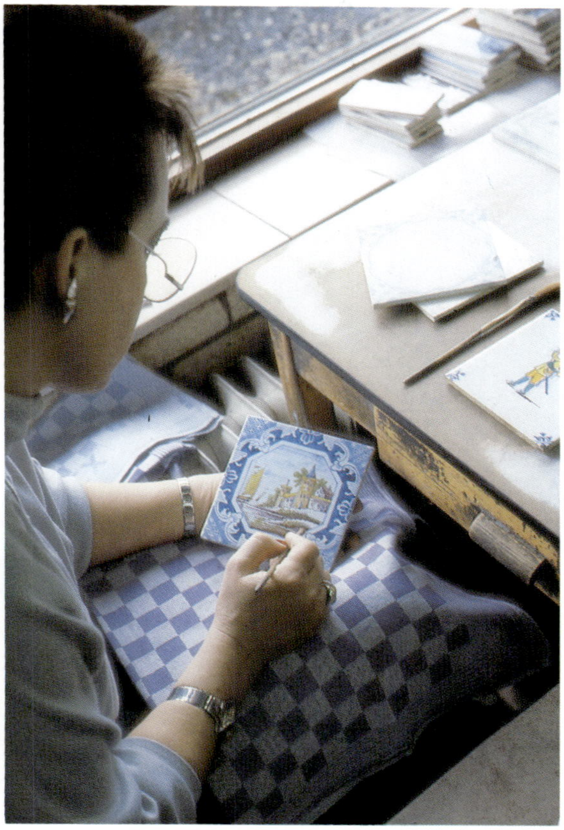

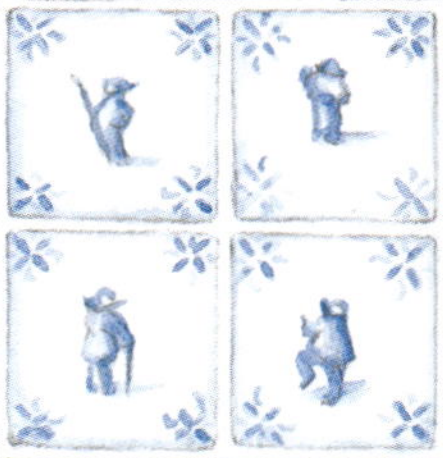

CHAPTER TWO

•

FAR LEFT *The tin-glazing process.*

LEFT *A Dutch woman tile-painter at work on a Delftware tile. Painting on unfired tin glaze requires great sureness of touch, since mistakes cannot be rectified.*

The tiles were then allowed to dry slowly and evenly to avoid warpage. When leather-hard they would be trimmed with a knife. Some 17th- and early 18th-century Dutch and English tiles have two small nail holes in opposite corners of the finished front surface, resulting from the tiles being fixed, face downward, to the cutting board. Later the nails were found to be unnecessary, thus few tiles made after about 1750 have nail holes. 18th-century tiles customarily had their edges chamfered to slope inward toward the back of the tile: this allowed them to abut neatly when fixed in their final position.

Inlaid tiles were made by stamping a design into the tile surface and filling the depression with milky liquid clay, or slip. This would fire to a light yellowish colour, in contrast to the reddish colour of the clay background. An alternative to relief or inlaid decoration was sgraffito, in which the whole tile surface was coated with slip and the design later scratched into it to reveal the darker clay body underneath.

Many types of tiles, particularly those of the medieval period in England, were lead-glazed and fired only once. In the early period the glaze was applied in the form of powdered sulphide of lead, which fired to a clear transparency. It gave a yellowish hue to white slip and could be made green by adding copper sulphide to the lead ore. Pale green resulted from such a tinted lead glaze being applied to a slip-coated surface, while a higher concentration of copper resulted in a darker — sometimes almost black — shade of green. Liquid lead glazes were developed in the 18th century, but by this time almost all tiles were fired twice.

Firing took place in a chamber or kiln specially constructed with a system of vents and holes that not only allowed high temperatures to be reached (about 1832°F/1000°C for 30–40 hours), but also gave the best possible control of heat from the fire box. The tiles and other wares within had to be carefully arranged both to gain maximum benefit from the furnace and to avoid damage during firing. While the construction and size of kilns varied considerably in different places and periods, these

18TH-CENTURY TILE PRODUCTION

The picture illustrated here is a copy of a tile picture, dated 1737, in the Rijksmuseum, Amsterdam, showing a Friesian pottery. It gives a fascinating insight into the various stages of traditional tile production in 18th-century Friesland. The 'pottery' is divided into three floors.

Ground-Floor
On the right can be seen a horse driven pug-mill, which is being fed with clay that is then mixed within the mill and squeezed out through a hole in the bottom. This clay mixture is then taken either to the first floor, the throwers' loft, or to the second floor, the tilemakers' loft. Next to the pug-mill stands the glaze grinding mill, which is also horse-driven and glaze is first crushed and then processed in the mill to obtain a fine powder.

On the left can be seen the decorators' room and on the shelves above painted tiles are stacked ready for glost firing. Stacks of wood lie ready for stoking the kiln which rises through the centre of the tile picture.

First Floor, The Throwers' Loft
On the right and left a thrower is depicted sitting at a wheel, assisted by a boy who is preparing lumps of clay ready for throwing. Another assistant is placing the thrown objects, mostly dishes, onto a shelf in the drying rack.

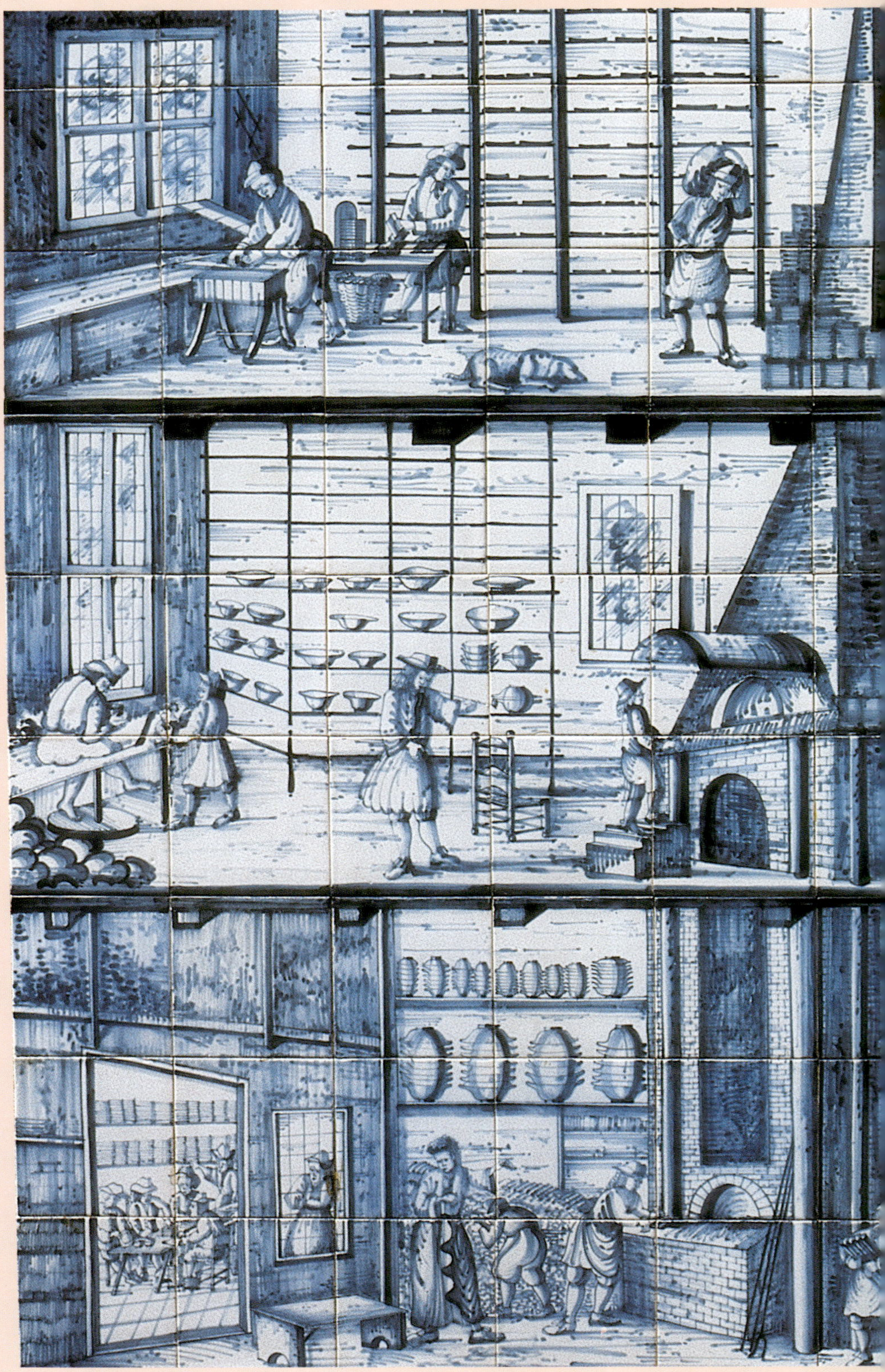

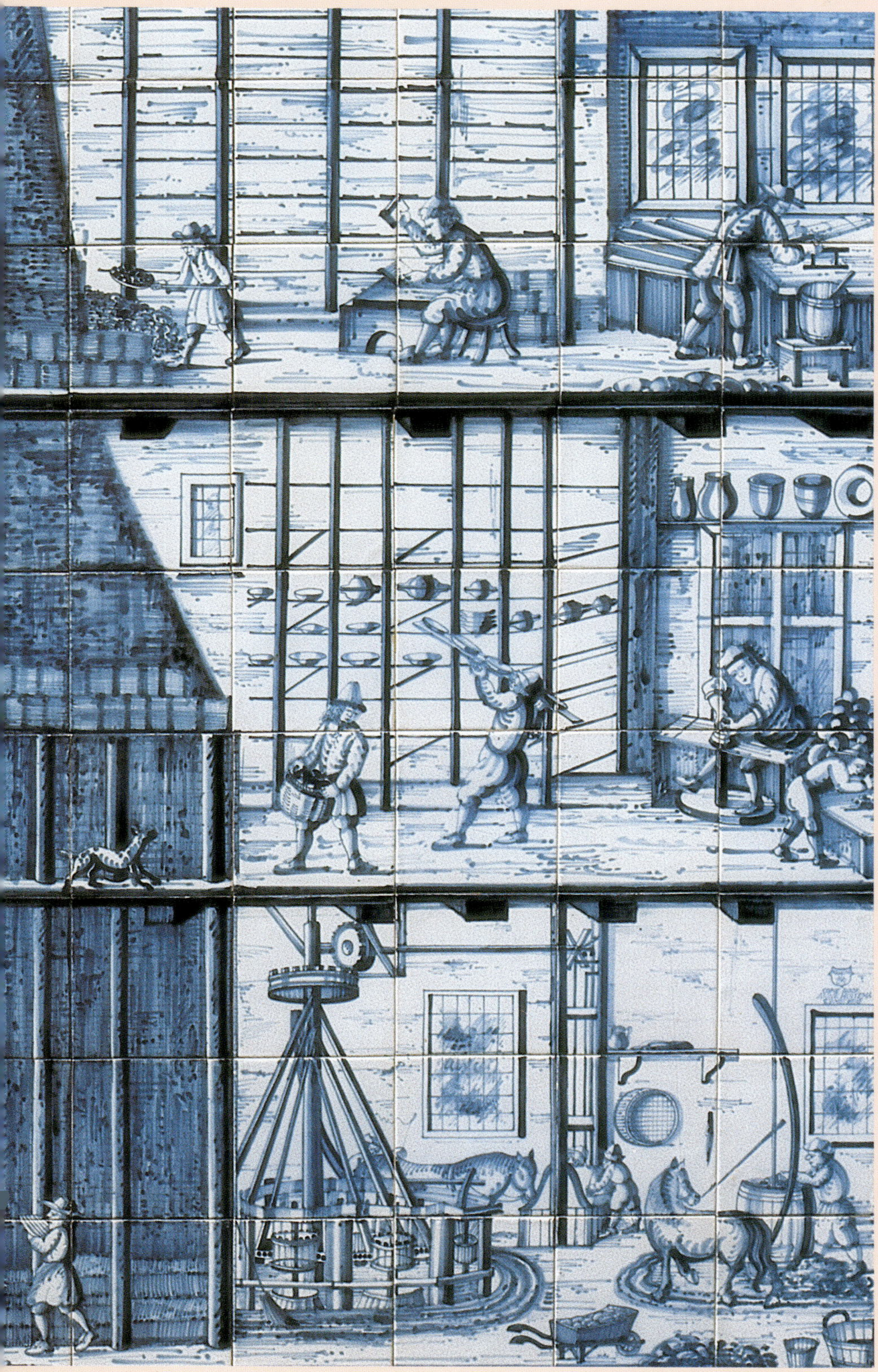

Second Floor, The Tilemakers' Loft
At either end a tilemaker is at work at a tile frame. The man on the right is sprinkling sand on the table in preparation for his frame which he would then fill with clay, smoothed out with a rolling stick. The boy to the right of the kiln is disposing of any excess clay. Once the tile has been formed, it is removed from the frame and put on a shelf to dry.

The second man on the right is stacking up the half-dried tiles with alternate sides up – once dry the tiles are flat but no longer perfectly square. The second man on the left corrects this – he places the tiles on a table, covers them one by one with a 5 in (13 cm) square board, and then trims the excess material thus exposed. The tiles are finally stacked to complete the drying process.

The Kiln
The kiln, with walls 3 ft (1 m) thick, is practically a building within a building. On the ground floor, two boys are depicted collecting wood for the firer to feed into the kiln through the half-round fire opening. The fire is drawn upward through holes in the vault over the hearth to the chamber – the middle part of the kiln – where the tiles, together with the dishes, are fired first to biscuit ware and secondly to glost ware. The articles are moved in and out of the chamber through a large door which is bricked up during the firing process.

objectives remained the same, and kiln construction and arrangement were highly skilled and critical matters. Mistakes could spell financial ruin for a pottery.

Tin-glazed tiles required more than one firing, and were given an unglazed, or biscuit, firing before being covered with the opaque-white tin glaze that was the basis of the painted decoration. Tin glaze was basically a transparent lead glaze made white by the addition of tin oxide. It was applied in an aqueous state to one side of each tile and the water was absorbed by the clay, leaving the front surface coated with a layer of powdered glaze. When dry this was painted and then fired again to fuse the pigments to the glaze. Before firing, Dutch tiles and certain others were given a final thin coat of transparent lead glaze — called *kwaart* — over the painting, to impart a more lustrous sheen to the finished surface.

Some early tin-glazed wares were painted before being glazed, and pigments such as cobalt blue were strong enough to show through the tin glaze after firing. However, the maiolica painting technique, with its subtle variations of colour and tone, demanded that the paint be applied on top of the glaze: this became normal practice for all tin-glazed, or faïence, wares. The colours came from metallic oxides: blue from cobalt, green from copper, purple from manganese, yellow from antimony and lead, and reds and browns from iron. The pigments were ground into powders and applied in a liquid form.

Great skill and lightness of touch were needed by the maiolica painters, especially if they worked freehand, and the decoration of tiles, particularly in the Netherlands, was generally made easier — and quicker — by the use of pounces, or pricked transfers. Powdered pumice or charcoal was driven through the holes in the paper pattern laid on top of the tile, thus forming the design in dotted outline. This could then be painted over with a *trekker*, or fine brush, and the shades or colours filled in.

Coloured grounds were achieved by covering the parts of the tile to be left white or painted, and sprinkling powdered pigment — invariably manganese in the Netherlands, but other colours as well in England — on the exposed parts of the surface; occasionally a coloured ground was painted in with a brush. Once the tiles had been painted they were given their second firing, during which the colours and the glaze fused together on the surface. Sometimes a third firing, at a lower temperature, was necessary, if low-firing pigments such as gold or red were used or if lustre effects were required.

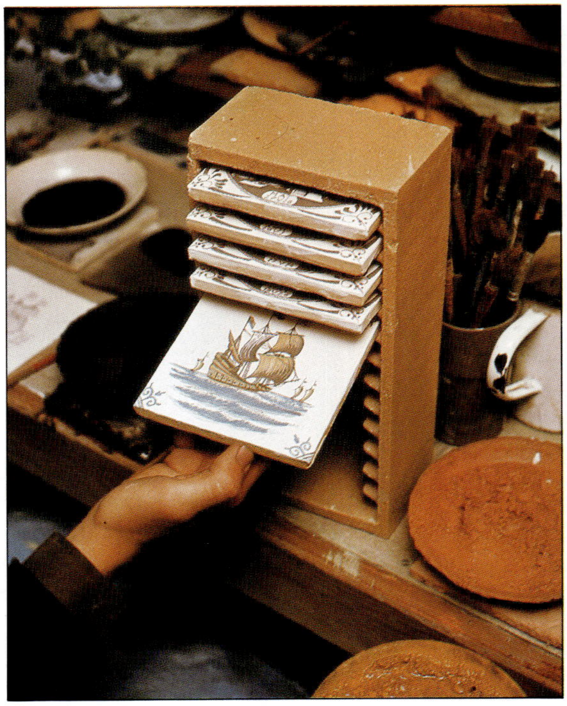

RIGHT *Painted tiles ready for glost firing: this will fix the tin glaze and its painting to the earthenware tile.*

The transfer prints of Liverpudlians Sadler and Green were applied to ready-glazed tile blanks of various types. The design, in enamel colours mixed with white lead and linseed oil, was transferred from the wood block or engraved copperplate onto tissue paper that was then laid face downward onto the tile. Having been pressed down hard enough to ensure that the print had registered on the tile, the paper was then soaked off and the printed tile fired in a low-temperature kiln. This relatively quick firing represented further savings of time and risk, on top of the advantage gained from the vastly increased rate of decorating tiles by transfer-printing rather than hand-painting methods.

During the 19th century both tile-making and decorating processes were refined and

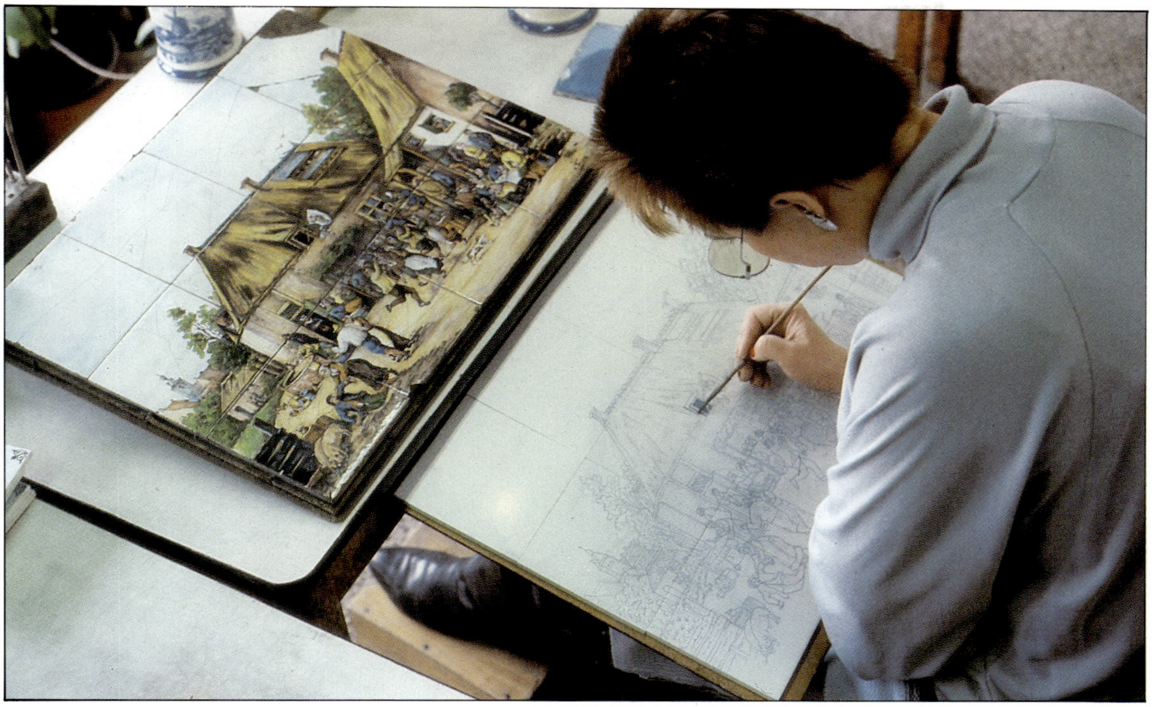

LEFT *A Dutch woman tile-painter working on a Delftware panel. A charcoal sketch has been pounced onto a panel of 12 Delftware tiles, to act as an outline guide for the painter.*

mechanized to meet the needs of a huge industry, and the contrast with earlier types is obvious. Victorian encaustic tiles are sometimes criticized for their perfection: there are none of the irregularities of shape, inaccuracies in pattern or unpredictability of colour that give so much charm to medieval examples. Similarly, transfer-printing processes were greatly advanced. To begin with, tiles produced by the dust-pressing method developed during the 19th century were already smooth and white enough to be decorated before being glazed. Transfer prints were applied to the unglazed tile body and covered with a transparent lead glaze. Colour could be applied by hand both over and under the glaze. Some of the best-quality tiles of the 1870s and 1880s have transfer-printed outlines with added hand-colouring.

While many firms had their own engraving departments, some used designs supplied by specialist printers, which is why the same designs may be seen on the tiles of a number of different 19th-century factories. Other supplies, like ready-mixed colours and glazes, could be obtained from firms like Wengers of Etruria, which supplied the late 19th-century pottery industry with all kinds of materials and equipment. This was a great advance over earlier periods, when potters had to mix their own colours and work out their glaze chemistry.

Block-printing enabled flat areas of colour — not just outlines — to be laid down. This method (also known as 'New Press') was patented in 1848 and was at first used exclusively by Minton and by other companies later. It was eventually superseded by the multicolour lithographic process in this century. Nowadays, silk-screen printing is used in preference to these other mechanical methods of decoration.

Several different methods of producing tiles are available to modern commercial tile-makers. As well as the traditional form of cutting tile slabs from plastic clay, the dust-pressing method developed by the Victorians is much used. Slip-casting and plastic-pressing (like dust-pressing but with wetter clay) are also employed commercially. A wholly modern development, mainly used for heavy-duty tiles, is extrusion, in which a slab of clay is drawn through a machine that cuts grooves down the middle and then chops off each tile length. When the extruded slab is split along its grooves it becomes a pair of 'twin tiles'. Drying, glazing and firing follow in the usual way.

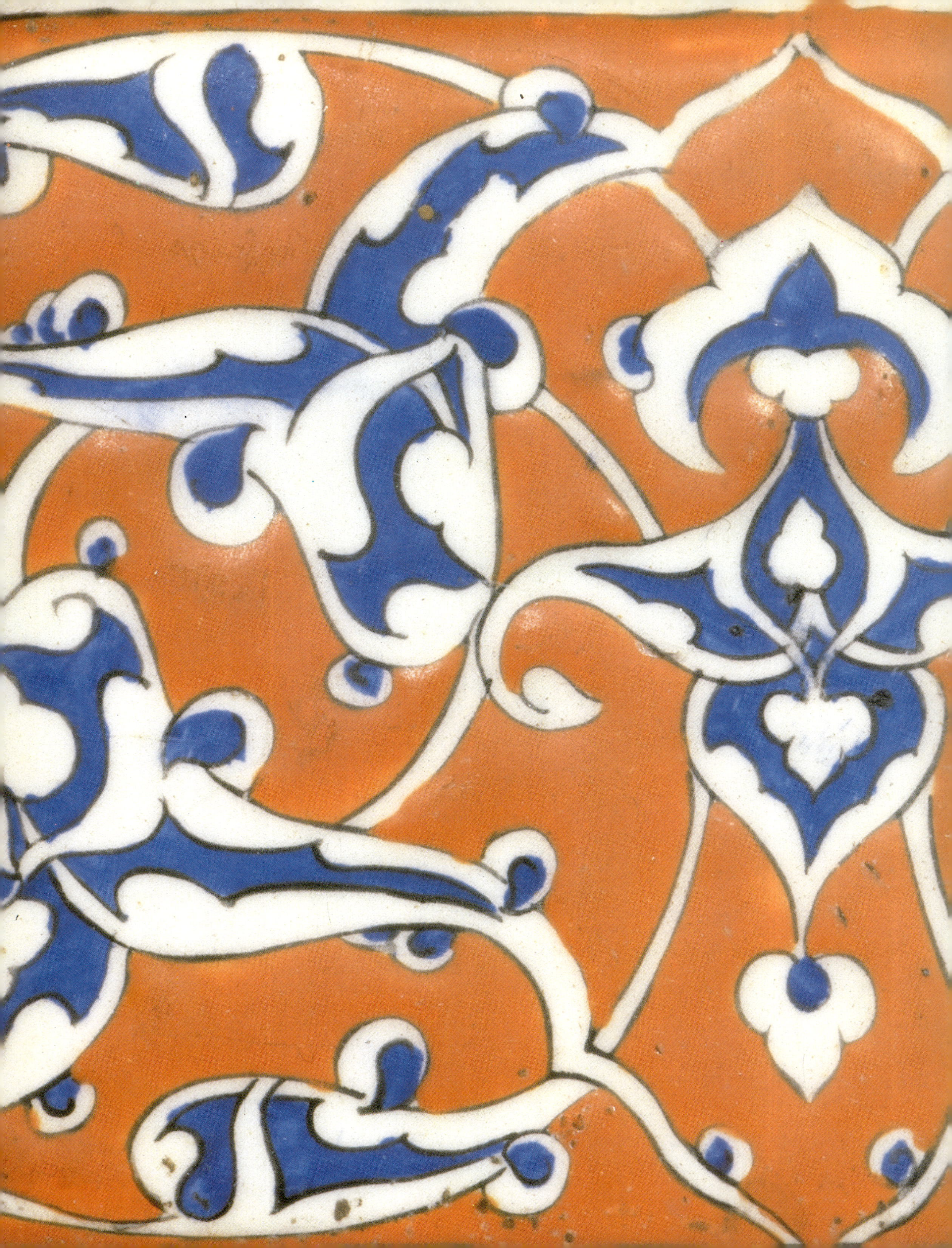

CHAPTER THREE

TILES OF ISLAM

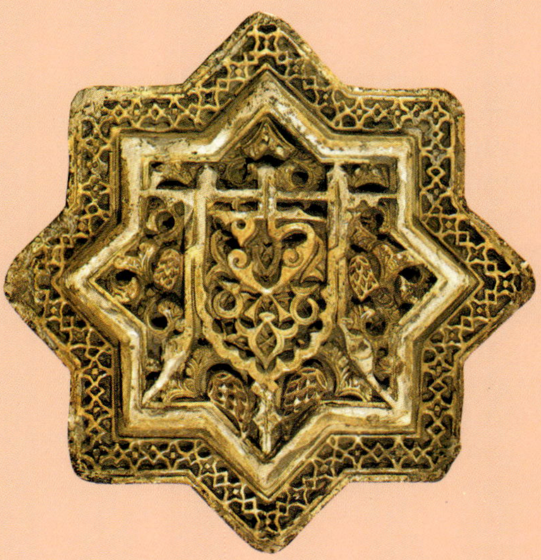

TWO GREAT arts of the Islamic world are architecture and calligraphy. Ceramic tiles — often decorated with calligraphic inscriptions — played a major part in the embellishment of buildings from an early period. Wall tiles dating from the second half of the 9th century AD were excavated from palaces in Samarra in Mesopotamia, and similar tiles are still to be seen in the Great Mosque of Kairouan in Tunisia. They were probably exported from Baghdad, one of the two main pottery-making centres in Mesopotamia; the other was Basra on the Persian Gulf.

OVERLEAF (BACKGROUND) *An Iznik border tile, c. 1575.*

OVERLEAF (INSET) *Lustre pottery star tile, c. 1262, said to have come from Imamzada Yahya in Veramin.*

RIGHT *Persian lustre tile with Koranic inscription in Naskhi script, 13th century.*

BELOW RIGHT *Spanish star-shaped tile of stucco or carved plaster, 13th or 14th century. An inscription forms the central emblem: the letters of the foliated Kufic script intertwine to produce the lobed arch that is the main feature of the decoration.*

ALTHOUGH utilitarian pottery had been produced in the Arabic world for many years, it was not until the 8th and 9th centuries, when an identifiable Islamic culture was emerging, that the aesthetic possibilities of fine ceramics began to be appreciated, largely due to Chinese influence. During the middle of the 8th century, the ruling Abbasids defeated a Chinese army that had occupied the area of Persia beyond the Oxus River at the eastern end of their domain, and cultural contacts began to grow between T'ang China and the Islamic world. Chinese prisoners introduced many artistic techniques, including the making of fine ceramics, into Mesopotamia, and a taste for imported Chinese wares developed. Highly prized T'ang porcelain came to Mesopotamia both overland by the Silk Route and by sea, across the Indian Ocean and up the Persian Gulf to Basra. Demand for these luxurious Chinese ceramics soon outstripped supply, and native craftsmen were encouraged by their rich patrons, the caliphs and princes, to set up workshops producing copies of the white Chinese porcelain and earthenware.

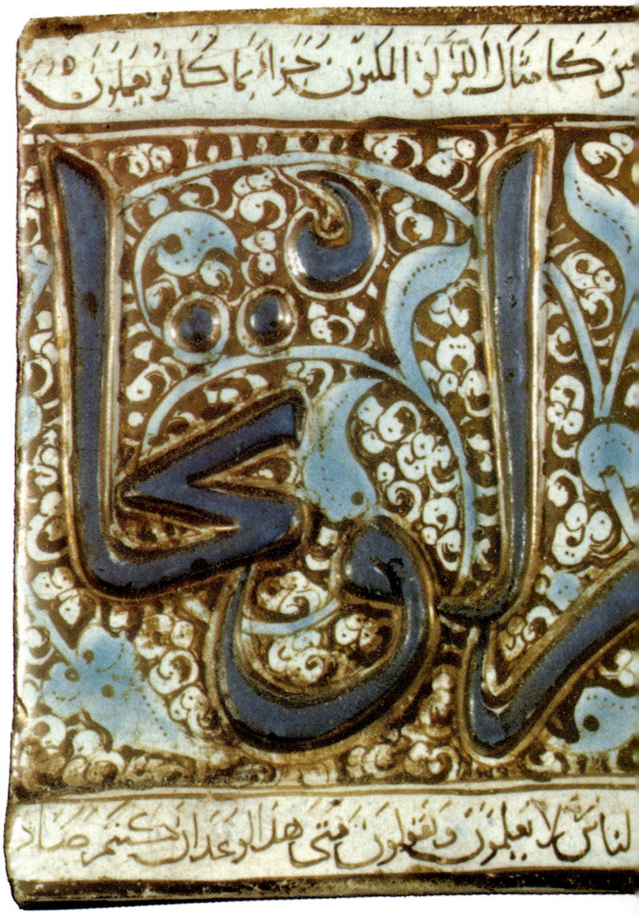

Although the Mesopotamian potters were unable to discover how to make true porcelain, they produced very creditable imitations by covering their buff earthenware with opaque-white tin glaze. Within a short time, they developed their skills beyond the mere copying of Chinese originals, and began to produce a range of ceramics in an unmistakably Islamic style. They used both opaque-white tin glazes and transparent lead glazes.

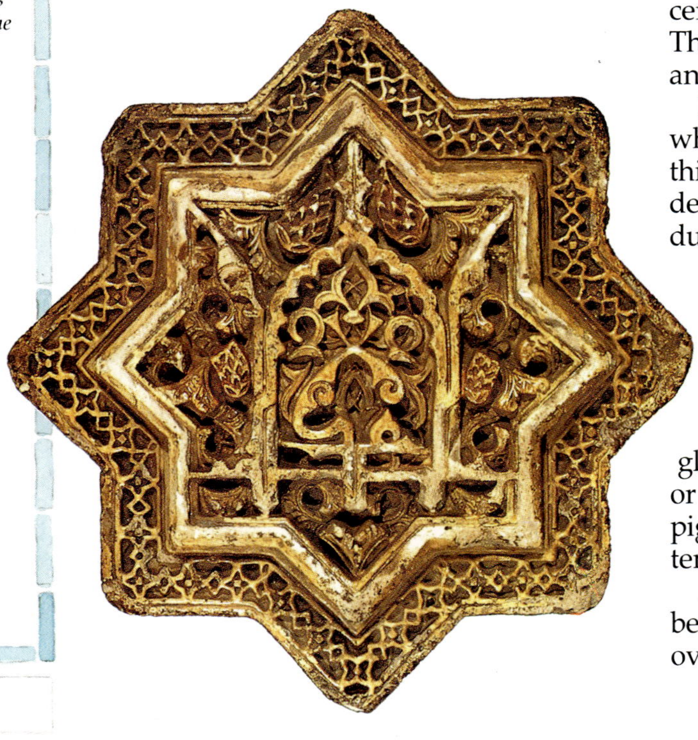

Painted patterns in blue and green on white tin-glazed backgrounds are typical of this period, but the most important development was that of lustre-painting during the 9th century. Possibly drawing inspiration from lustre-painted glass made in Egypt and Syria nearly a century earlier, the Islamic potters exploited the technique and it remained exclusively theirs for many years. The method involved painting the fired tin-glaze or lead-glaze surface with either silver or copper oxides, and fixing these metallic pigments by a second firing in a low-temperature muffle kiln.

At first, relief-moulded vessels that had been lead-glazed were simply lustred all over — evidently to simulate metalwork —

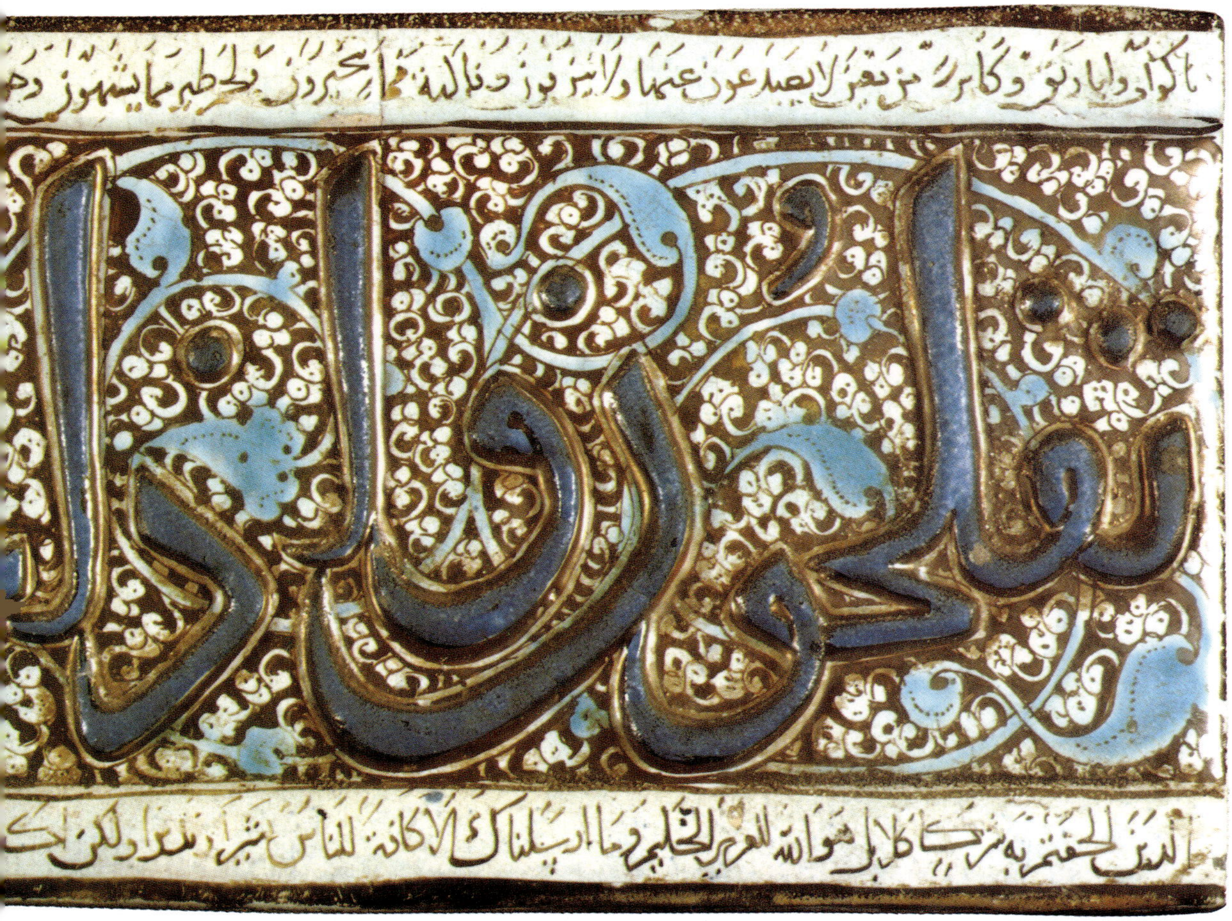

CHAPTER THREE

but later lustre was used on smooth white tin-glaze surfaces. The iridescent lustre pigments ranged in tone from vivid ruby through brown and yellow, and potters in the early period sometimes exploited this spectrum by using different toned lustres on the same piece, producing an almost polychrome effect. The tiles found at Samarra and those in the Great Mosque of Kairouan are of this polychrome lustre type, but a little after they were made, during the second half of the 9th century, the lustre palette was reduced to monochrome, while the designs became more complicated.

The early polychrome lustre tiles were decorated with chevron patterns, dots, cross-hatching, palmettes, the so-called Sasanian wing motif and, occasionally, naturalistically portrayed cocks and eagles. It was only later, in the late 9th and 10th centuries, when the colours of Mesopotamian lustre wares were simplified, that humans and animals regularly began to appear.

By the late 10th century, the lustre-painting technique had reached Egypt, probably brought there by immigrant Mesopotamian potters escaping political unrest in Basra. Al-Fustat and Al-Bahnasa are known to have been pottery-making centres of some importance during the Tulunid dynasty and later under the Fatimids (969–1171), but it is uncertain whether tiles were produced there.

During the 12th and 13th centuries, in the remote and mountainous north and north-western districts of Persia bordering the Caspian Sea, pottery wares unlike any others in the Islamic world were being produced. They were decorated with incised lines in coloured slip and their patterns showed pre-Islamic Sasanian influence.

One type of this incised slip pottery produced in the Garrus district included tiles as well as vessels. The ground was cut back to the clay so that the light-coloured slip formed a low-relief pattern against a dark brown or black background, and the tiles were covered in transparent green glaze.

RIGHT *Persian moulded lustre tile from Kashan, first half of the 13th century.*

These pieces, generally known as *champleve*, or Garrus ware, were decorated with simple scrolling patterns, roundels, palmettes, interlaced bands or cross-hatching. Many had Kufic inscriptions. Kufic was the monumental and angular form of Arabic script that was the first to be developed as a calligraphic art. Later, during the 14th century, the more curvaceous Nashki script was developed in Persia and was also much used in the decoration of ceramics.

During the late 12th and the 13th centuries the chief centres of Islamic pottery production were in Mesopotamia and Persia, by this time part of the Seljuk empire. They included Rayy, Kashan, Sava, Rakka and Sultanabad, of which Kashan was by far the most important. Far-reaching technical and artistic developments took place, again under the influence of Chinese imported wares; this time, it was the white Ting porcelains of the Sung dynasty (960–1279 AD) that stimulated imitation, both in the composition of the pottery body and in its decoration.

It was probably the potters of Kashan who were the first in Persia to develop the technique of underglaze painting in the early 13th century. Whereas painting on a tin-glazed surface led to blurring of the colours during firing, and slip-painting was limited in its decorative possibilities, it was discovered that coloured pigments such as cobalt and manganese remained stable under alkaline glazes. As well as painting in black and blue under colourless or tinted glazes, the Persian potters soon developed their methods even further, by painting over the glaze in enamel colours that were fixed by a second firing; this overglaze

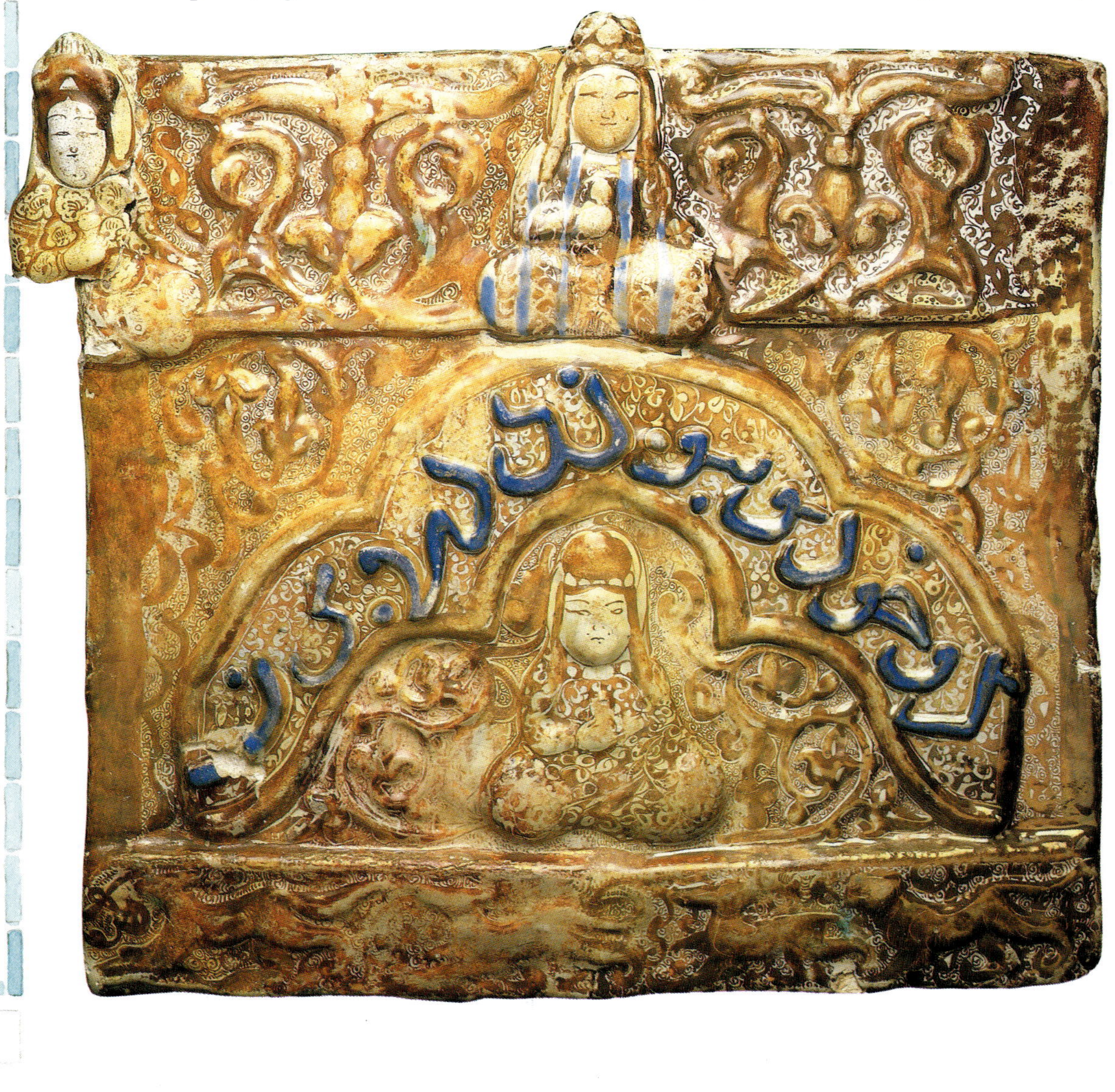

painting was known as *mina'i*. By using a combination of underglaze and overglaze painting, the potters were able to extend their palette to as many as seven colours.

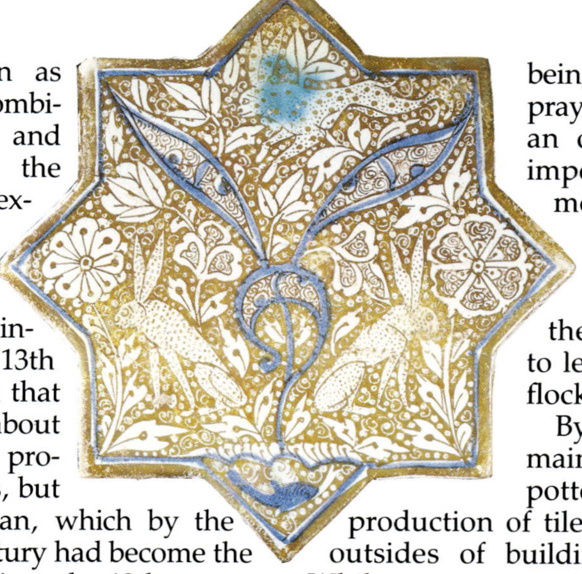

Successive Mongol invasions during the 13th century, starting with that of Genghis Khan about 1220, halted pottery production in many areas, but it continued in Kashan, which by the second half of the century had become the major tile producer. Since the 12th century, tiles — usually blue and black — had been used to adorn the outside brickwork of the domes of mosques and other important buildings, but a century later they were also being used to decorate the prayer-niche, or mihrab, an object of preeminent importance inside the mosque: it is in front of the mihrab, which indicates the direction of Mecca, where the imam (priest) stands to lead the prayers of his flock.

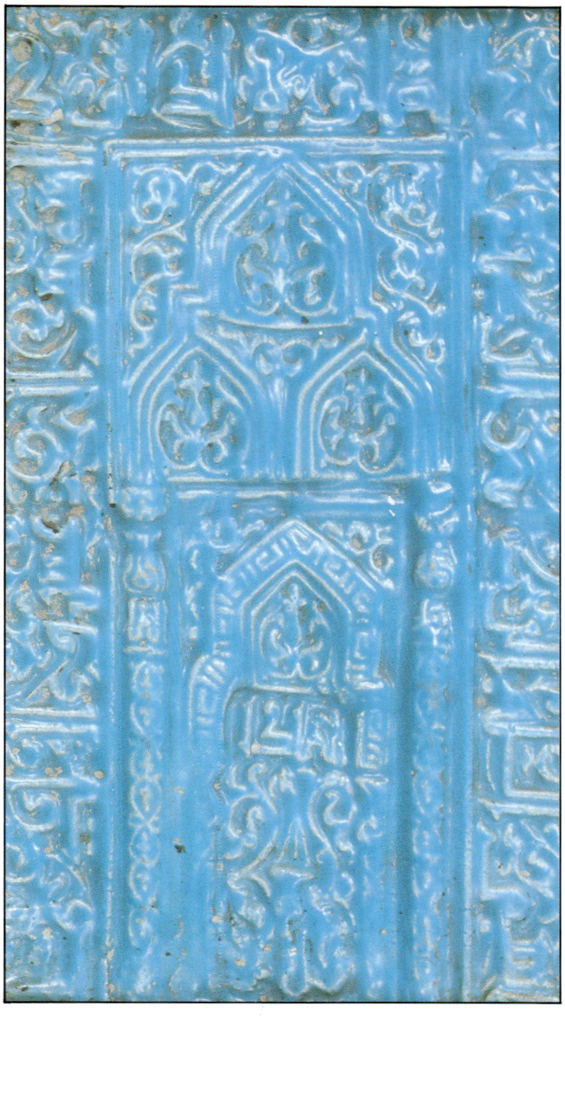

By the 13th century, the main thrust of the Kashan pottery industry was the production of tiles for the insides and outsides of buildings all over Persia. While most were designed for mihrabs, tombstones, architectural friezes and various religious purposes, some were undoubtedly made to adorn palaces, baths and other secular buildings. Methods of decoration included lustre-painting and relief-moulding, but colours, especially cobalt blue and turquoise, were also used under, in and over the glaze.

Tiles were made in many shapes: square, rectangular, star, cross and variants of these. In many cases, compositions were made from several tiles linked together. For example, a tomb chamber might be covered with panels of alternating stars and crosses; architectural borders could be formed by rows of square tiles; a mihrab might be made from a set of tiles that might include a large pair with triangular tops placed together to form the upper section, with a central piece and flanking inscriptions. Individual tiles ranged in size from stars with a diameter of about 8 in (20 cm) to large panel sections as high as 30 in (76 cm).

Decoration included swirling arabesques, scrolling plants, dots, palmettes, flowers, leaves, birds, animals and human figures. Inscriptions from the Koran were common and these could form border decorations or be part of the central design of a tile panel: in these cases they were often moulded in relief. Both Kufic and Nashki characters were used.

Some tiles were inscribed with dates and even the names of makers, which have been helpful elements in the identification of different types. For example, at least

LEFT *Kashan lustre star tile depicting spotted hares above a fish pond, 13th century.*

BELOW LEFT *Persian monochromatic moulded mihrab tile with Koranic inscription, 12th to 13th century.*

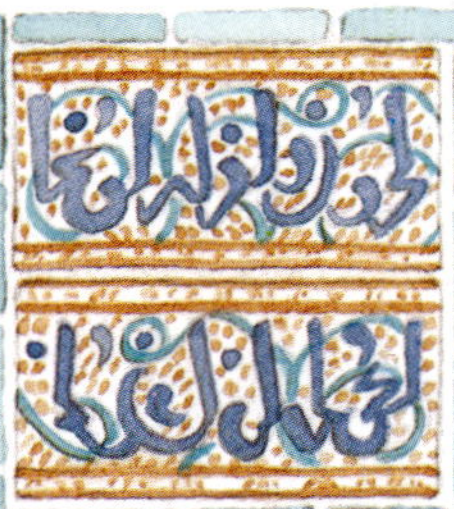

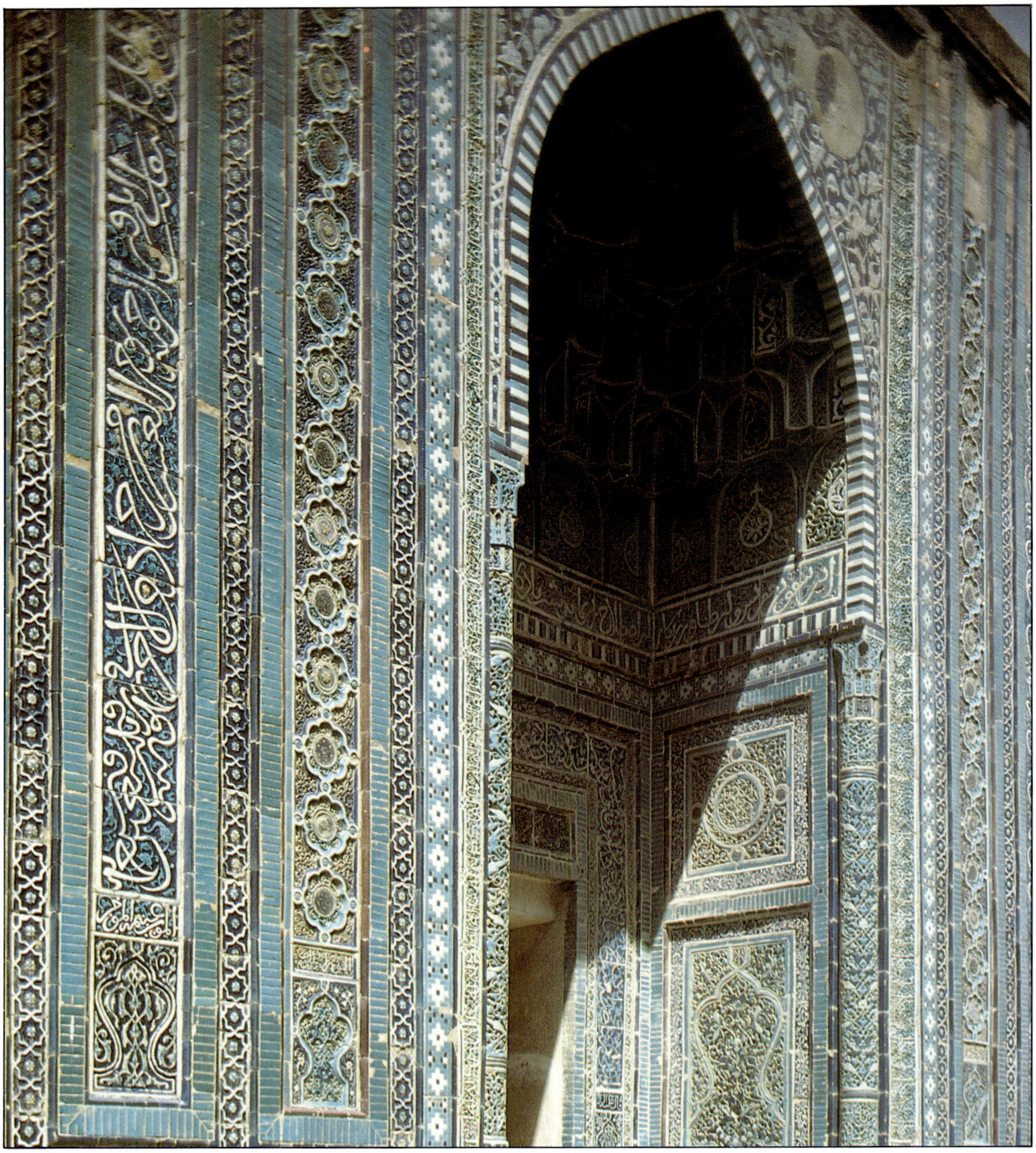

RIGHT *A view of the tiled portal of the Turkan-Aka Mausoleum, Shah-e Zinda, Samarkand.*

seven lustre-tiled mihrabs have survived from a family of potters headed by Abu Tahir who, with his children and grandchildren, produced tiles in Kashan over a 100-year period, from the early 13th to the early 14th century.

As well as lustre-decorated tiles, whose production at Kashan appears to have ceased after about 1340, a type of coloured ware known as *lajvardina* has been associated with Kashan and with the Sultanabad region during the late 13th and early 14th centuries. In effect it was a simplified form of the *mina'i* technique: relief-moulded designs were painted in red, white and black enamel and gold leaf over a brilliant cobalt- or turquoise-blue glazed ground and fixed with a second short firing. Tiles of various shapes, including hexagonal and cruciform, have been found decorated in the *lajvardina* technique.

Samarkand, capital of the Timurid empire from 1378 to 1506, was a major tile-producing centre during this period in Persia.

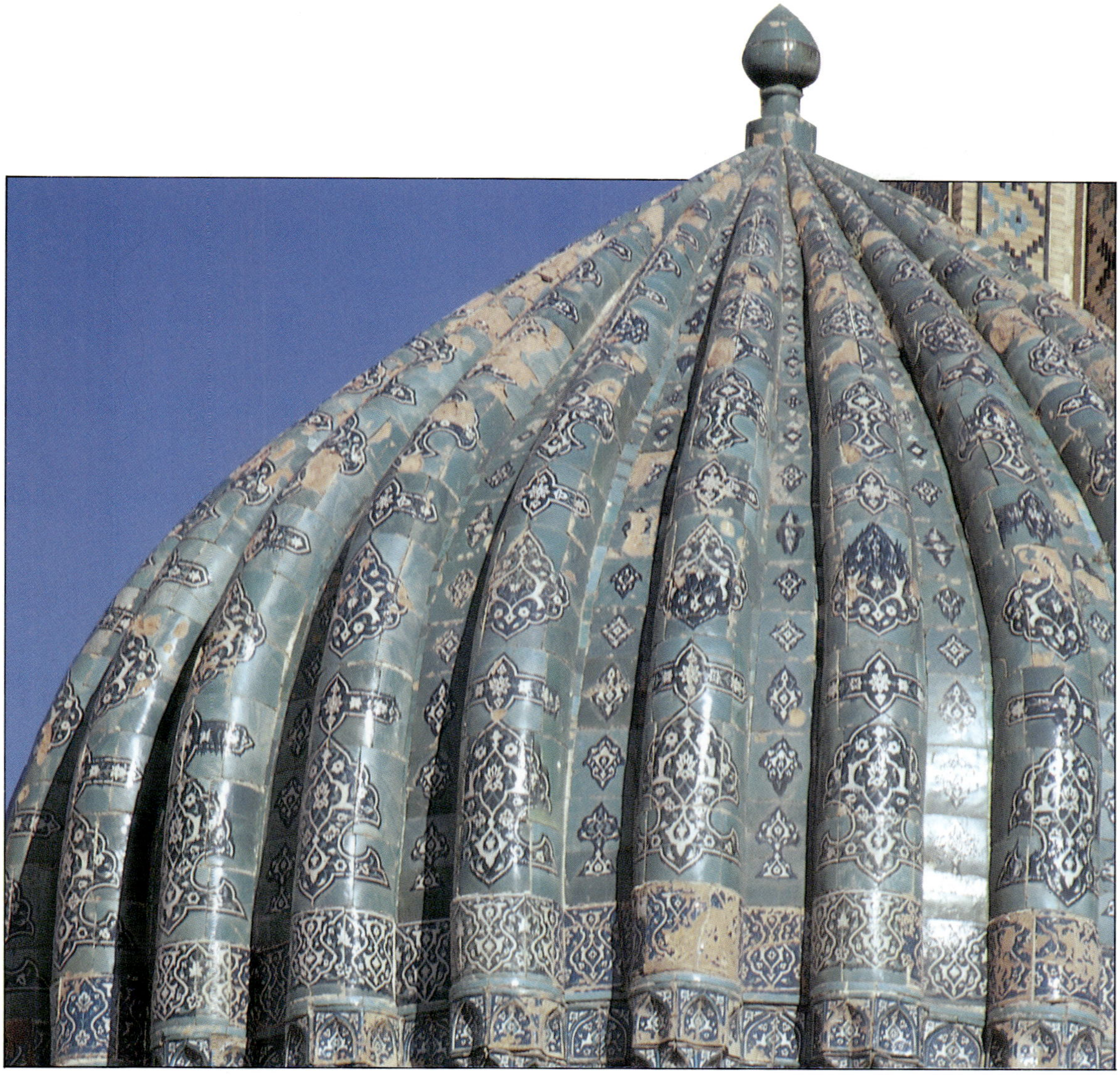

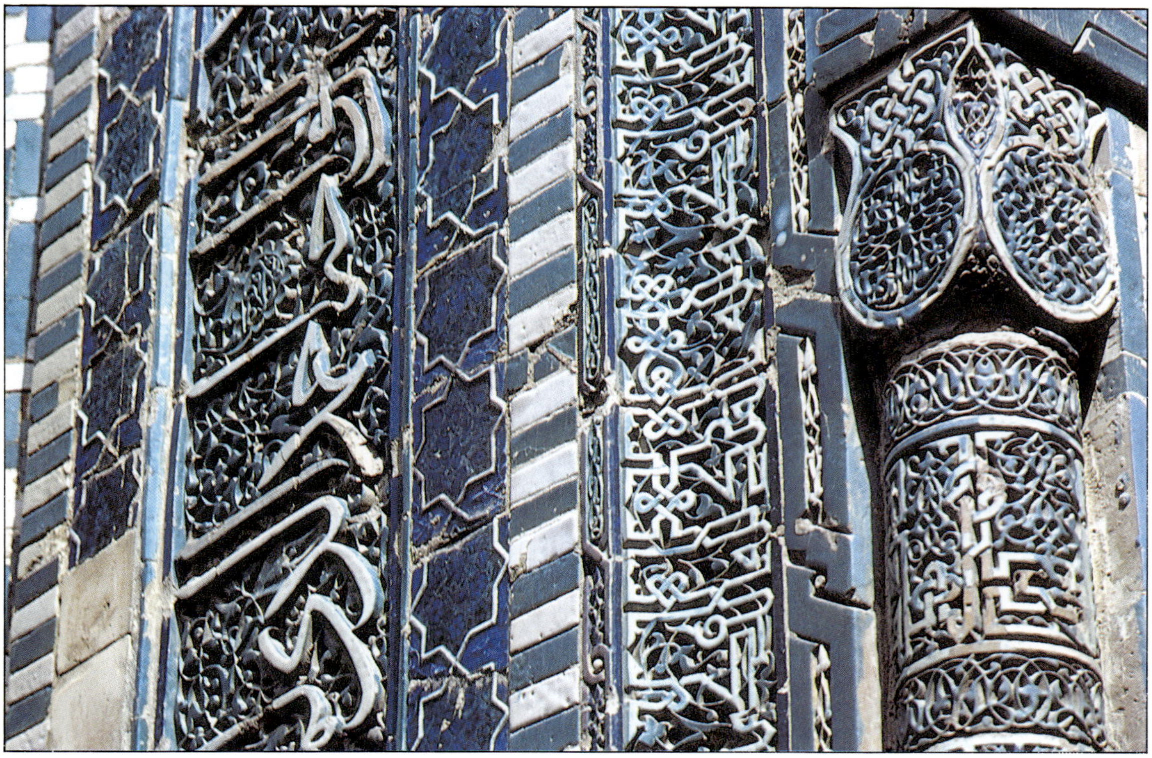

CHAPTER THREE

•

LEFT *The lobed dome of Shir-Dor madrasah, Registan, Samarkand.*

BELOW LEFT *Undercut and other tiles from the Hodja Akhmed Mausoleum, Shah-e Zinda, Samarkand.*

TILE ART

•

RIGHT *View of the dome in the entrance to the Royal Mosque, Isfahan.*

BELOW RIGHT *Syrian blue-and-white pottery tile depicting a peacock, c. 1425. The square shape was less common than the hexagonal during this period.*

BELOW FAR RIGHT *A rare Ottoman* cuerda seca *pottery tile, 16th century.*

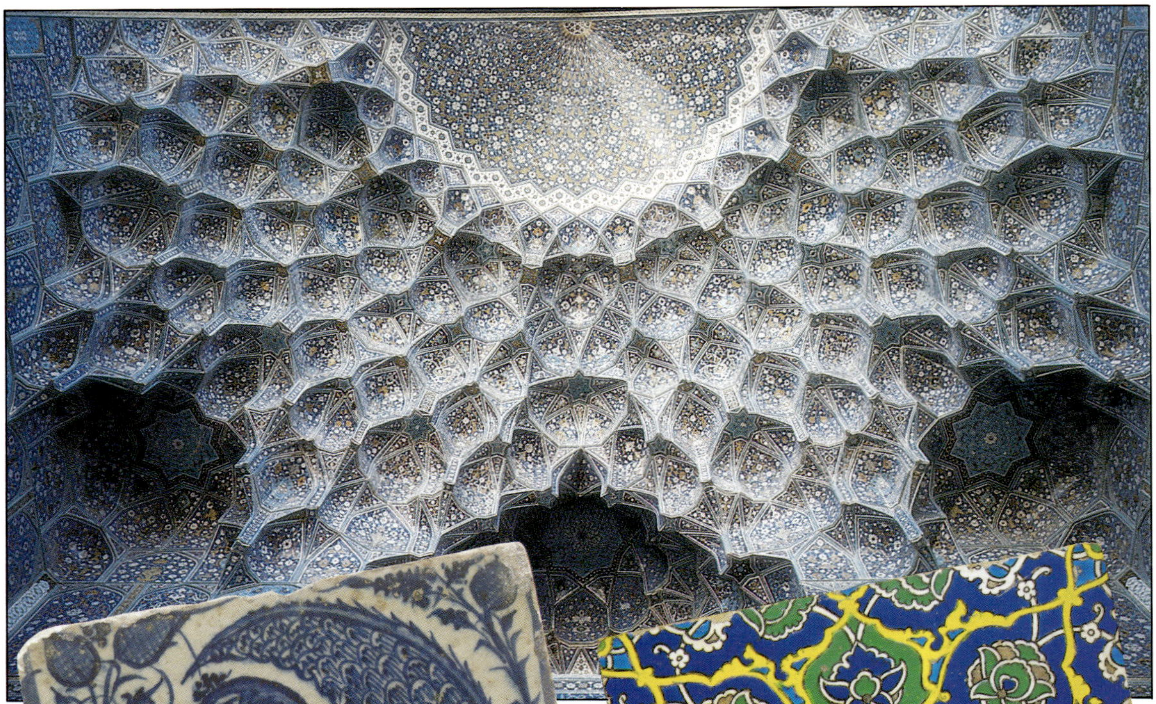

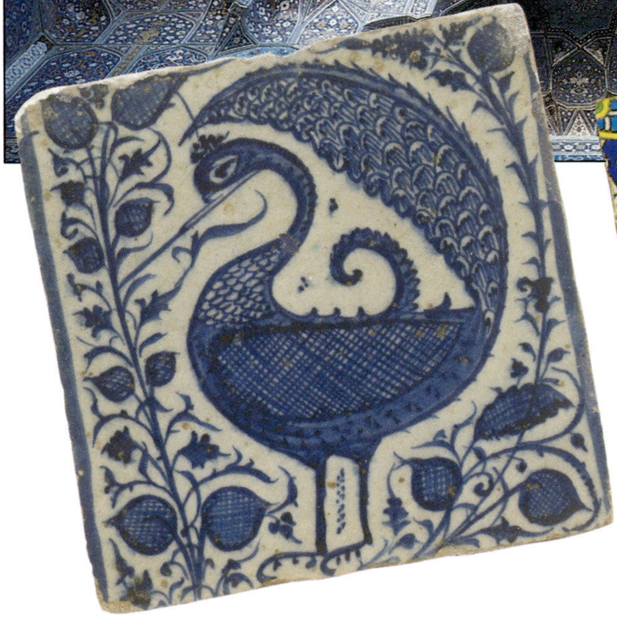

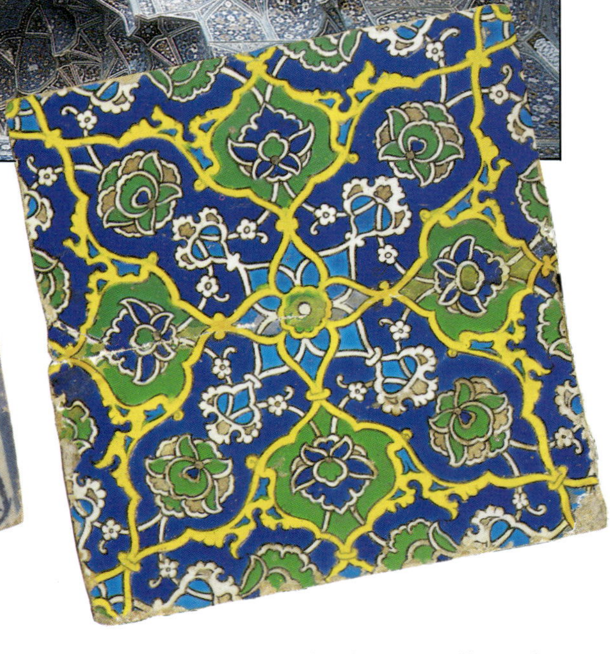

The great emperor Tamerlane built a large tomb complex for family members around the shrine of the Muslim saint Shah-e Zinda, and the façades of the mausolea are covered with tiles made in a range of techniques, including relief-carving under coloured glazes. Tiles like these, made to imitate stucco work, are known to have been used earlier on buildings in and around Bukhara, but the relief-carving technique was brought to perfection in late 14th-century Samarkand. Many kinds of buildings — mosques, *madrasahs* (schools, often attached to mosques), mausolea and palaces in Herat and Meshed as well as in Samarkand itself — were faced with brilliantly coloured tiles of carved openwork, their scrolling designs of arabesques, palmettes and inscriptions painted in blues, greens, purple and yellow. The exterior of Tamerlane's own mausoleum in Samarkand, the Gur Emir, finished in 1434, was completely covered in mosaic titles whose brilliant turquoise hues even extended over the huge lobed dome. Both this type of dome and the all-over tiling of exterior surfaces became usual for important buildings throughout the empire from this time.

Although the pottery industry in Persia was generally in decline during the 15th and 16th centuries, tiles continued to proliferate as architectural decoration. The blue-

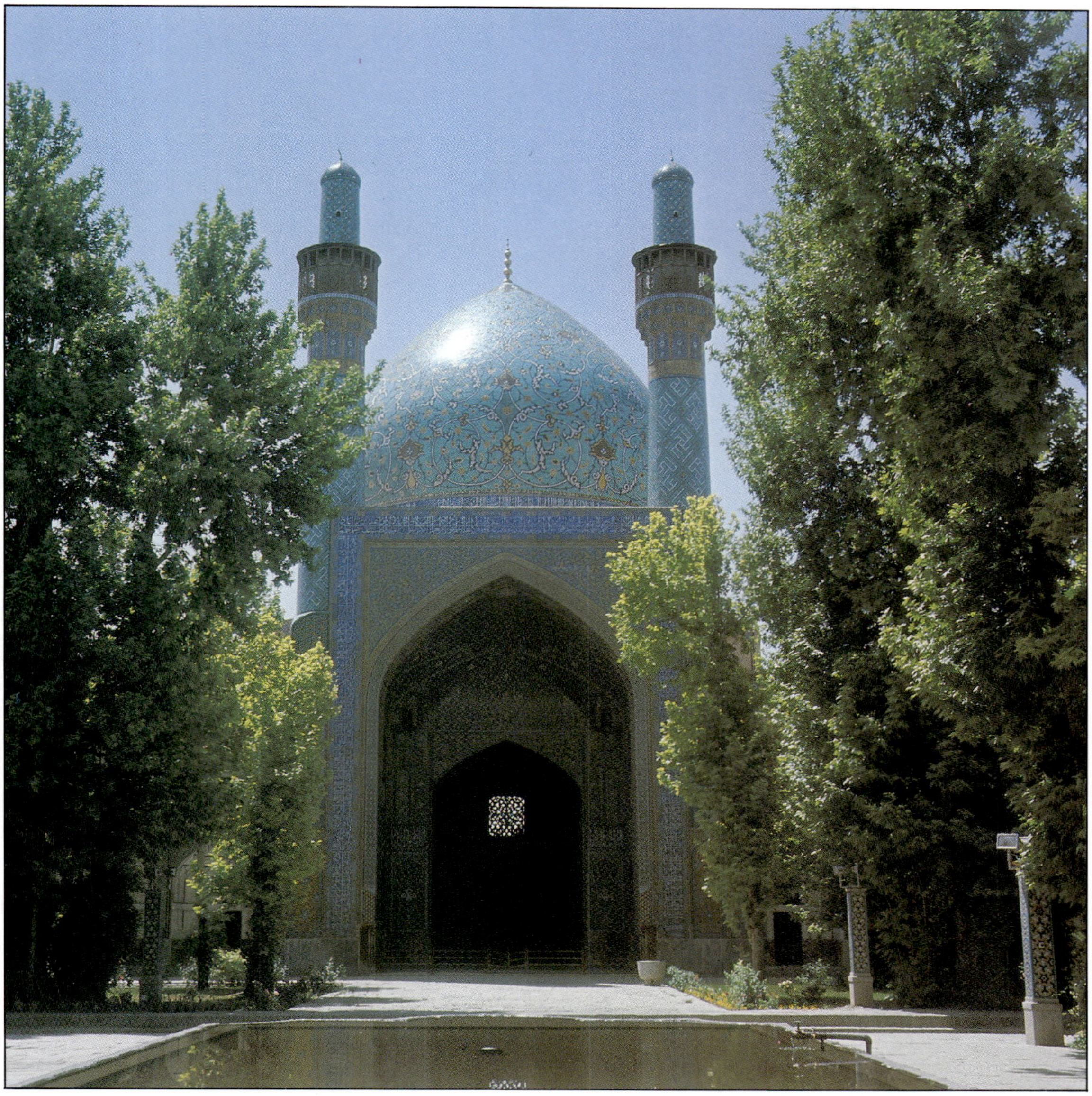

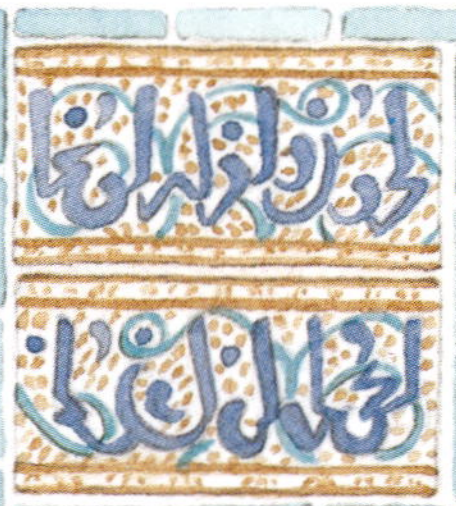

CHAPTER THREE

•

LEFT *View of the southern iwan and dome of the Madrasah Madar-n Shah, Isfahan.*

and-white porcelains of Ming China were by now a dominating influence and tiles made in both Persia and Syria during the 15th and 16th centuries were decorated with Chinese-inspired plant and animal forms, generally in black, blue or occasionally green under a clear glaze.

Outstanding tiled buildings from the 14th and 15th centuries can be seen in Samarkand, while the best examples from the 16th and 17th centuries are those in Isfahan, capital of the Safavid dynasty from 1506 to 1722. The brilliance of the tiles' blue colourings is largely due to their unusually thick glazes, which give an enhanced luminosity under the bright sunlight.

Tiles made by the *cuerda seca* (or dry cord) technique were used on the Imperial Mosque, Isfahan, in the early 17th century. This was a method known since the 11th century but not exploited in Persia until the 14th. The outlines of the design were drawn with a manganese and grease mixture that resisted the glaze, and the spaces were filled with white and coloured glazes. After firing, the glaze colours appeared within unglazed outlines.

Damascus continued to be a notable tile-producing city during the 16th and 17th centuries, coming under both Persian and Turkish influence. Tiles decorated in the *cuerda seca* technique and with underglaze

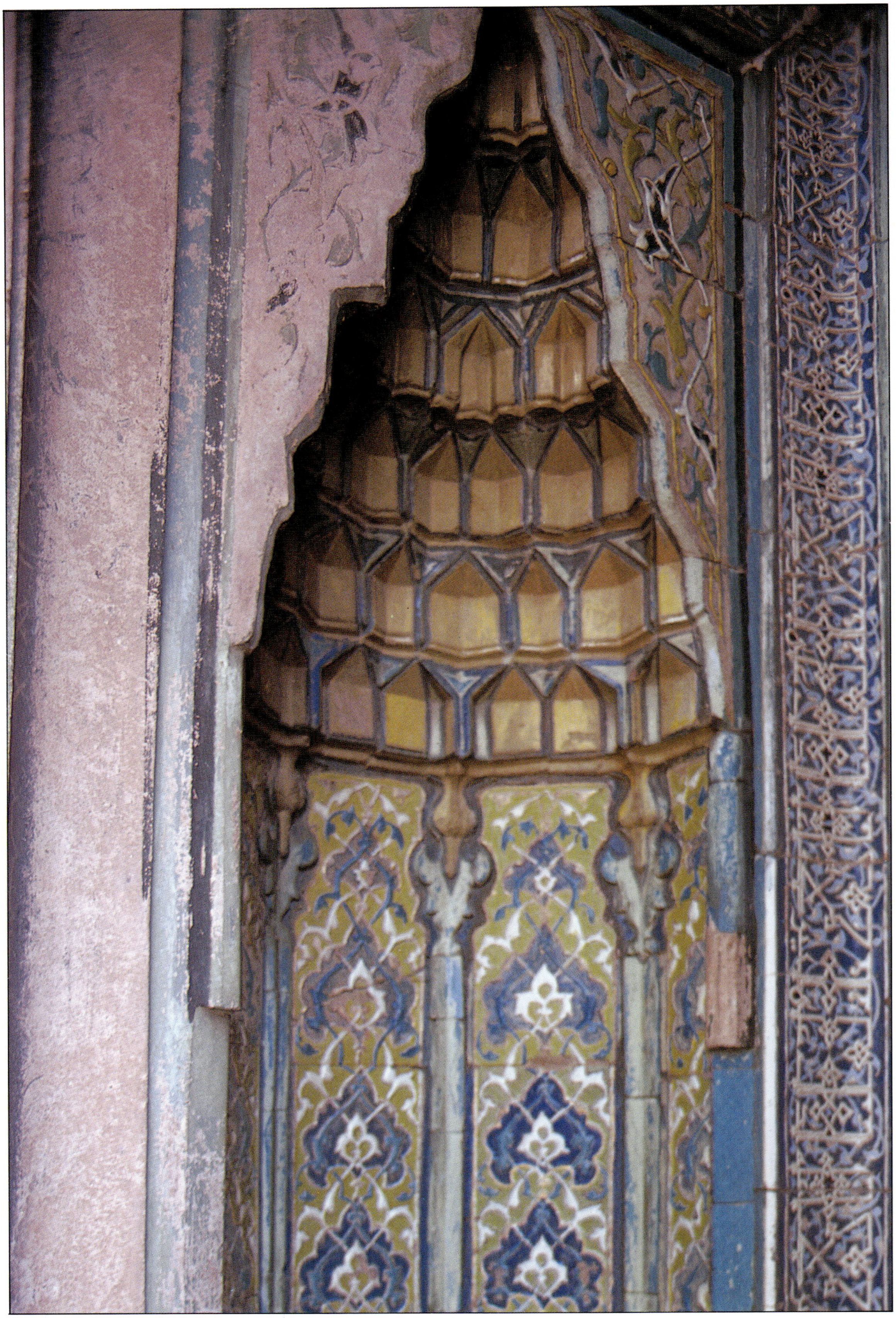

RIGHT *Tiled niche in the Green Mausoleum, Bursa.*

FAR RIGHT (TOP) *A blue-and-white pottery tile from Iznik, mid-16th century.*

FAR RIGHT (CENTRE) *An Iznik border tile, c. 1575.*

FAR RIGHT (BOTTOM) *A polychrome tile, from Iznik, mid-16th century.*

painting were produced there, and both types can be seen in the Dome of the Rock at Jerusalem, which was tiled under the orders of Suleiman the Magnificent in about 1545. Tiles of a similar type to those of Damascus were also made in Egypt in the 17th century.

At the western end of the Islamic world, in Asia Minor, tiles were made for architectural purposes from the 12th century onward. Like those of Kashan, they were made in a variety of shapes and with decoration that included arabesques, geometric patterns, and inscriptions in both Kufic and Nashki; their colours ranged from turquoise blues and greens to white and black. Many surviving examples of such tiles made during the 13th century are to be seen in mihrabs in various parts of Turkey. They are thought to have been made by Persian potters who fled westward from the Mongol invasions of the 1220s.

Persians continued to work in western Turkey for several centuries and were responsible for some of the outstanding tiled buildings of the 15th and 16th centuries, many of them decorated with *cuerda seca* tiles. Notable examples are the Green Mosque (1419–24) and the Green Tomb (*c* 1421), both in Bursa; others are in mosques at Edirne, Ankara and Istanbul.

It was at Iznik in western Anatolia that tiles and other wares of the highest quality were produced throughout the 16th century. Although pottery manufacture had been established at Iznik for 100 years or more, during which time blue-and-white-painted tiles are known to have been made, its greatest artistic impetus came when patronage of the Ottoman court began at the end of the 15th century. The pottery known today as Iznik ware is that produced from 1490 until about 1700, of a thick, loose-grained whitish composition, with painted decoration under a fine transparent glaze. Between 1490 and 1525, tiles were produced with blue-painted flowers, arabesques and inscriptions on white grounds, while the next group, dating from the period 1525–55, includes turquoise, green and, around the middle of the century, purple and blue in the painted decoration. By this time designs

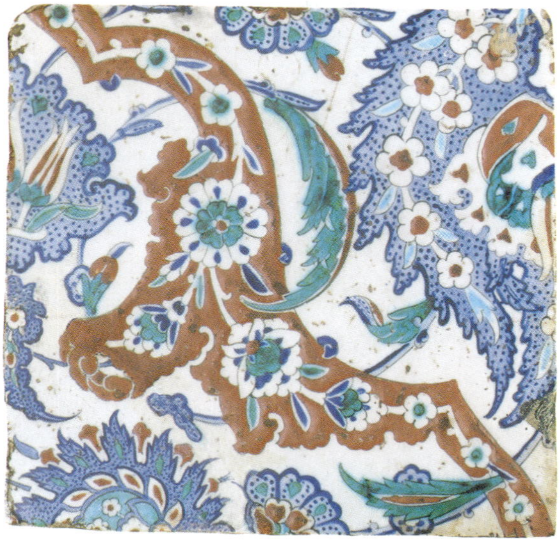

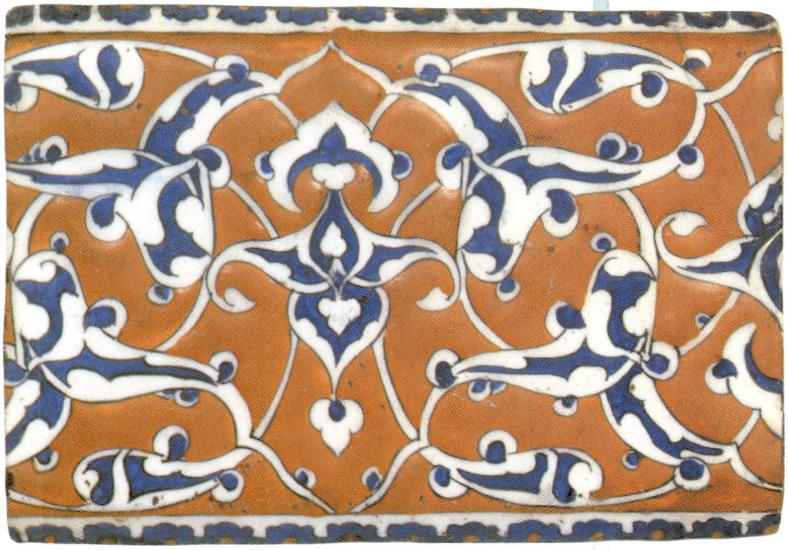

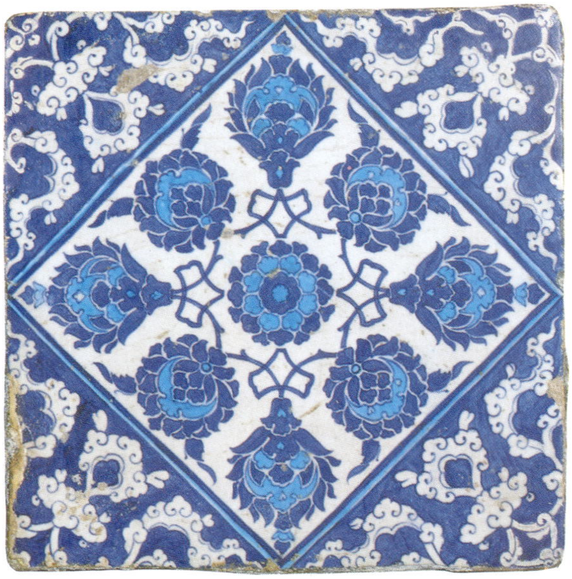

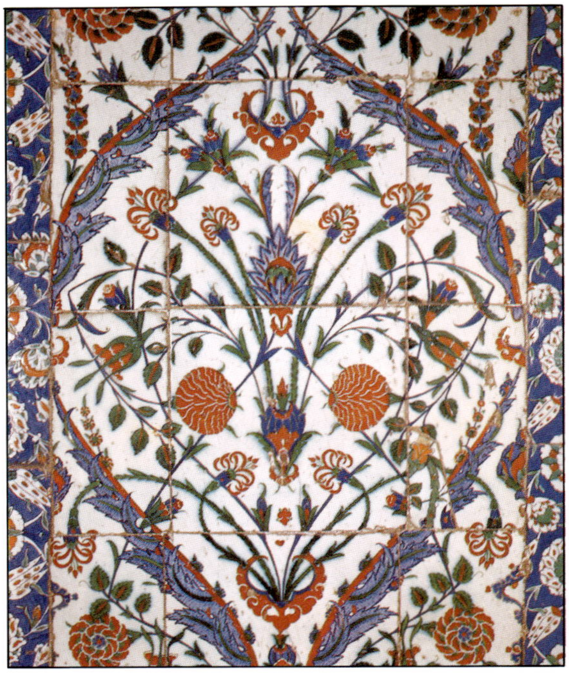

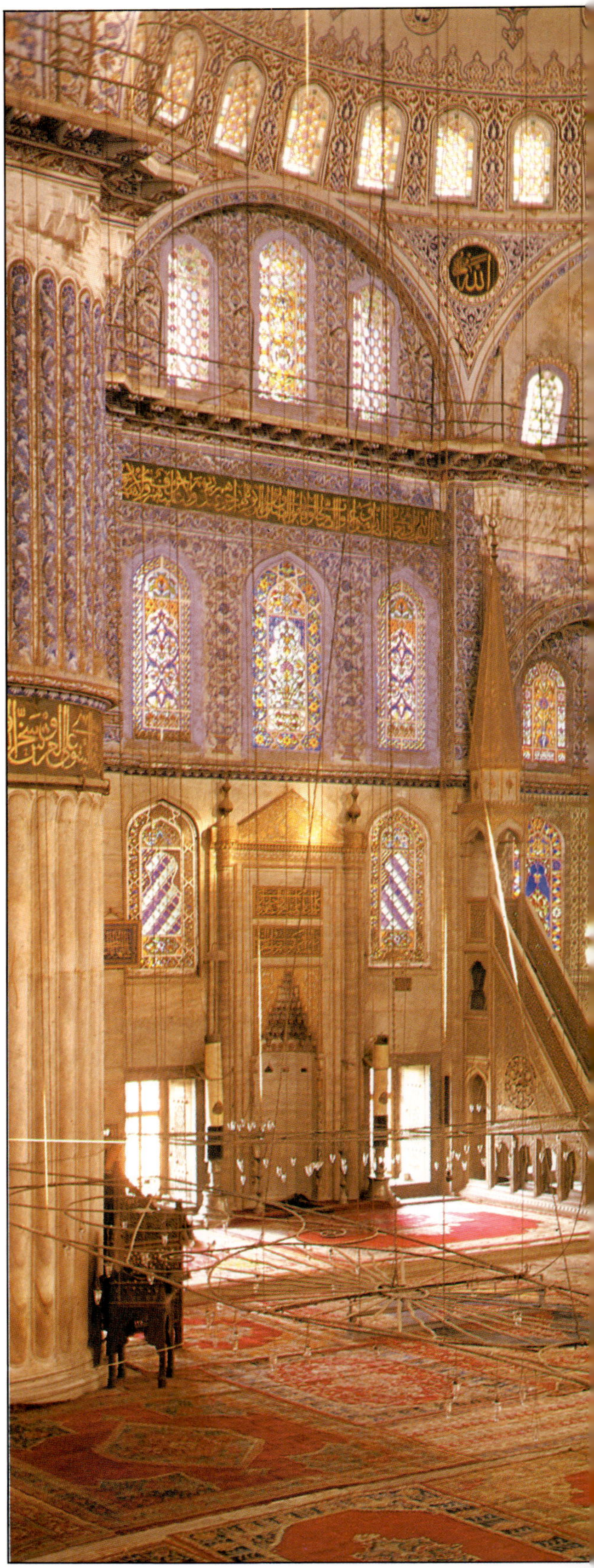

RIGHT *Tiled panel in the Mosque of Sultan Ahmet, Istanbul.*

CENTRE RIGHT *Interior of the Mosque of Sultan Ahmet, Istanbul.*

had become more naturalistic and included recognizable plants such as vines, tulips and carnations as well as the stylized arabesque motifs of the earlier period; inscriptions no longer appeared.

The greatest period of Iznik production was between 1555 and 1700, when vast quantities of wall tiles were made for the embellishment of mosques and palaces. A bright red now replaced purple in the palette, and typical subjects were realistically drawn flowers such as roses, tulips, carnations and hyacinths, often with scrolling plant borders, all outlined in black. Designs on paper were customarily provided by court artists in Istanbul and transferred onto tiles at the Iznik potteries.

Among the most spectacular examples of Iznik tiles of this period are those to be seen in Istanbul, notably in Sultan Suleiman's mausoleum (1566), the mosques of Rustem Pasha (*c* 1550) and Sokollu Mehmet Pasha (1571–2) and, most famous of all, the 'Blue Mosque' of Sultan Ahmet, built in 1609. Others are on view at the Victoria & Albert Museum, the Louvre and the Fundaçao Calouste Gulbenkian in Lisbon.

Although Iznik tile production continued throughout the 17th century, artistic standards declined, apparently with falling demand; by the end of the 17th century the

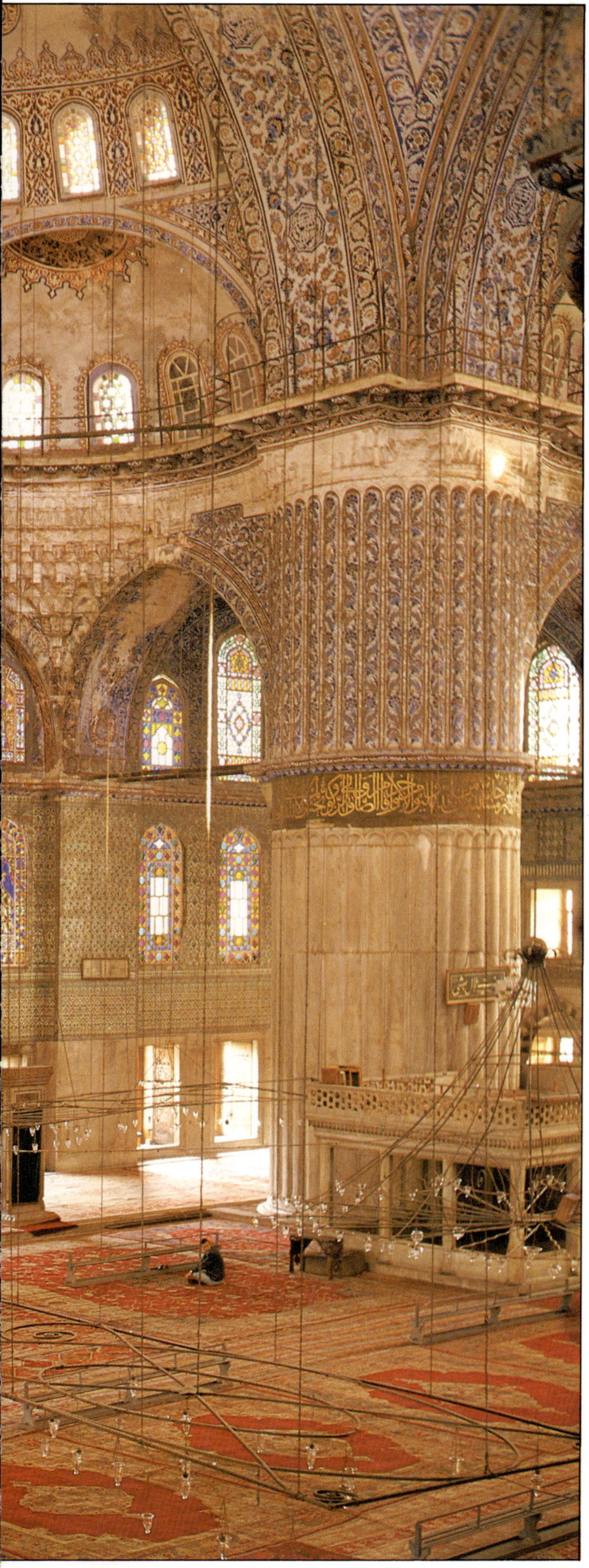

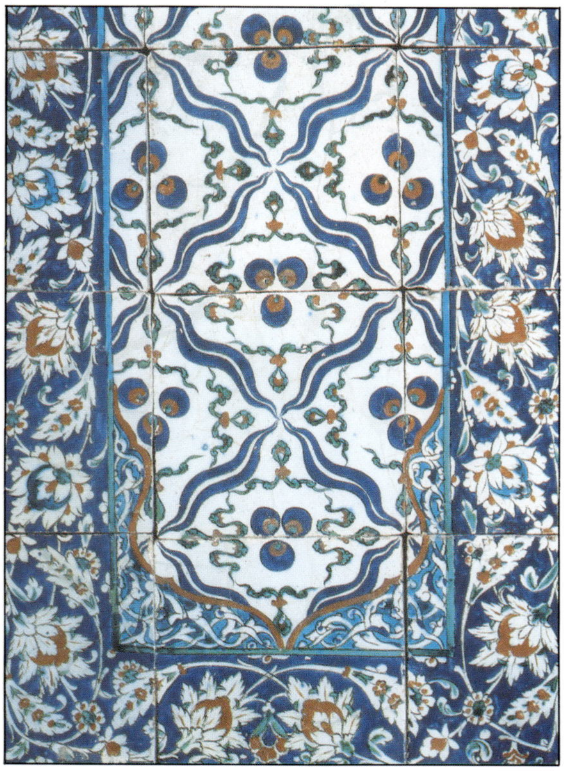

chief Turkish pottery centre was Kütahya, where Armenian potters made tiles and other vessels mainly for the Christian communities of the Ottoman empire during the 18th and 19th centuries. Tiles were also produced for mosques and palaces, but they never reached the excellence of the Iznik wares. Tiles decorated with Christian subjects made in this period are to be seen in the Armenian Cathedral of St James in Jerusalem and in other Armenian churches. The influence of both Iznik wares and European styles is to be seen in their naive but colourful designs.

In northern Persia during the 16th and 17th centuries a type of painted and lead-glazed ware was produced. It was known as Kubachi, after the town in the Caucasus where much of it was found, although it is thought to have been made in Tabriz. Early Kubachi decorated tiles, mostly depicting plants, animals and figures, were painted in blue and white in imitation of Chinese porcelain. By the early 17th century the designs included portraits of Europeans and the underglaze decoration was painted in the same polychrome palette as the contemporary Iznik wares.

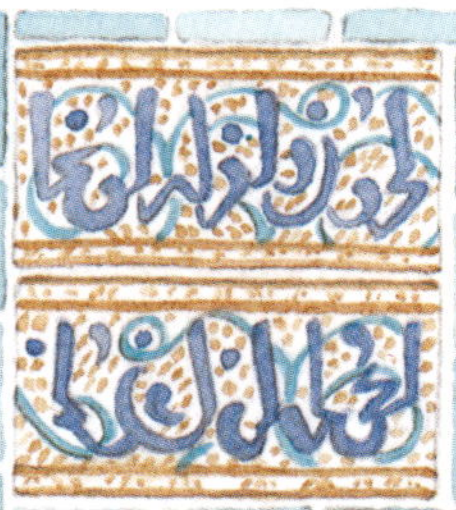

CHAPTER THREE

LEFT *Ottoman tile panel made c. 1731 in the Tehfur Saray factory, which was founded by the Vizier Daud Ibrahim in 1724 to revive Iznik tile production.*

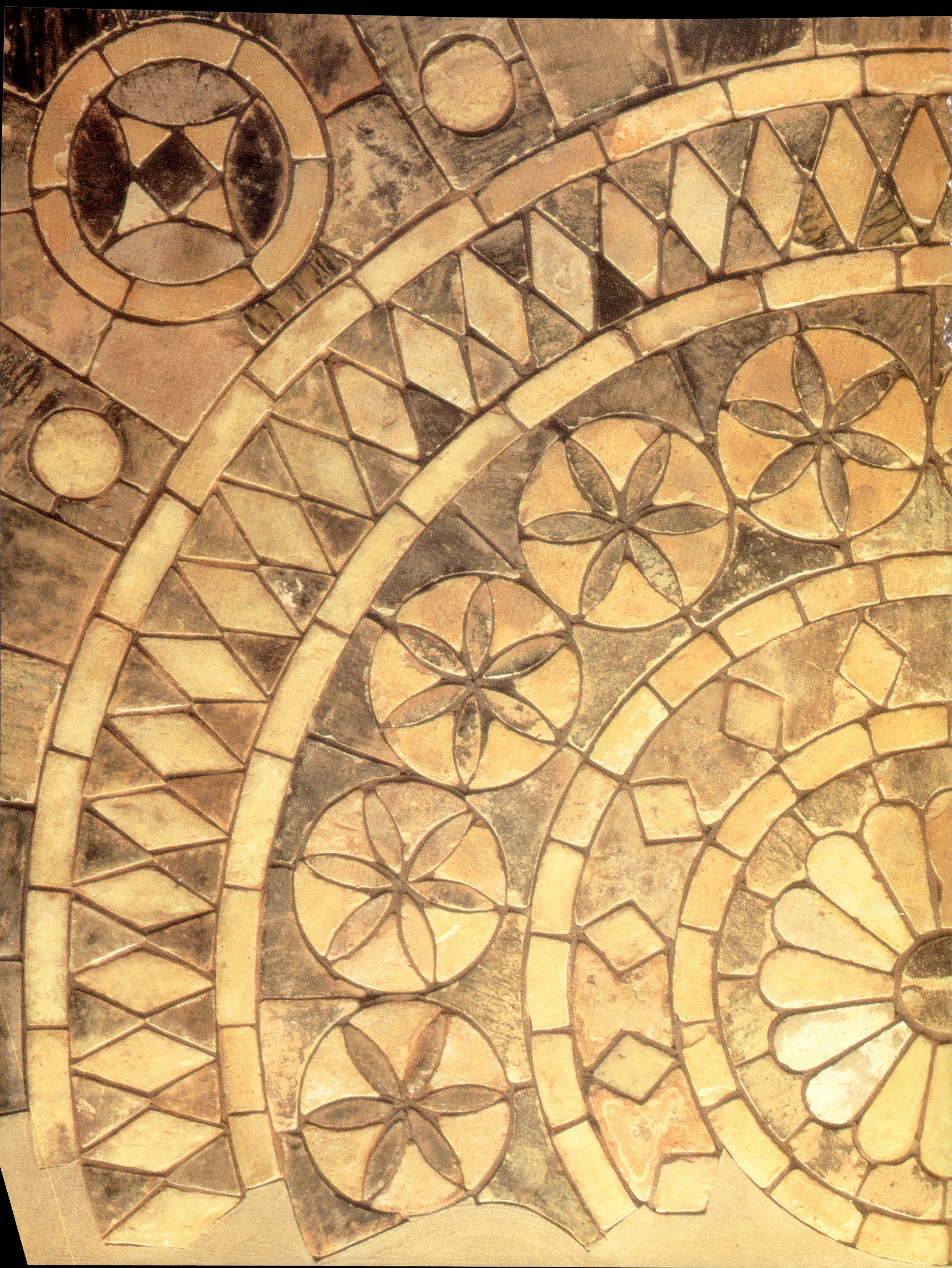

CHAPTER FOUR

BYZANTINE AND MEDIEVAL TILES

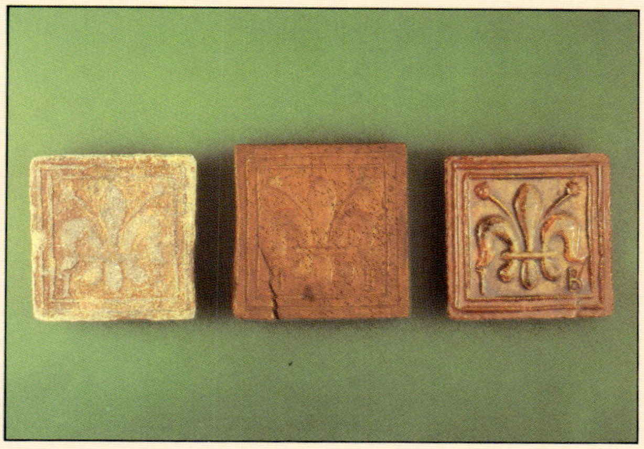

LIKE THEIR *Islamic contemporaries, the Christians of the Byzantine Empire used ceramic tiles for architectural decoration. One particular type of purpose-made tile, especially shaped for cornices, columns and other architectural uses, survives from the 9th to the 12th centuries. These tiles are characteristically thinner than Islamic examples of the same period, although of a similar whitish body, and it is clear that the Byzantine ceramic industry developed quite separately from the Islamic. At the same time there must have been considerable interchange between the two cultures, with the result that Oriental motifs — and even designs based on Kufi script — appear on some of these Byzantine wares.*

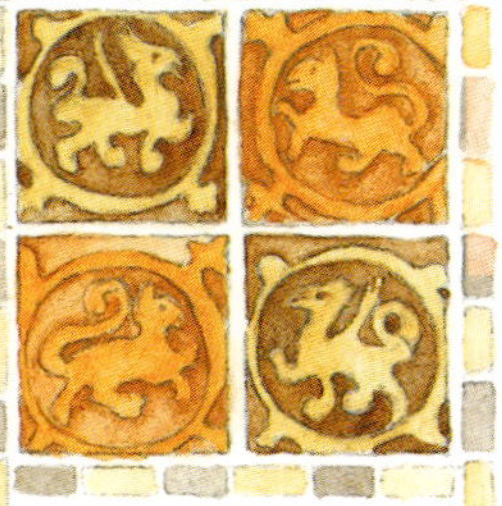

OVERLEAF (BACKGROUND) *Tile mosaic from Byland Abbey.*

OVERLEAF (INSET) *A fleur-de-lis decorated tile from Barnstaple, with the moulds used for impressing it.*

MOST Byzantine tiles were used in churches and many are decorated in polychrome with sacred subjects ranging from small medallions of saints to larger compositions of the Virgin and Child. Occasionally a religious picture was built up with a number of tiles. There are thought to have been tile-producing potteries in or near Constantinople (Istanbul), and there was also an important centre of production at Patleina in Bulgaria. Red-clay tiles decorated in relief with mythological animals were excavated from the site of the Carolingian imperial palace at Ulm, and other tiles, made of clay from the same area, have been excavated in Germany, suggesting that they all originated from a local workshop.

By the early 11th century the Mediterranean countries of Europe were beginning to show the influence of both Islamic and Byzantine pottery, and tiles, nearly always lead-glazed, were among the many wares that benefited from the greater diversity of ceramic craftsmanship that ensued. Because tiles have sometimes remained in the (usually ecclesiastical) buildings for which they were originally made, they can more often be dated and attributed than many other objects. Pavements of tiles with incised geometric patterns filled with green or brown glaze were laid in 12th-century Cistercian abbeys in France, while unglazed tiles with moulded decoration were being used for floors and walls in Germany and the Low Countries in the same period. Another type, dating from the mid-12th century, was found in the Basilica of St Denis: small monochrome tiles of various shapes were fitted together, mosaic-like, to form designs.

It was the spread of the Cistercian order to England that undoubtedly promoted first mosaic and later other types of decorative floor tiling in England. The Cistercians, the reformed ascetic order that broke away from the Benedictines under Bernard of Clairvaux in 1098, were dubbed 'the missionaries of Gothic architecture' and their grandiose if austere building schemes did much to disseminate the Gothic style throughout Europe.

At the remote English abbeys of Foun-

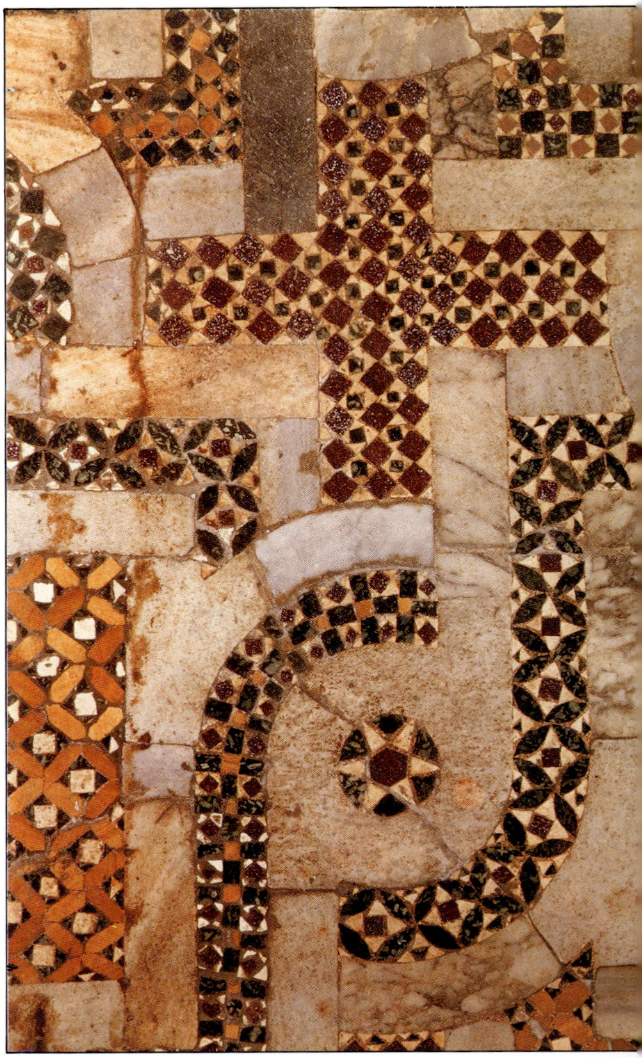

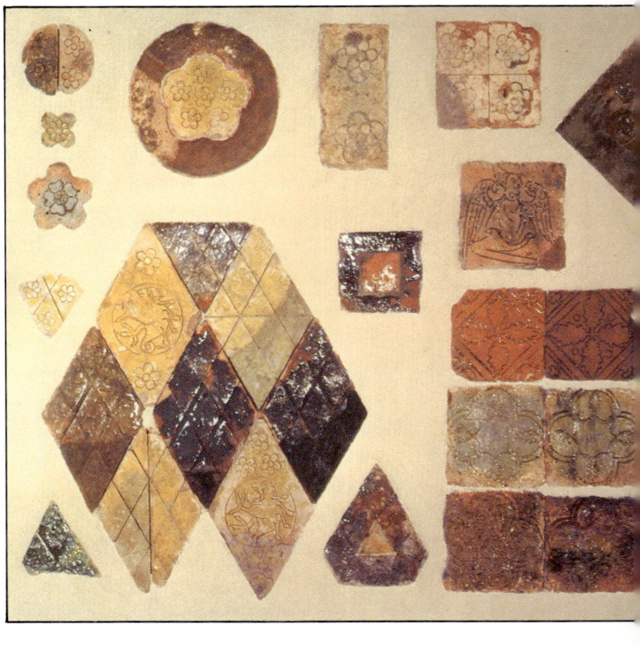

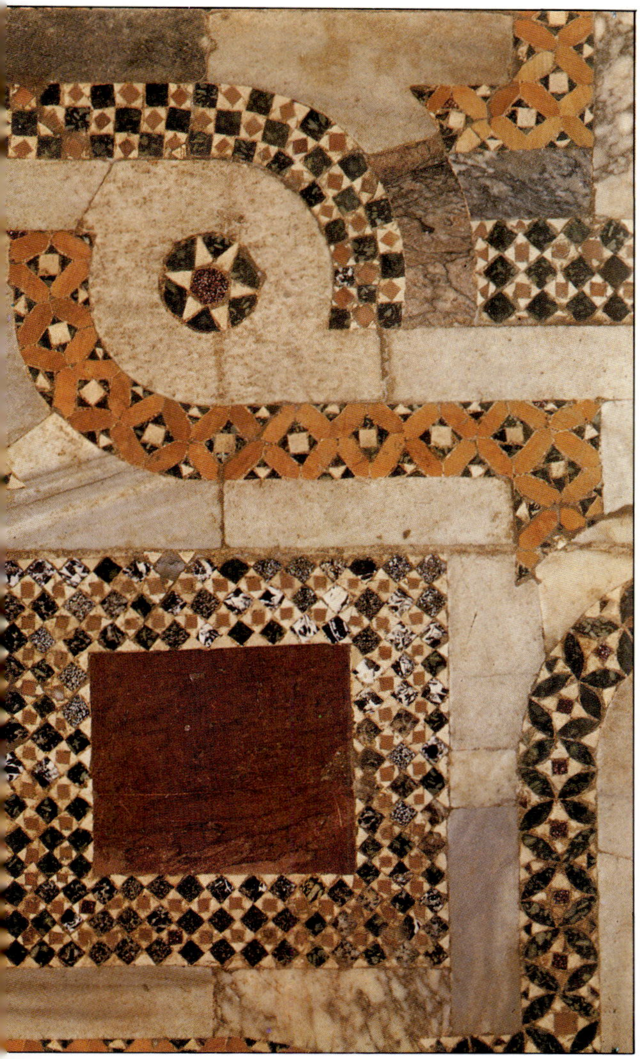

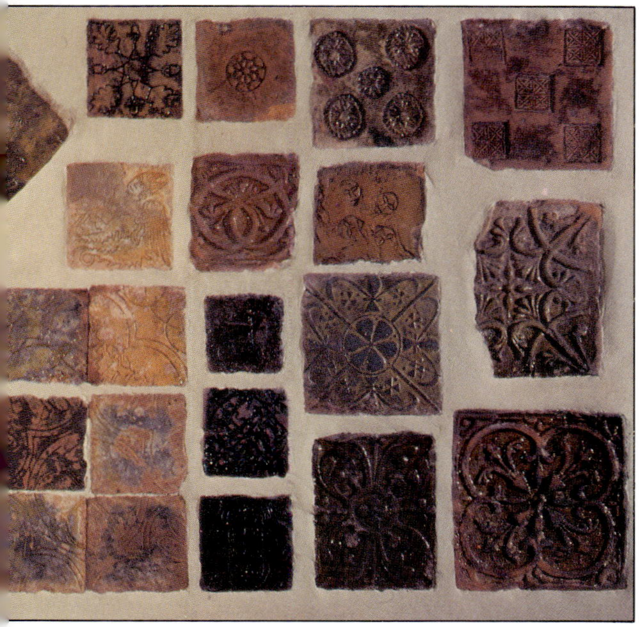

tains, Byland, Rievaulx, Melrose, Meaux and others, the Cistercians established tile-producing potteries and, during the 12th and early 13th centuries, employed large numbers of local people to make the complicated geometric floor tiles that have come to be regarded as the earliest examples of decorative tiling in England. Rectangles, rhomboids, triangles, circles, squares and more complicated lobed forms, polygons, florets and even fleurs-de-lis — all in shades of brown, yellow, green and grey — were set in astonishingly rich patchworks on monastic floors.

As with all north European medieval tiles, the colours in these were achieved by varying the clays and the lead glazes: no paints or enamels were used. Brown was obtained by applying a plain lead glaze to a red earthenware body; yellow by applying lead glaze over a slip of white-firing clay; green by adding copper to the glaze and applying this to white slip (light green) or red earthenware (dark green), and black by including a higher proportion of copper in the lead glaze and applying it to the red earthenware body.

The Cistercian style of mosaic tiling was apparently adopted at other potteries and persisted until the middle of the 14th century. One of the finest and latest examples is in Prior Crauden's Chapel at Ely, built in the 1320s, where some of the shaped mosaic tiles are further embellished with impressed patterns.

By this time the immensely complex mosaic designs were becoming simpler. Whereas in the early Cistercian pavements as many as 50 different tile shapes might be used at one site, the difficulties of firing the tiles successfully — shrinkage and warpage on these irregular forms of varying sizes must have been extremely difficult to predict, apart from the problems of glazing with relatively impure materials — eventually led their makers to look to easier methods of creating stylish effects.

Tiles of less varied shape but with line-impressed or relief decoration stamped on them like those in Prior Crauden's Chapel, were one development, and it was not long before these patterns impressed in the reddish-brown clay body were being inlaid

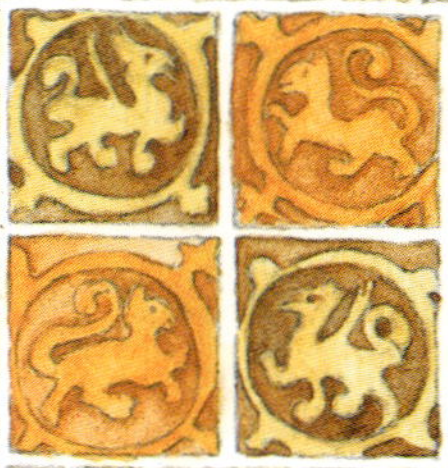

LEFT *Detail of the pavement in San Nicola, Bari, Italy.*

BELOW LEFT *Panel showing a selection of medieval impressed tiles.*

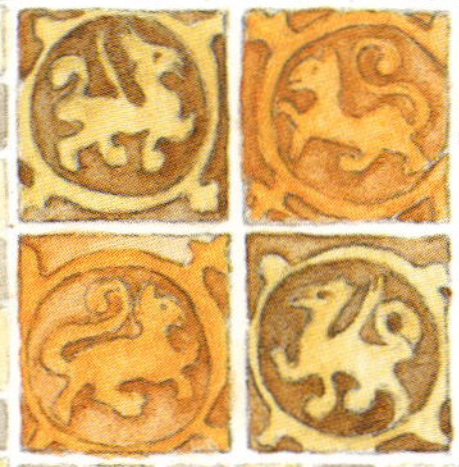

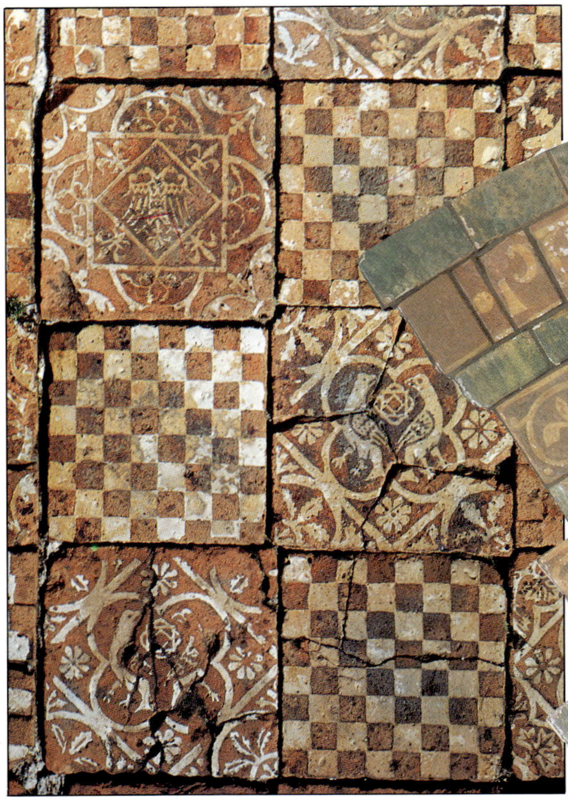

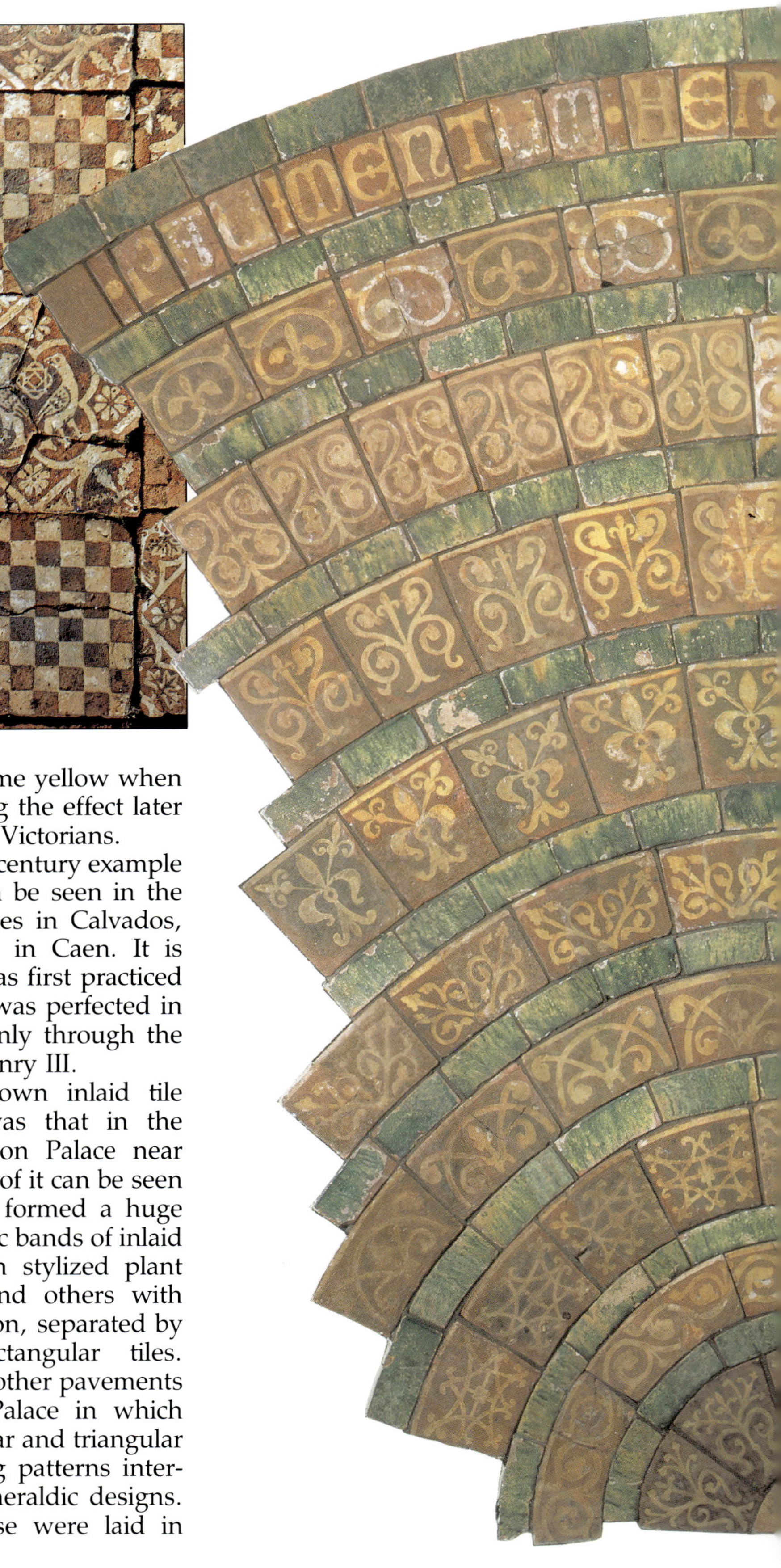

RIGHT *Inlaid tiles on the floor of the cloisters at Titchfield Abbey, Hampshire.*

CENTRE RIGHT *Part of the tiled pavement from Clarendon Palace.*

with a white slip that became yellow when glazed and fired, producing the effect later known as encaustic by the Victorians.

A late 12th- or early 13th-century example of this slip-inlaid tiling can be seen in the church of St-Pierre-sur-Dives in Calvados, and another at St-Etienne in Caen. It is likely that the technique was first practiced in northern France, but it was perfected in 13th-century England, mainly through the unstinting patronage of Henry III.

Among the earliest known inlaid tile pavements in England was that in the King's Chapel at Clarendon Palace near Salisbury, built *c* 1244. Part of it can be seen at the British Museum: it formed a huge circular pattern of concentric bands of inlaid tiles, some decorated with stylized plant motifs and fleurs-de-lis and others with letters forming an inscription, separated by smaller green-glazed rectangular tiles. Slightly later, in the 1250s, other pavements were laid at Clarendon Palace in which panels of square, rectangular and triangular tiles were laid in repeating patterns interspersed with animal and heraldic designs. Inlaid tiles similar to these were laid in

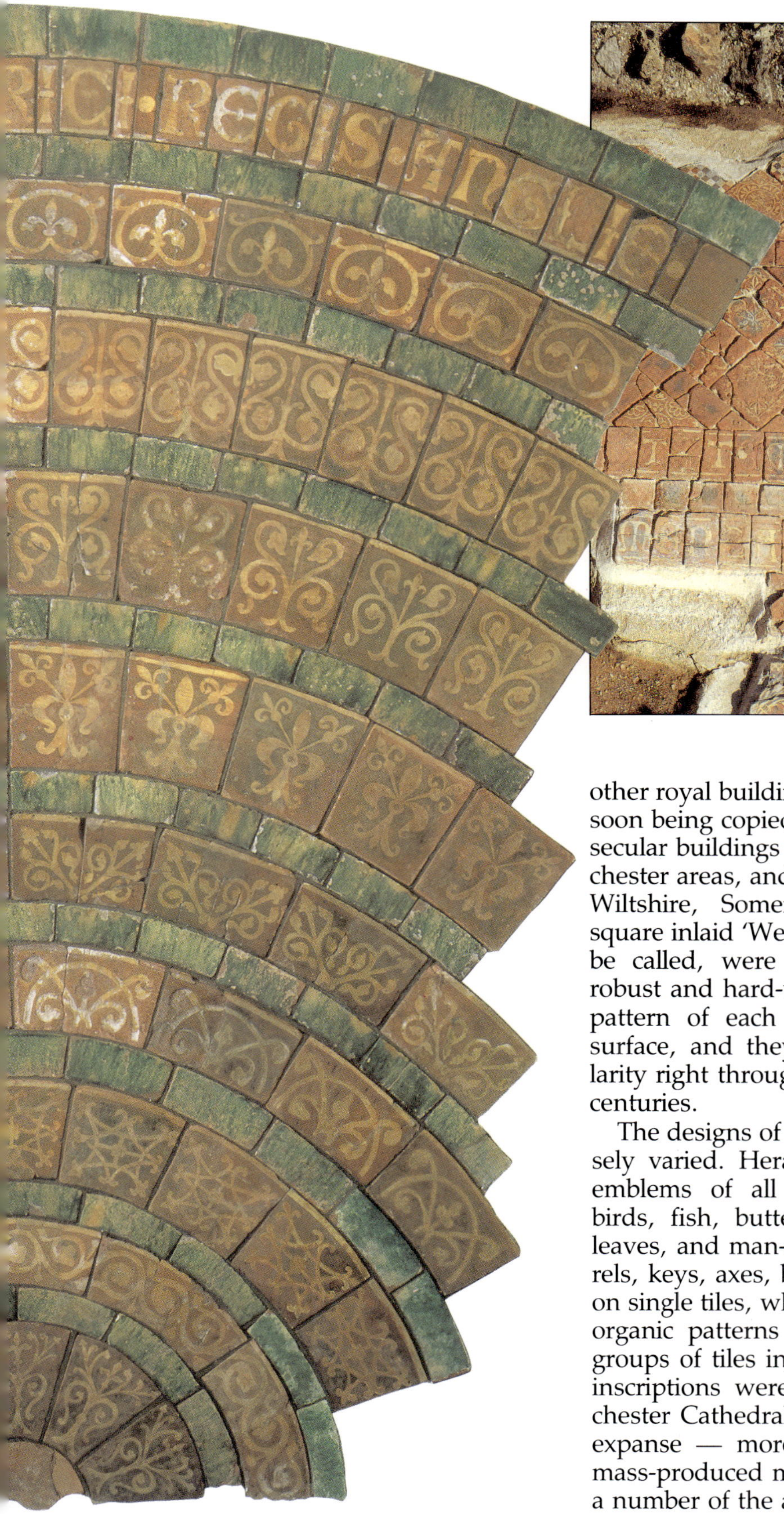

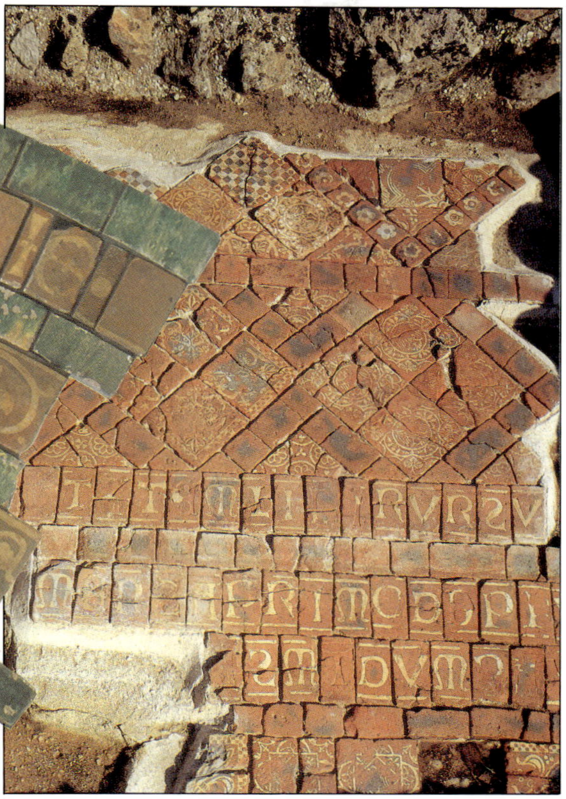

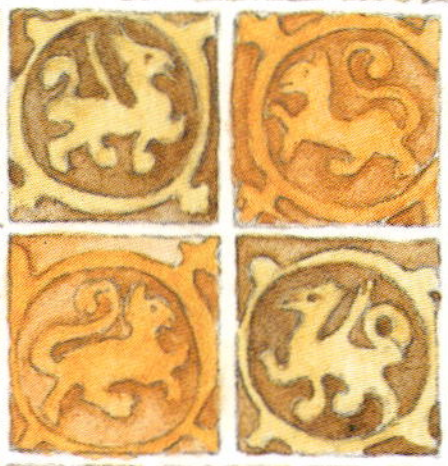

CHAPTER FOUR

•

LEFT *Plain and inlaid tiles from Titchfield Abbey cloisters.*

other royal buildings of Henry III, and were soon being copied in both ecclesiastical and secular buildings in the Salisbury and Winchester areas, and later all over Hampshire, Wiltshire, Somerset and Dorset. These square inlaid 'Wessex tiles', as they came to be called, were not only decorative but robust and hard-wearing, as the inlaid slip pattern of each tile was flush with the surface, and they maintained their popularity right through the 14th and early 15th centuries.

The designs of Wessex tiles were immensely varied. Heraldic and pseudo-heraldic emblems of all kinds abound; animals, birds, fish, butterflies, fruit, flowers and leaves, and man-made objects such as barrels, keys, axes, bells and buildings appear on single tiles, while geometric and stylized organic patterns were often used to link groups of tiles in composite arrangements; inscriptions were used occasionally. Winchester Cathedral has the largest surviving expanse — more than 5,000 — of these mass-produced medieval inlaid tiles. While a number of the abbeys and priories appar-

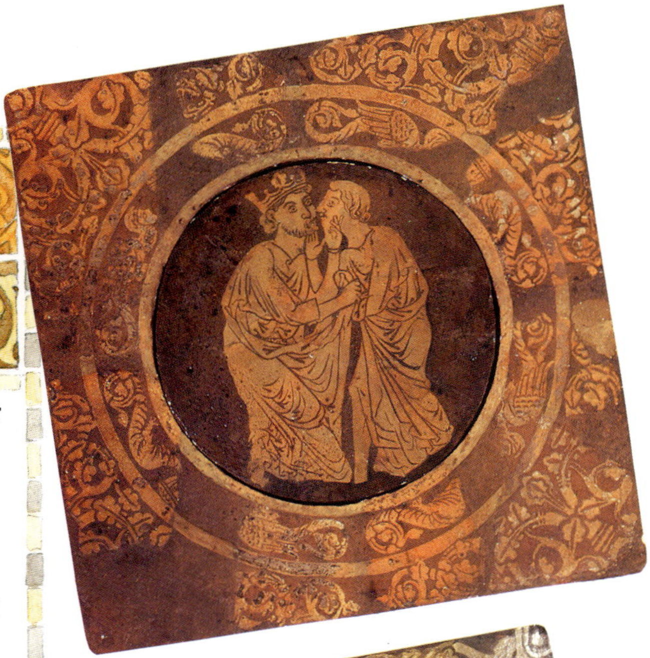

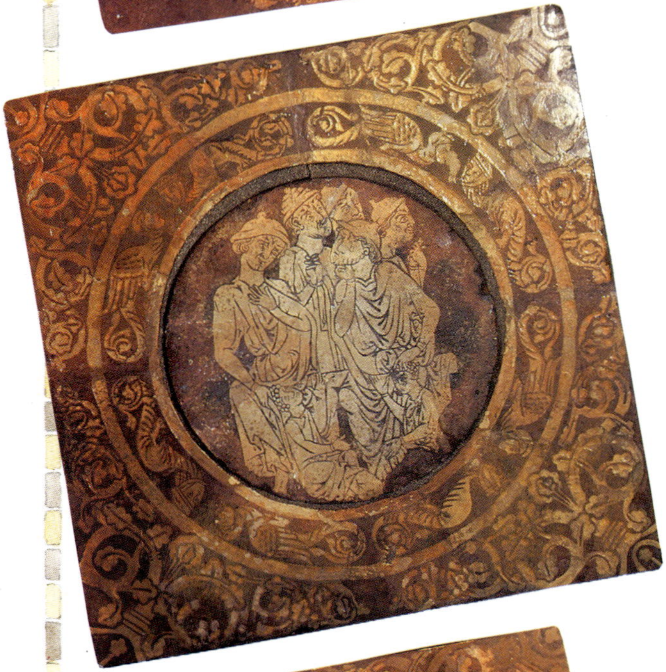

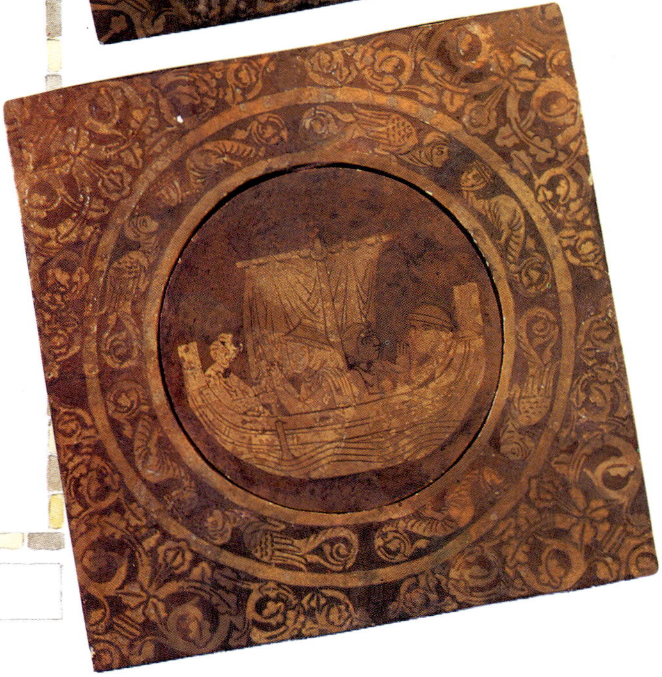

RIGHT *Three of the famous inlaid tiles made at Chertsey Abbey, Surrey, during the 1260s and 1270s.*

ently had their own tile workshops, many of these tiles were made by itinerant craftsmen who travelled around the area taking their design stamps with them and setting up kilns and workshops wherever a major paving commission demanded.

Tiles of a similar type were made in France and the Low Countries during the 13th, 14th and 15th centuries, generally by itinerant craftsmen. They were decorated with heraldic motifs, fleurs-de-lis, animals, birds and fishes, while human figures became common from the 14th century onward. Scenes of hunting and falconry, and of jugglers and tumblers provide glimpses of contemporary life, and a few are inscribed with the names of makers or donors, or with medieval maxims.

The highest peak of excellence in inlaid tiling was reached in the tiles made at Chertsey Abbey in Surrey during the 1260s and 1270s. They illustrate the romance of Tristan and Isolde and scenes from the exploits of Richard Coeur de Lion in roundels surrounded by shaped tiles inlaid with scrolling patterns and mythological beasts, sometimes with inscriptions. These mosaic-type tiles (since they relied upon their shape as well as their surface decoration for their patterned effect) were used at Chertsey Abbey itself, as well as at Westminster Abbey, and conform to the courtly style apparent in other manifestations of Henry III's wide-ranging artistic patronage.

Chertsey-type decorated tiles were used at Hailes Abbey in Gloucestershire and at Halesowen Abbey in Warwickshire and, in the same way that the Clarendon Palace tiles led to a widespread diffusion of similar inlaid tiles in the south and west of England, these Chertsey-Westminster tiles were influential in the area north of the Thames. Major tile industries were established in Warwickshire and Nottinghamshire in the 14th century, and their products have been found on sites all over the Midlands and in parts of Yorkshire.

During the middle decades of the 14th century tiles were also produced on a commercial scale in the Chilterns, notably at Penn in Buckinghamshire, where a more commercial method of decoration, possibly developed earlier in Nottinghamshire or

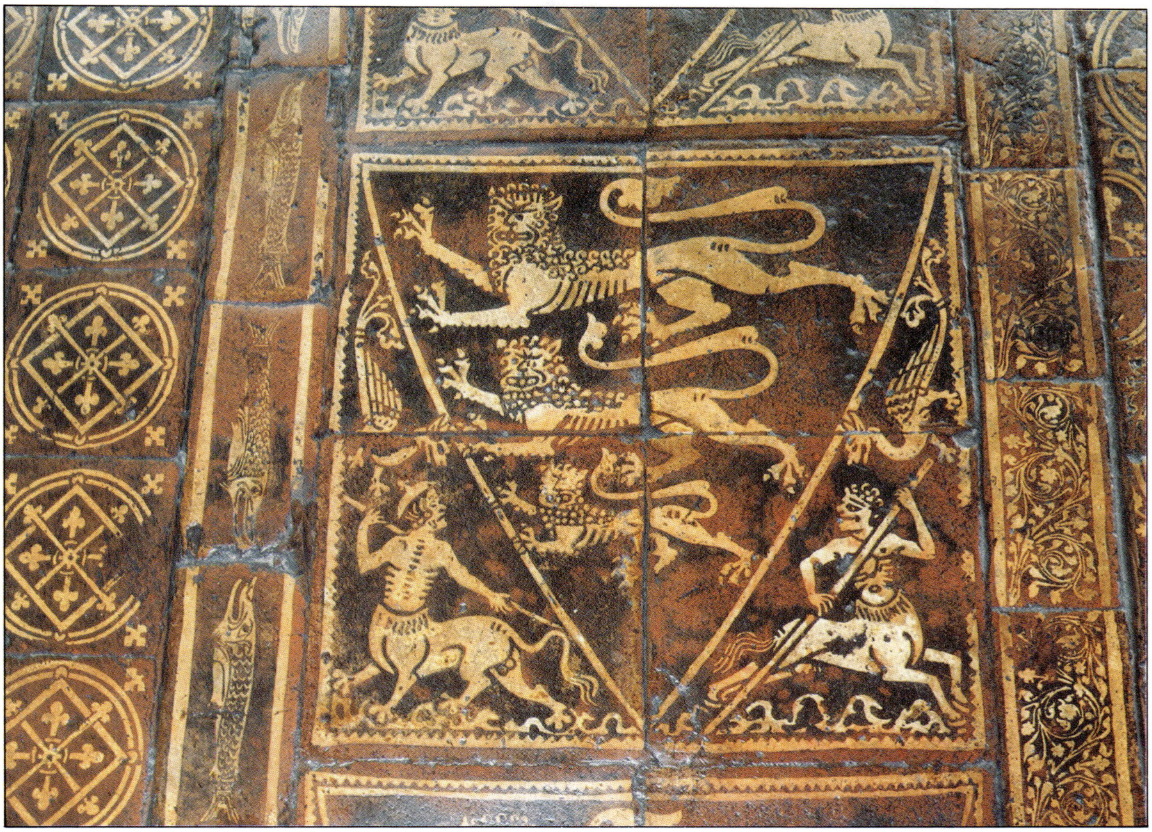

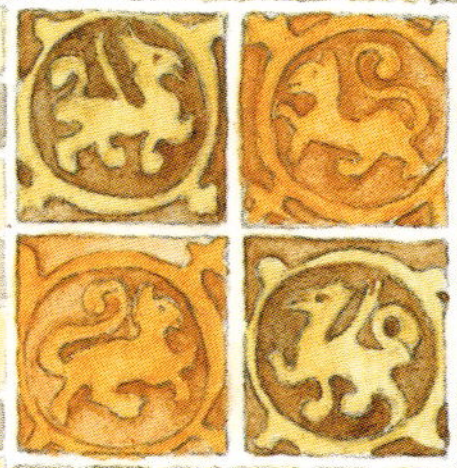

CHAPTER FOUR

•

LEFT *Inlaid tiles from Westminster Abbey, 13th century.*

Warwickshire, was used. Instead of inlaying the white slip into the pre-stamped tiles, the two processes were combined by 'printing', or stamping the tiles with a die dipped into slip. This was obviously a much quicker and more economical way to decorate tiles and the Penn tile-makers further decreased their material costs by reducing the size of the tiles themselves. This meant that the tiles could be made thinner without danger of warping in the kiln, with the same ease of firing and transport as in smaller, lighter tiles. Their one disadvantage was that the surface decoration was less hard-wearing than that of the inlaid Wessex-type tiles. These mass-produced tiles from the Chilterns area, often referred to as Penn tiles although they were made in a number of locations, were not only supplied to many of the local parish churches but also to royal households and important abbeys.

Late in the 14th and during the early years of the 15th centuries, printed tiles were being made in and around London, possibly by workers who had moved from the Chilterns when the industry there began to decline. Another type was made in the Midlands in the later 15th century but these appear to be unconnected with the Penn-style tiles; typically, they are decorated with heraldic motifs similar to those on earlier Midlands tiles.

In the Severn basin inlaid tiles of the old Wessex type were still being made in the mid-15th century. Known as Malvern School tiles (both tiles and a tile kiln were found at Great Malvern), they have been found all through the Severn area and into Warwickshire, and as far west as St David's in Wales. They are characterized by their chunky size and by their architectural style of decoration, often covering the whole surface of the tile. Some are rectangular. A number of these rectangular, castle-decorated tiles, once forming part of a wall panel surrounding the high altar in the priory church at Great Malvern, can be seen at the British Museum, and so can the magnificent Canynges Pavement, so called because it came from the house of William Canynges, a leading Bristol merchant. It is

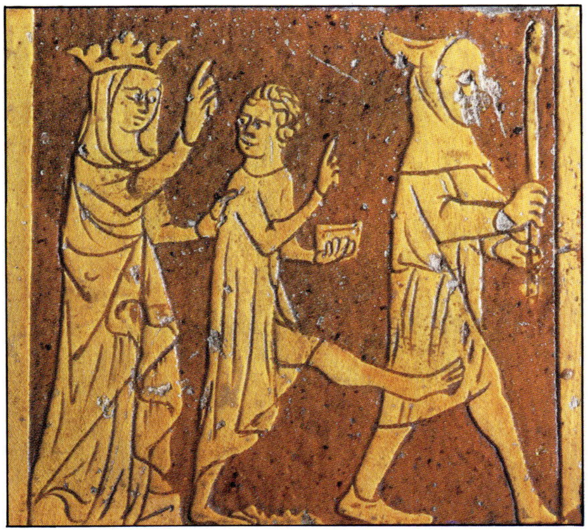

RIGHT *One of the sgraffito-decorated Tring tiles depicting scenes from the apocryphal stories of Christ's childhood.*

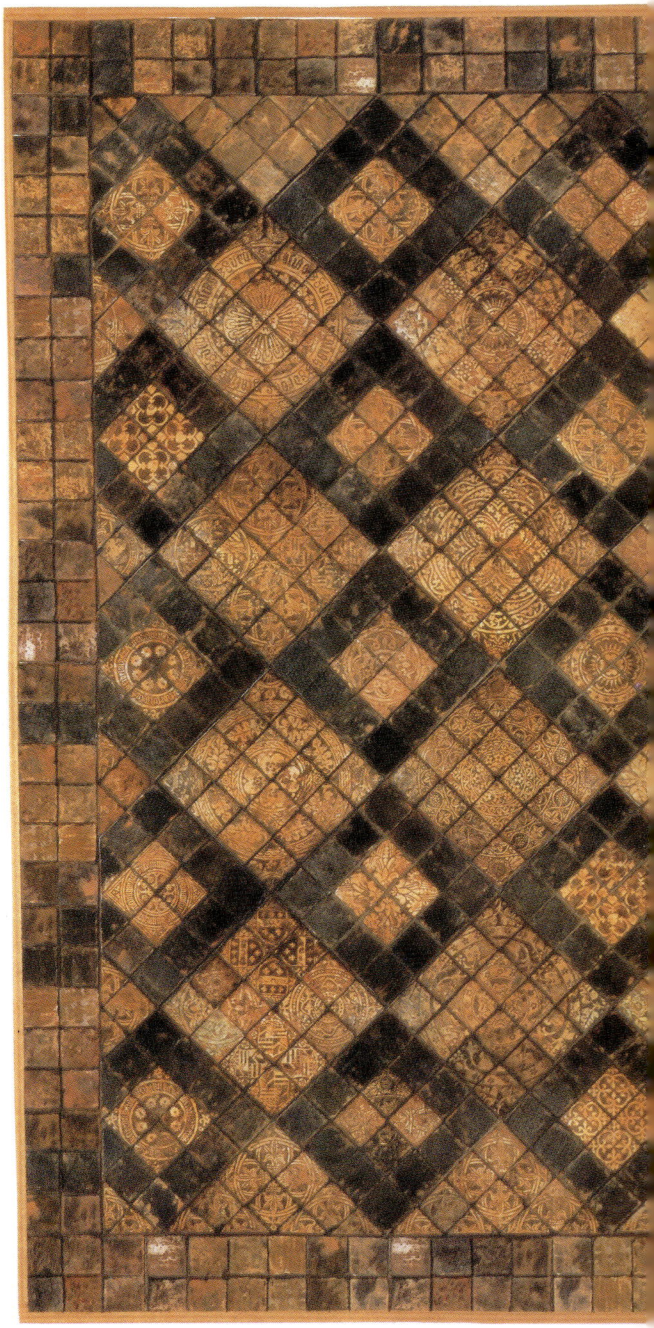

thought to have been laid about 1460 and consists of 16- and 4-tile patterns framed by dark tiles. The designs are secular — roses, grapes and vine leaves, stylized plants and tendrils, animals and heraldic emblems. Tewkesbury Abbey also has many inlaid medieval tiles, including good examples of the Malvern School in particular.

Malvern-type tiles in a modified form and of varying quality were made in the Gloucestershire, Warwickshire, Leicestershire and Buckinghamshire areas during the early 16th century, but the dissolution of the monasteries from the 1530s effectively put an end to the production of inlaid medieval floor tiles on any major scale.

Apart from the two-colour inlaid and printed tiles of the medieval period, relief-decorated tiles in monochrome — in the later period usually glazed yellow or dark green but sometimes light green or brown — were produced in many parts of Europe from the 13th to the 16th century. They were made from blocks that stamped the design onto the tiles either in relief or counter-relief. The earliest relief tiles were unglazed, and were made in the Alsace region in the second half of the 12th century. The technique later spread southward to Switzerland and Austria, northward through the Rhineland and Friesland, and eventually to England.

A flourishing glazed relief tile industry is known to have existed at Bawsey near King's Lynn in Norfolk in the latter half of the 14th century. Designs include heraldic motifs, inscriptions, animals, birds and stylized plants. Another group, dating from the later 15th or early 16th century, comes from Leicestershire, and a still later production, in Barnstaple, Devon, can be dated as late as the 17th and early 18th centuries.

There was another type of decoration on medieval tiles that was atypical and, as far as we know, not used for floor tiles. A famous frieze of 14th-century wall tiles known as the Tring tiles (now in the British

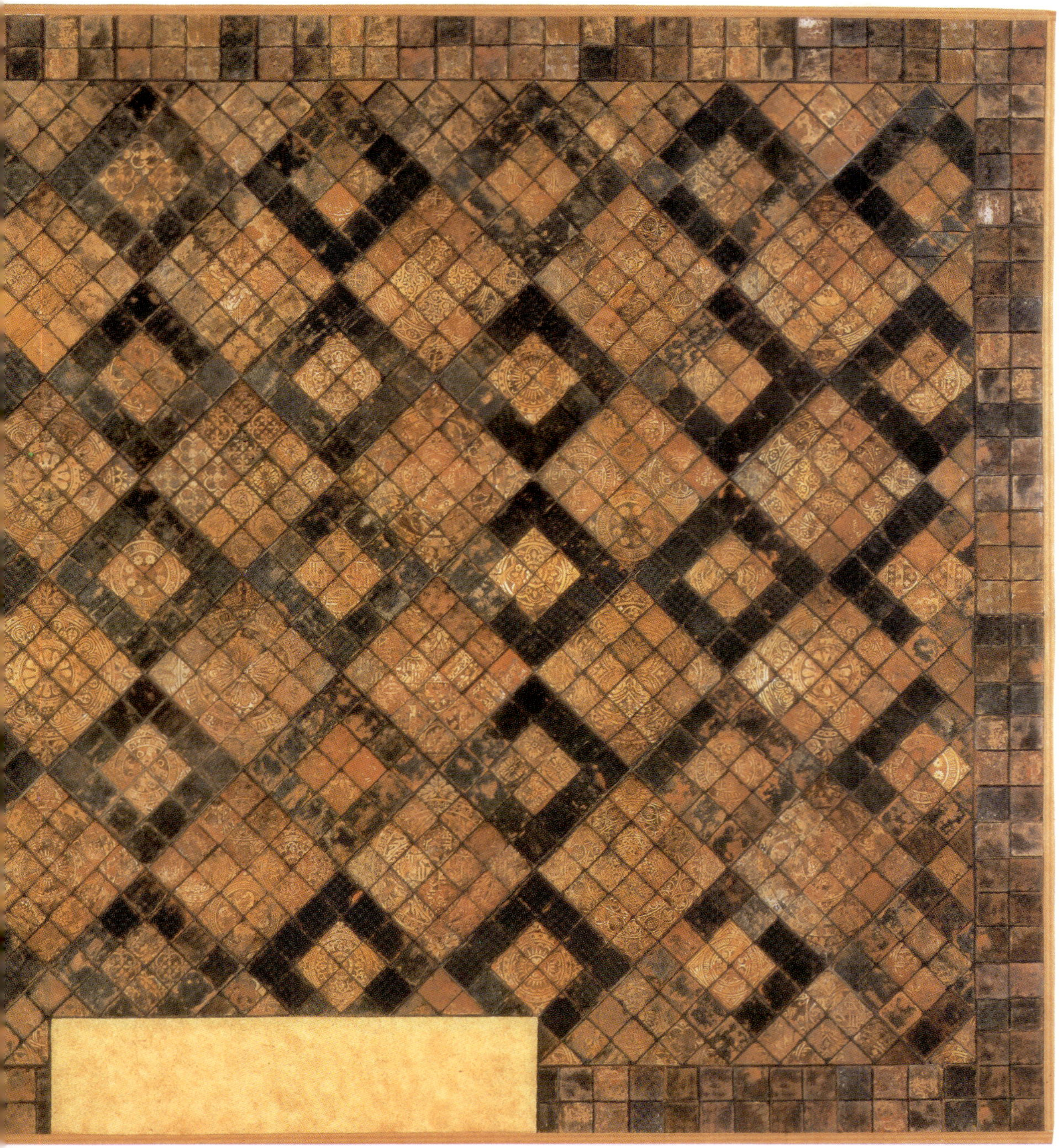

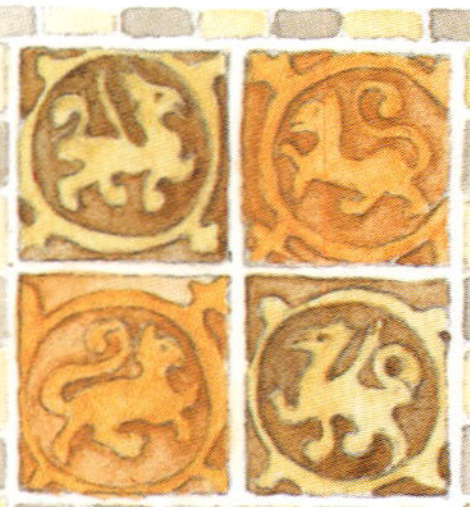

CHAPTER FOUR

•

LEFT *The tiled pavement originally laid in William Canynges' house in Bristol, c. 1460.*

Museum) is decorated by the sgraffito method with scenes from apocryphal stories of the childhood of Jesus. The design was incised onto a slip-coated tile and the background slip was then removed, leaving the yellowish glazed design raised on a brown background. The method was in use for domestic pottery at this time, but if it had been used for floor tiles, it is unlikely that such raised designs could have survived the wear and tear of so many years.

By the early 16th century fashions were changing. Apart from the practical upheavals caused by the Reformation, and in particular the dissolution of the monasteries in England, Renaissance influence was percolating to the north of Europe. Like everything else, the ceramics industry was affected, chiefly by the introduction of the tin-glazing, or maiolica, technique from Italy and Spain, which had a far-reaching effect on the tile industry.

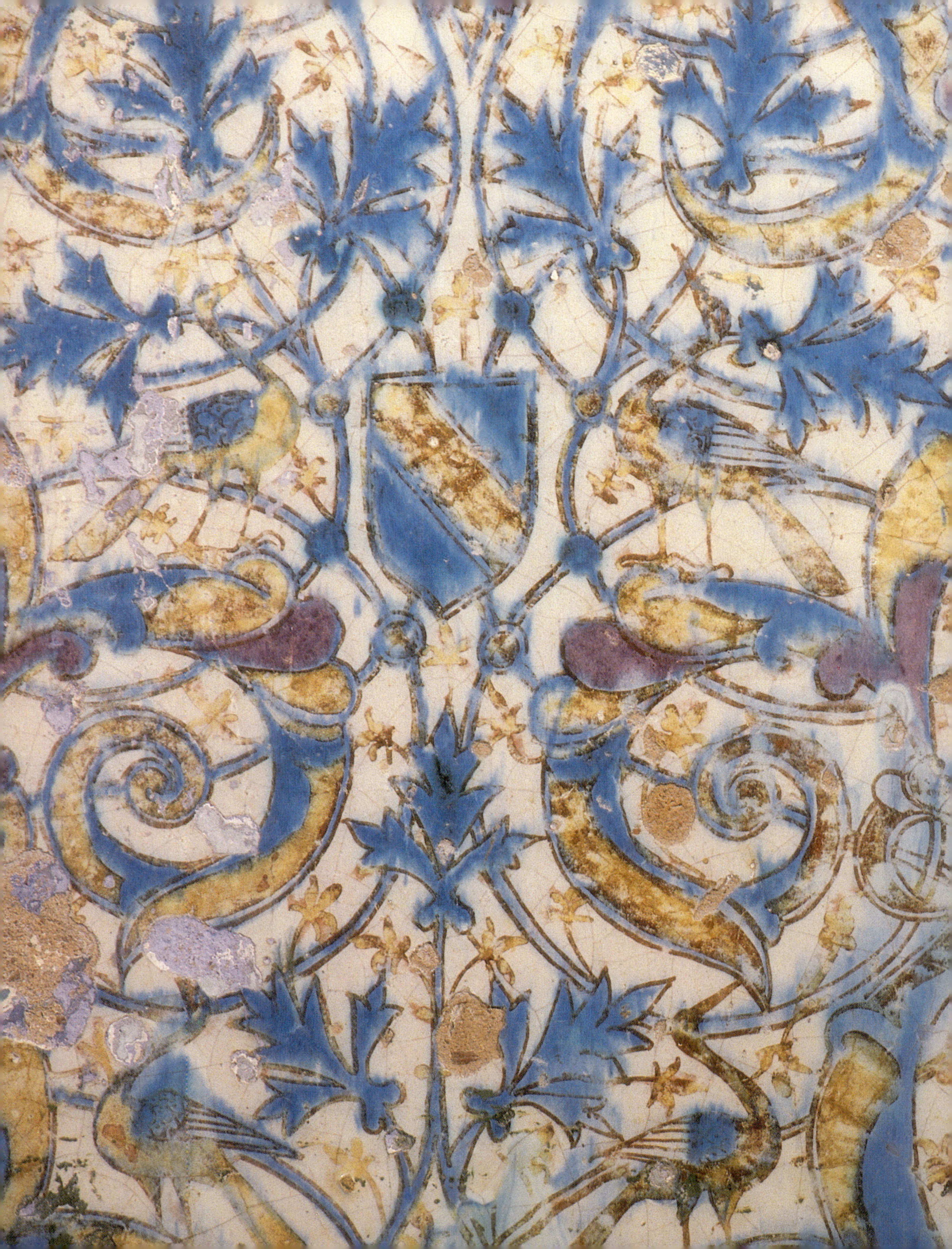

CHAPTER FIVE

EARLY EUROPEAN TIN GLAZING

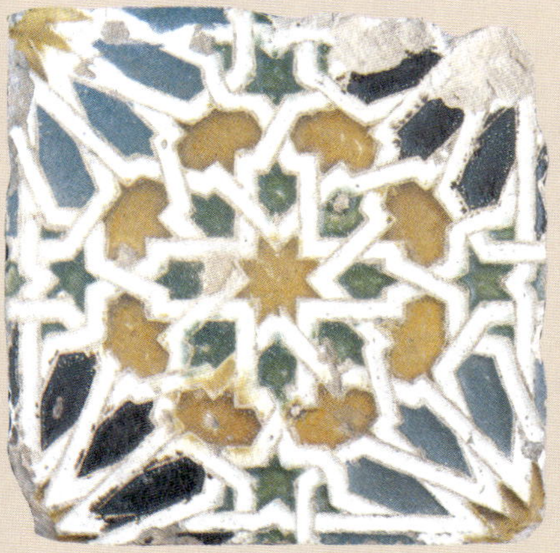

As might be expected, the technique of tin-glazing earthenware, so effectively practiced in the Islamic world, came to Europe through the Iberian Peninsula, one of the last outposts of Islam in an otherwise Christian sphere of influence. Tin-glazed wares are known to have been made in southern Spain in the early 11th century, but the first regular production was probably established in the 13th century at Malaga. The introduction of cobalt in the early 13th century was a major milestone in the history of European ceramics: the blues now available to potters did much to emphasize the whiteness of the tin glaze, and were admirably combined with lustre pigments. Malaga and other Andalusian potteries became famous for lustre and blue pottery, a good deal of which was exported from an early period.

OVERLEAF (BACKGROUND) *Tile, probably from the Alhambra Palace, Granada, 14th century. Enclosed in the foliage design are the arms of the Nasrid kings.*

OVERLEAF (INSET) *Spanish tile decorated by the* cuenca *technique.*

RIGHT *Detail of the tiling on the walls of the Patio de los Arrayanes, Alhambra Palace.*

THE IMPORTANCE of Malaga was further enhanced by the provision of tiles and other wares for the buildings of the Nasrid kings of Granada, notably the Alhambra Palace in the second half of the 14th century. Many of the dado panels still to be seen there consist of *alicatados*, or small geometric-shaped tiles of green, black, greyish-blue, brown and yellow set in repeating patterns against white-tile borders, as well as more complex designs formed from fragments of larger tiles set into a plaster backing. Stylistically these are derived from the 13th-century mosaic tile work of the Seljuks, the best examples of which may be seen at Konya in Turkey, but neither Malaga nor the other pottery centres in Andalusia produced exclusively Islamic wares.

Lustre-decorated tiles were used to cover the walls and pavements of important buildings in many parts of 13th- and early 14th-century Spain, and evidence of artistic contact with the surrounding Christian communities is often strong. Muslim motifs and designs based on Kufic script are combined with European subjects such as jousting knights, heraldry and other medieval themes, and demand from the Christian communities, which provided many commissions, led to an increased introduction of European stylistic elements.

From Malaga, even in this early period, tin-glazed earthenwares were exported to other parts of Europe, notably France, Italy and England, as well as to different regions of the Islamic world, and knowledge of tin-glazing techniques was beginning to spread within Spain itself. Other lustre potteries were established in the region of Valencia, where that of Manises superseded Malaga in importance by the opening years of the 15th century. Spanish lustre wares were especially popular in Italy from about 1450 onward, and important pieces were prized status symbols among the nobility. It was at this time that they began to be known as 'maiolica' wares, because they passed from Valencia to Italy via the island of Majorca.

Square tiles known as *losetas* and long-shaped hexagons called *alfardones* were made in the more northerly towns of Manises, Paterna and Teruel in Aragon,

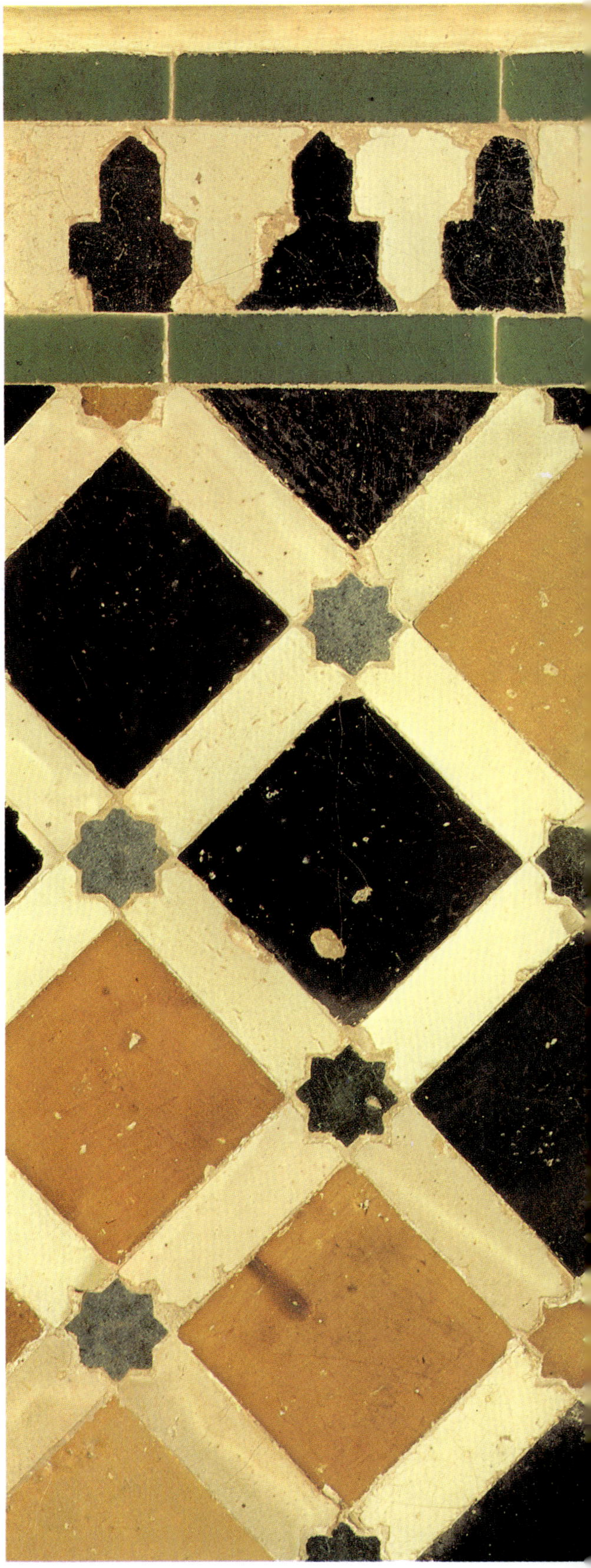

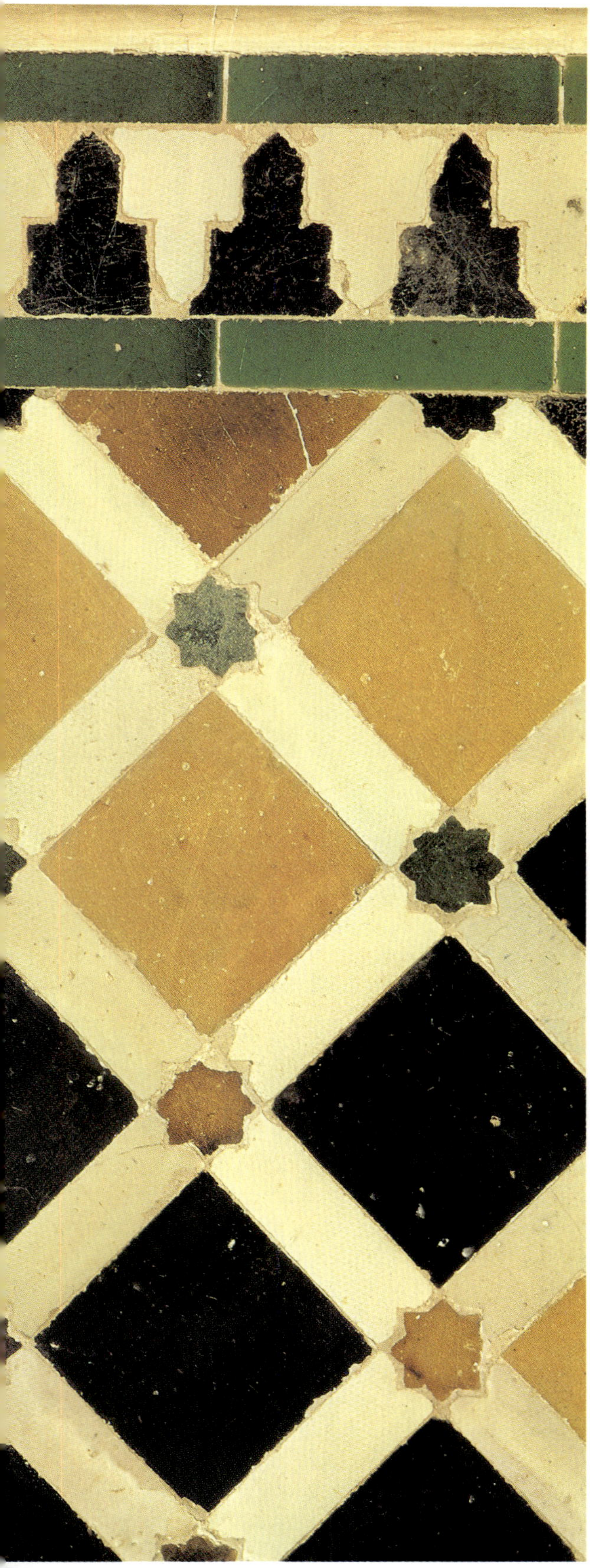

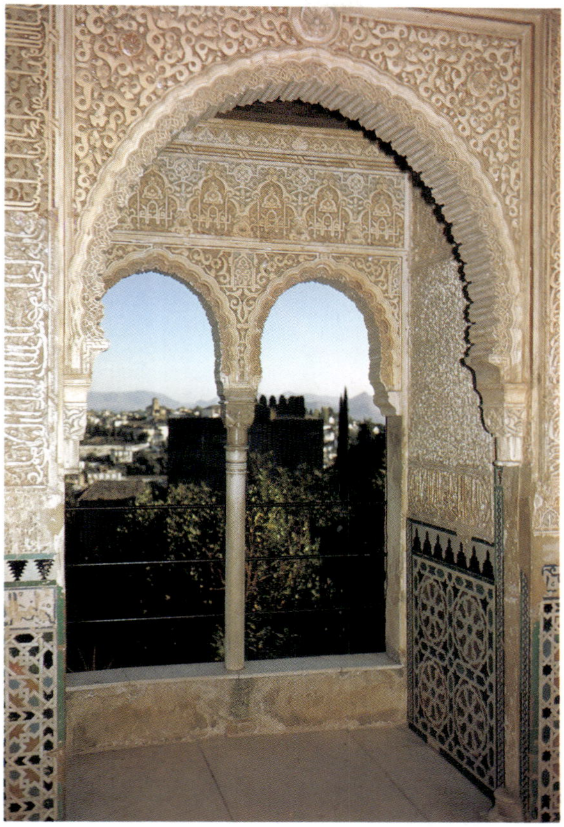

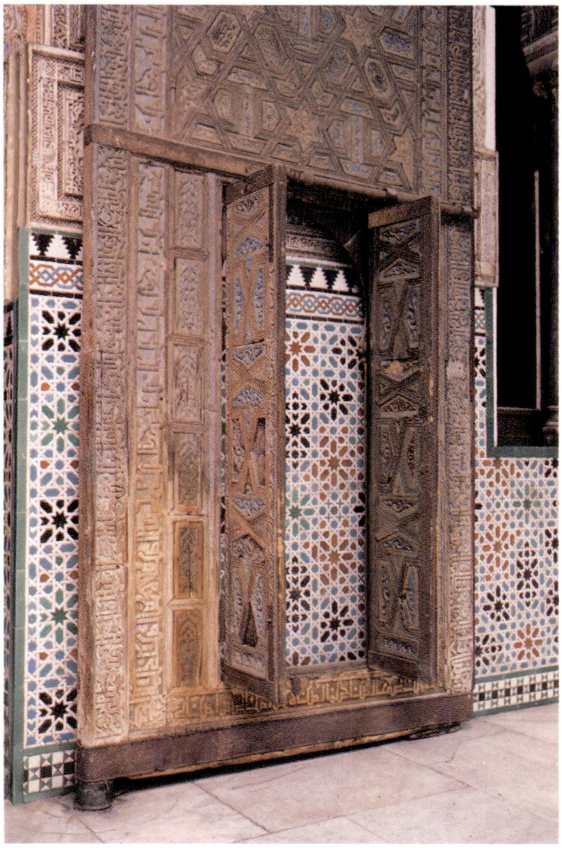

CHAPTER FIVE

•

LEFT *Tiled dado panels and view from the Alhambra Palace.*

BELOW LEFT *Panels of alicatados in the Court of the Maidens, Alcazar, Seville.*

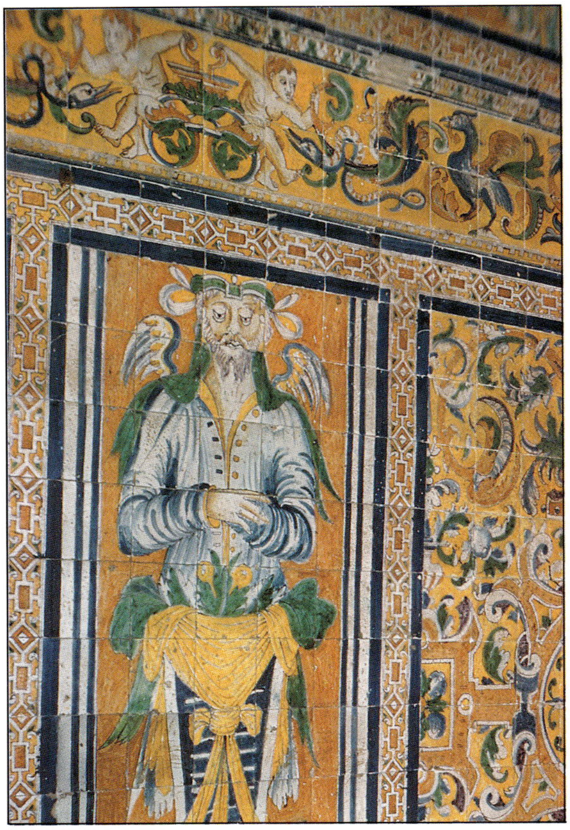

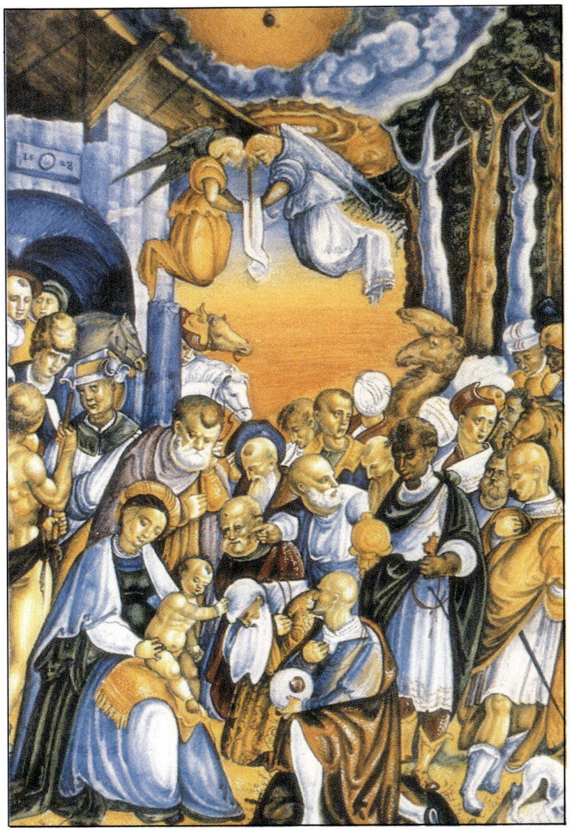

RIGHT *Tiles by Cristobal de Augusta, 1577-79, in the Hall of Charles V, Alcazar, Seville.*

FAR RIGHT *Italian maiolica* istoriato *plaque depicting the Adoration of the Magi, made in Faenza,* c. *1528.*

and in Barcelona and Manresa in Catalonia. The mingling of Moorish with Christian-Gothic designs continued, and was known as the *mudejar* style.

Toledo and Seville were important centres of production for architectural ceramics, including tiles, during the 15th and 16th centuries, and the small geometric *alicatados* were by this time replaced by the larger *azulejos*, a name also adopted in Portugal for decorative wall tiles.

One of the methods of decoration used at Seville and Toledo was *cuerda seca*, a technique imported from the Near East but known in Spain since the 11th century. *Cuerda seca* was used extensively for tiles in the late 15th and early 16th centuries.

In Spain during the early 16th century, however, the *cuerda seca* technique began to give way to the *cuenca*, in which the tile design was impressed with a mould, leaving indentations bordered by raised lines. The coloured glazes were held in these depressions and divided from each other during firing by the raised outlines. The softly textured surface resulting from this is reminiscent of *champlevé* enamels. *Cuenca*-glazed tiles, decorated with Moresque geometric and plant motifs, were used for dados and pavements in southern Spain, and were also exported in large quantities to Portugal, the West Indies and Italy during the middle decades of the 16th century.

For several centuries, until the reign of Philip II (1556–98), the Moors and the Christians of Spain had co-existed, culturally speaking, and both had benefited from a healthy exchange of ideas and craftsmanship. This was exemplified in the Hispano-Moresque pottery of the 15th and 16th centuries, which continued to play an influential part in ceramic developments all over Europe until the Counter-Reformation and its aftermath. From the mid-16th century onward, the Moors were increasingly hounded and finally, in 1610, they were expelled from the Iberian Peninsula, to the detriment of the pottery industry. Spanish lustre ware never regained its respected position among European ceramics, and from this time Spain became the recipient rather than the provider of foreign influences.

Meanwhile, in Italy the art of maiolica was reaching its peak. The first tin-glazed wares to be made in Italy date from the 11th or 12th century, but the art's great flowering, on tiles as on most other wares, took place in the late 15th century. This was as much due to the enormous progress in enlarging the palette of colours available to the pottery artist as to the development and perfecting of his techniques. Most important of all, there was a profusion of patrons wealthy and discerning enough to create a demand for these prestigious works of art — for the best maiolica wares of Renaissance Italy were, for the first time in European ceramic history, elevated to an artistic level equal to jewellery and silver.

The first manifestations of the new richness of colour and design in Italian maiolica appeared in the style known as 'Gothic floral', which was best seen on tiles. Central subjects such as portraits, plants, animals, heraldic emblems, sacred symbols, musical instruments, weapons and objects from everyday life are surrounded by borders in which a combination of classically inspired Renaissance motifs and Islamic-rooted decoration is brought together in dazzling harmony. Both square and hexagonal tiles were laid in pavements, and an outstanding example is still *in situ* in the basilica of San Petronio, Bologna. It consists of more than 1,000 hexagonal tiles made by Petrus Andrea of Faenza, dating from about 1487. These tiles, with their spectacular range of design and pattern ideas, must have been to pottery artists what samplers were to needlewomen, and their patterns reappear in later generations of decorative pottery all over Europe.

Faenza was at the forefront of ceramic innovation and was outstanding for both the sheer number of its workshops and the volume of its output; indeed the city was eventually to give its name to the tin-glazed earthenware of both France and Germany. But many other Italian cities were renowned for maiolica production, and tiles were produced in Florence, Siena, Casteldurante, Pesaro, Deruta and Perugia, among others. It is not often possible, however, to distinguish the tiles produced in one town from those of another, as craftsmen travelled about, taking their designs from workshop to workshop.

Portraits, heraldic devices, mottoes, grotesques and motifs symbolic of the new humanism were favourite subjects on 15th-century tiles. Typical of these are the square tiles made for Isabella d'Este for her apartments in the Palazzo Ducale in Mantua (*c* 1494), which can be seen today in the Victoria & Albert Museum, London. Both octagonal and irregular polygonal tiles were used in a pavement laid in the church of San Francesco at Forli in the early 16th century. They were probably made by an artist from Faenza and many of them — portraits, landscapes, animals, trophies, monsters and other motifs within borders — can also be seen in the Victoria & Albert Museum.

16th-century Siena is particularly associated with tiles decorated with grotesques, often on a black background. Sienese tiles also show a greater variety of shapes, including circles, lozenges and triangles as well as squares and hexagons, than others. One of the finest Sienese pavements was laid in the Palazzo Petrucci in 1509, some of whose tiles are now in the Victoria & Albert Museum.

A pavement made for the church of San Angelo in Deruta in 1524 (and now in the Museo Civico) is composed of cruciform and star-shaped tiles strongly reminiscent of Persian designs. The crosses are decor-

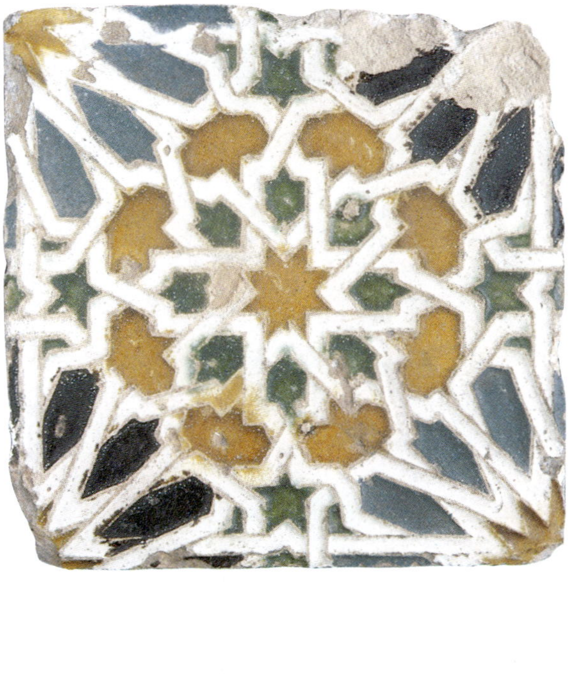

BELOW LEFT *Spanish tile decorated by the* cuenca *technique.*

RIGHT *The Luca Della Robbia relief plaques on the façade of the Ospedale degli Innocenti, Florence.*

BELOW RIGHT *Maiolica tile with the emblem of the Ordelaffi family, c. 1480-90.*

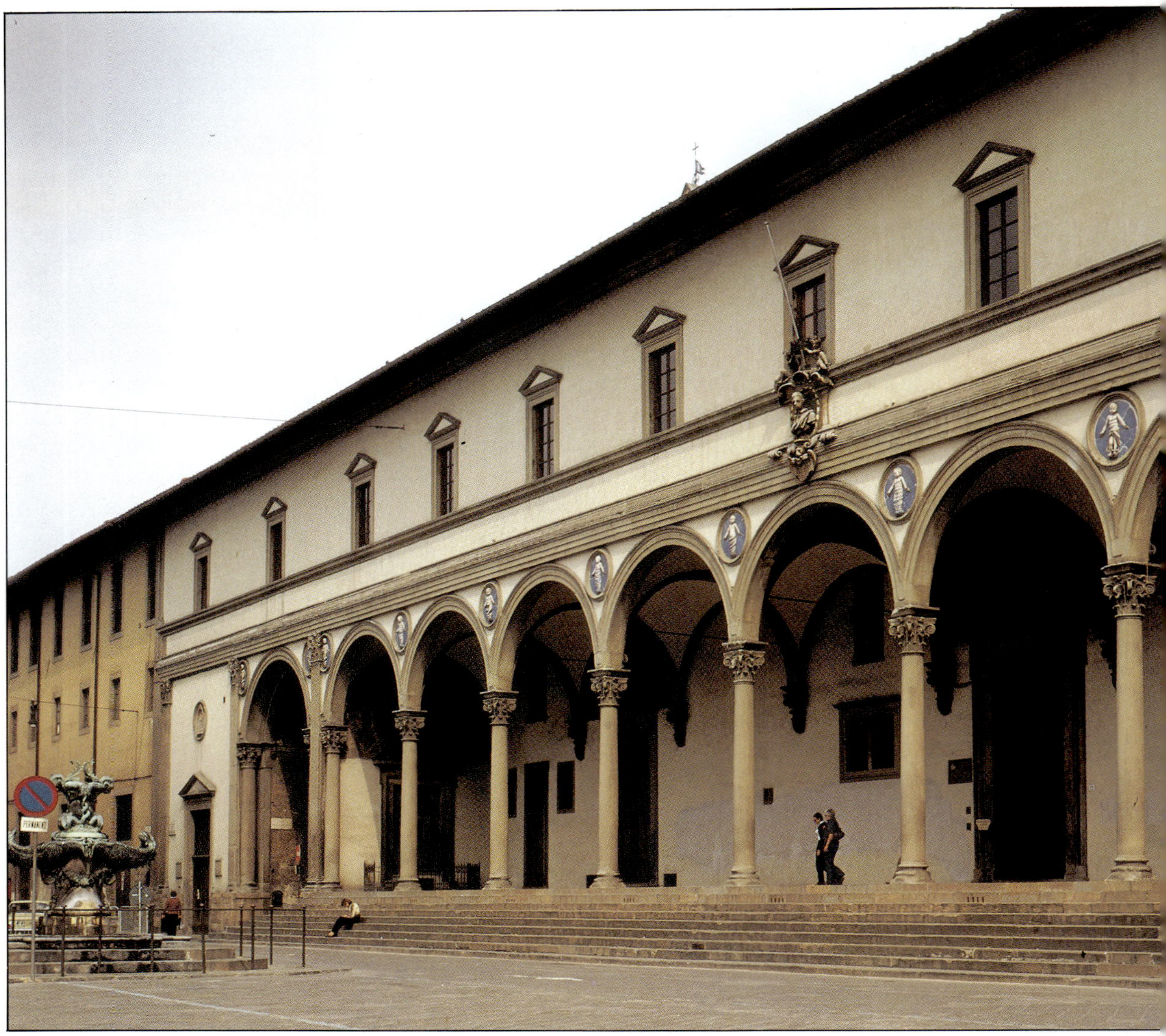

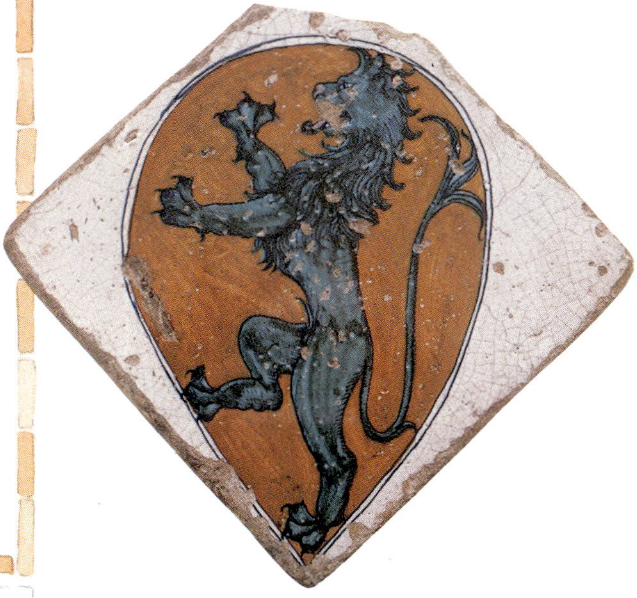

ated in white and yellow arabesques on a blue ground, and they surround the figurative scenes — mythological, sporting and religious — on the stars.

The Della Robbias of Florence, famous for their tin-glazed terracotta sculptures of the late 15th and 16th centuries, also produced tiles and wall panels, invariably of a religious nature. Their work stands apart from the mainstream of maiolica production: they used less vitreous glazes and thicker colours, and followed a different style. Above all, the work of the Della Robbias was a sculptural phenomenon, in contrast to the two-dimensional discipline of other maiolica artists. They were extremely influential, not only in Italy but abroad, and one of them, Girolamo, travelled to both

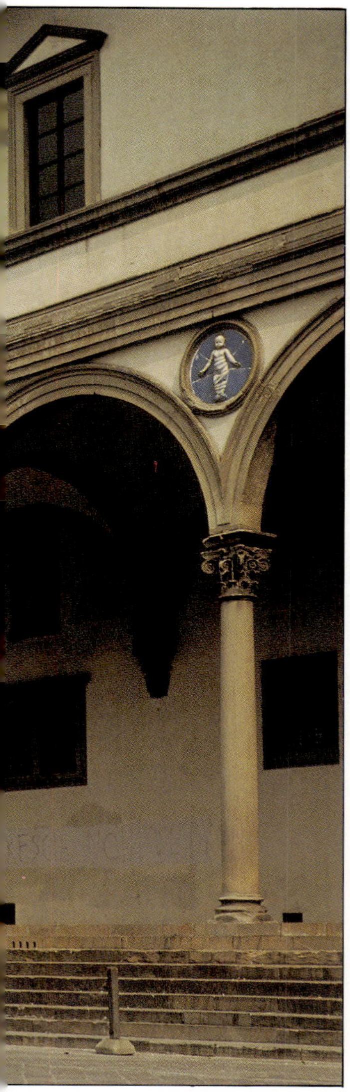

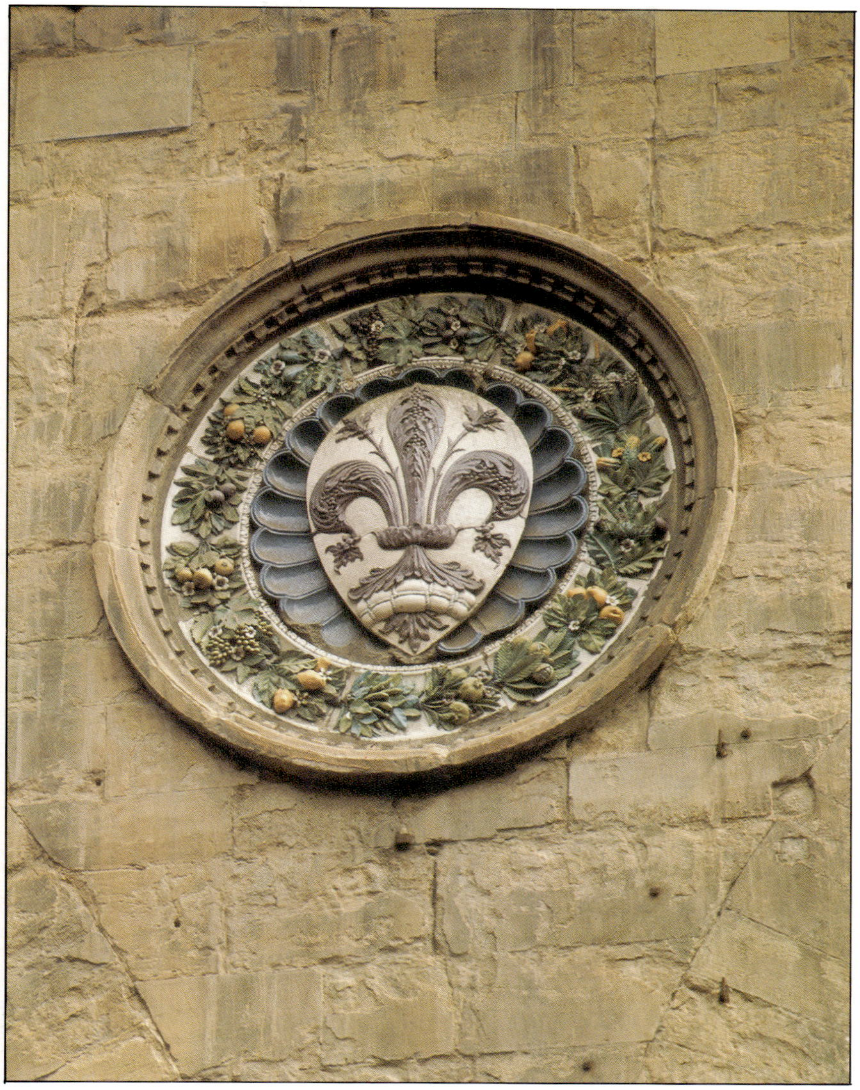

CHAPTER FIVE

•

LEFT *Della Robbia plaque with the arms of Florence on the outside wall of Orsanmichele, Florence.*

Spain and France.

By the early 16th century, artists from Faenza were beginning to paint narrative scenes on maiolica panels, and this soon developed into the *istoriato* style, the high point of Italian maiolica production, in which religious, historical and allegorical scenes were translated from contemporary engravings onto pottery. The *stile istoriato* is to be seen at its most splendid on the large dishes of the early to mid-16th century, but it also lent itself successfully to tiles, wall panels and plaques. It could be said that the use of mural medallions set into walls led to the development of the show-piece dish decorated in the *istoriato* style. Luca Della Robbia's relief plaques on the façade of the Ospedale degli Innocenti in Florence (finished in the 1440s) are early examples. Later, ceramic discs decorated with coats of arms or religious subjects were similarly displayed, often in honour of a building's owner or benefactor; it was a short step to the idea of the movable plaque, or dish, displayed inside a building.

While Italy was never as wholehearted as Spain and Portugal in the use of tiles for large-scale architectural decoration, they were used for walls, ceilings and church floors in various parts of the region well into the 16th century. Liguria, the area around Genoa, was particularly known for *laggioni*, or wall tiles, which were used in churches in much the same large-scale way as in early 16th-century Spain. This may well have been the result of Spanish influence in this

RIGHT *Dutch tiles, c. 1520, in the chapel at the Vyne, Hampshire.*

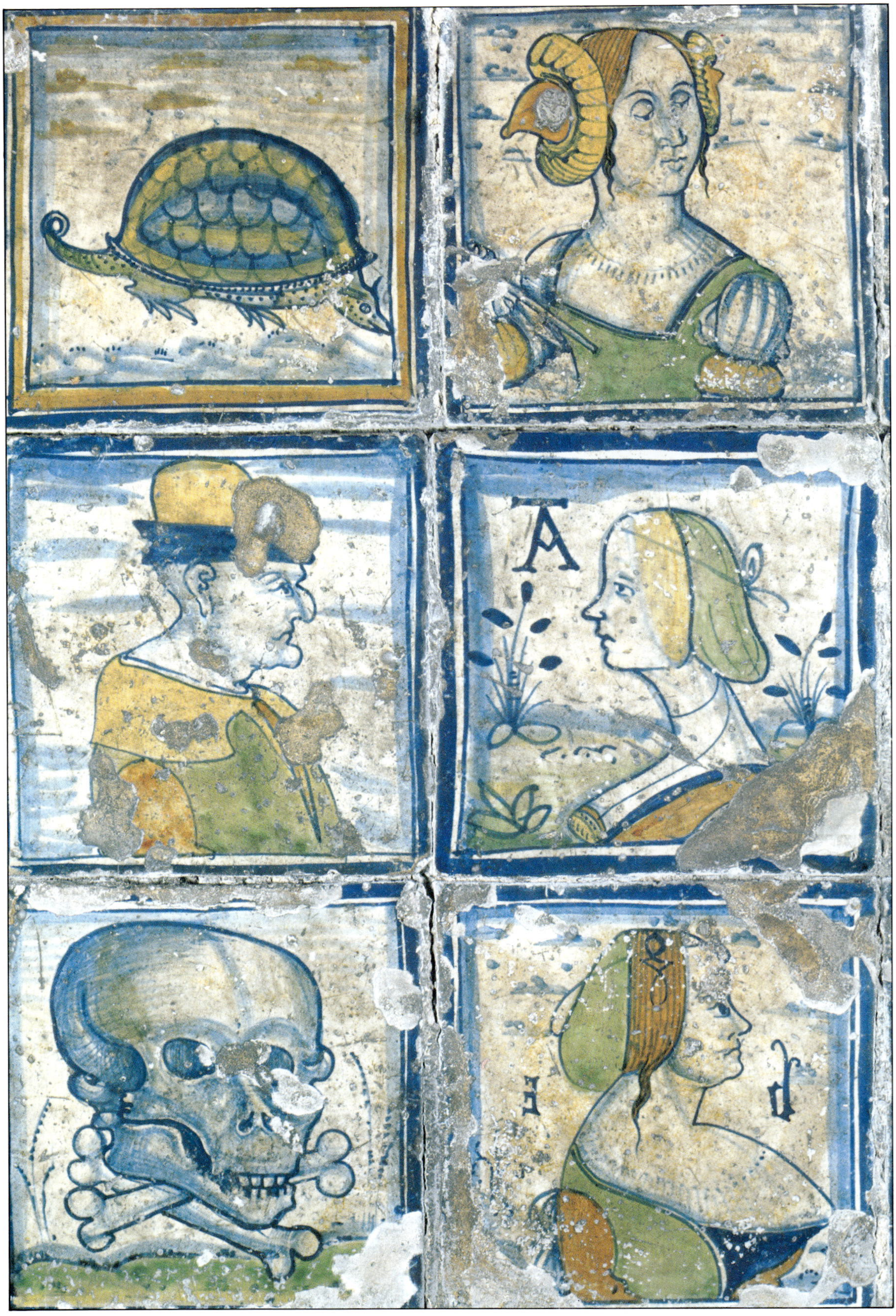

traditionally receptive region whose ports were very often the first stopping places for foreign merchants and immigrant craftsmen as well as exotic goods from all over the world. In the tile panels of the Botto Chapel in the church of Santa Maria di Castello, Genoa (*c* 1524), an interesting mixture of the Italian *istoriato* style with Spanish-influenced designs executed in the *cuenca* technique can be seen. Tiles were also produced in the Sicilian towns of Caltagirone and Sciacca, where both Genoese and Spanish influence was strong as a result of commerce; wall tiling became prevalent in that region in the 1500s.

The 16th century saw a massive export, not only of maiolica wares from Italy, but also of the craftsmen themselves, who took their techniques to all parts of Europe. Wherever they went, new tin-glazing industries were established, each developing along different lines, as dictated by particular local conditions and needs. Italian potters are known to have been working in Lyon in 1512, and a maiolica industry was well established there by the 1550s. Italians from Albisola in Liguria set up workshops in Nevers about 1578, and at Rouen. Between about 1528 and 1564 Masseot Abaquesne, a French craftsman who had worked on tiles with Girolamo Della Robbia in Madrid, was the master of one of the Rouen potteries producing tiles in the Italian style. Among the outstanding schemes carried out by these Rouen potters was the tiled pavement in Brou church (*c* 1530) and a series of wall and floor tiles for the Château d'Ecouen (1542). Abaquesne was closely associated with the art of the Fontainebleau school, fostered at the court of François I, which translated the Italian Mannerist style into a distinctively French form. Examples of his work can be seen in the Musée des Beaux-Arts at Rouen and in the Musée Royal de Cinquantenaire in Brussels.

Early in the 16th century, a certain Guido da Savino (later to be known as Guido Andries) of Casteldurante set up workshops in Antwerp that were to be carried on by his sons. For the development of pottery-making generally and tile-production in particular in the area this was to have momentous consequences. Among the pavements of maiolica tiles associated with these early Antwerp potters was that laid in the Abbey of Herckenrode near Liège (1526) and the series of tiles at the Vyne in Hampshire, dating from about 1520, which is thought to have come from the factory of Guido Andries.

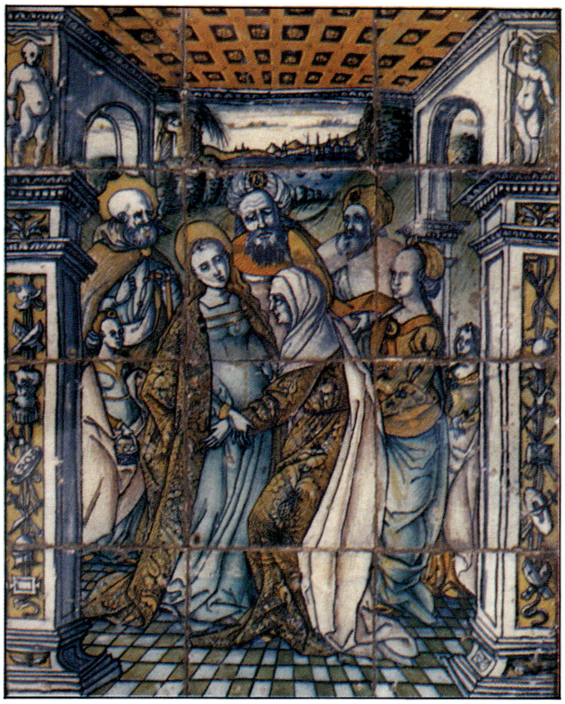

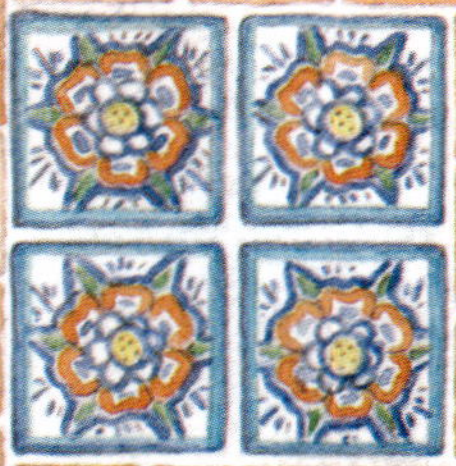

LEFT *Tile panel,* c. *1505, depicting the Visitation; signed Niculoso Italiano.*

Southern Germany and Austria had always had close commercial links with the potteries of northern Italy, and particularly the Venice and Faenza areas, and maiolica wares were being produced around Nuremberg in Bavaria and the South Tyrol from the 1520s. While their technical inspiration came from Italy, they drew heavily on German engravings for their designs. Switzerland in particular adopted the maiolica technique for making stove tiles early in the 16th century.

Even before this, Italians were introducing their techniques into Spain, and notably Seville, where a maiolica painter called Francisco Niculoso Pisano (the Pisan) was working by 1500. He was responsible for a number of altarpieces, altar frontals and wall tombs covered with smooth-surfaced picture tiles between 1503 and 1520. In these he combined the Italian maiolica *istoriato* style, which he had probably

RIGHT *Tiles in the Royal Palace, Sintra, Portugal.*

FAR RIGHT *Tiles of 'diamond point' pattern with border,* c. *1600, based on late 16th-century examples from Seville.*

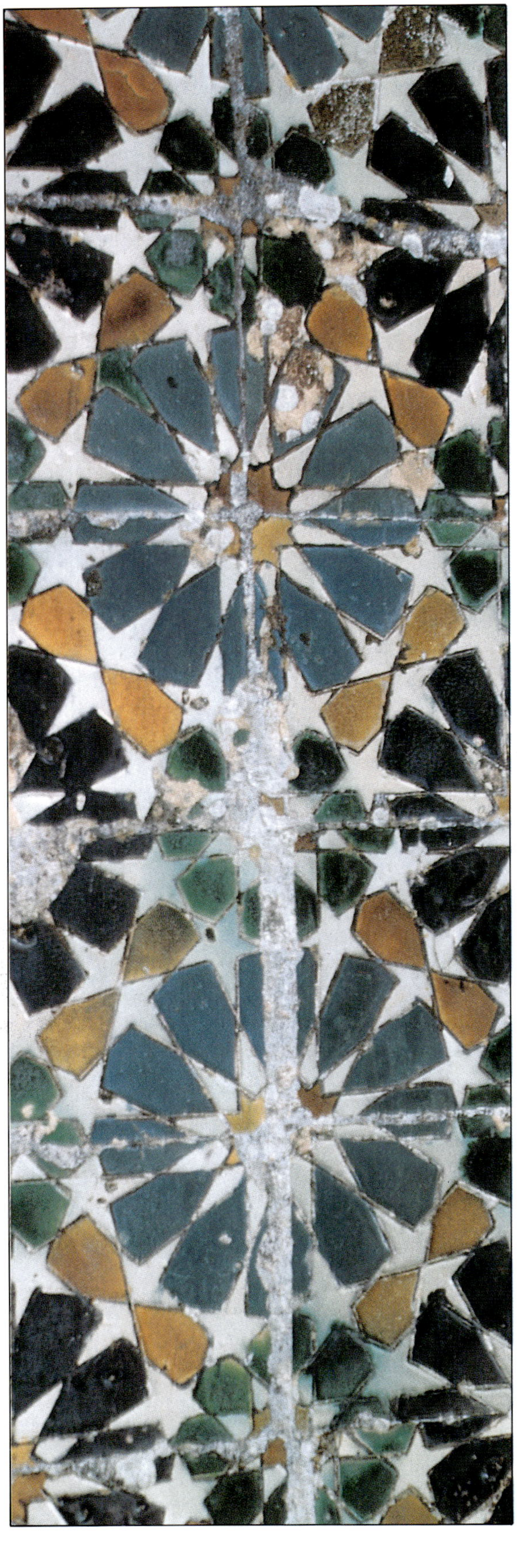

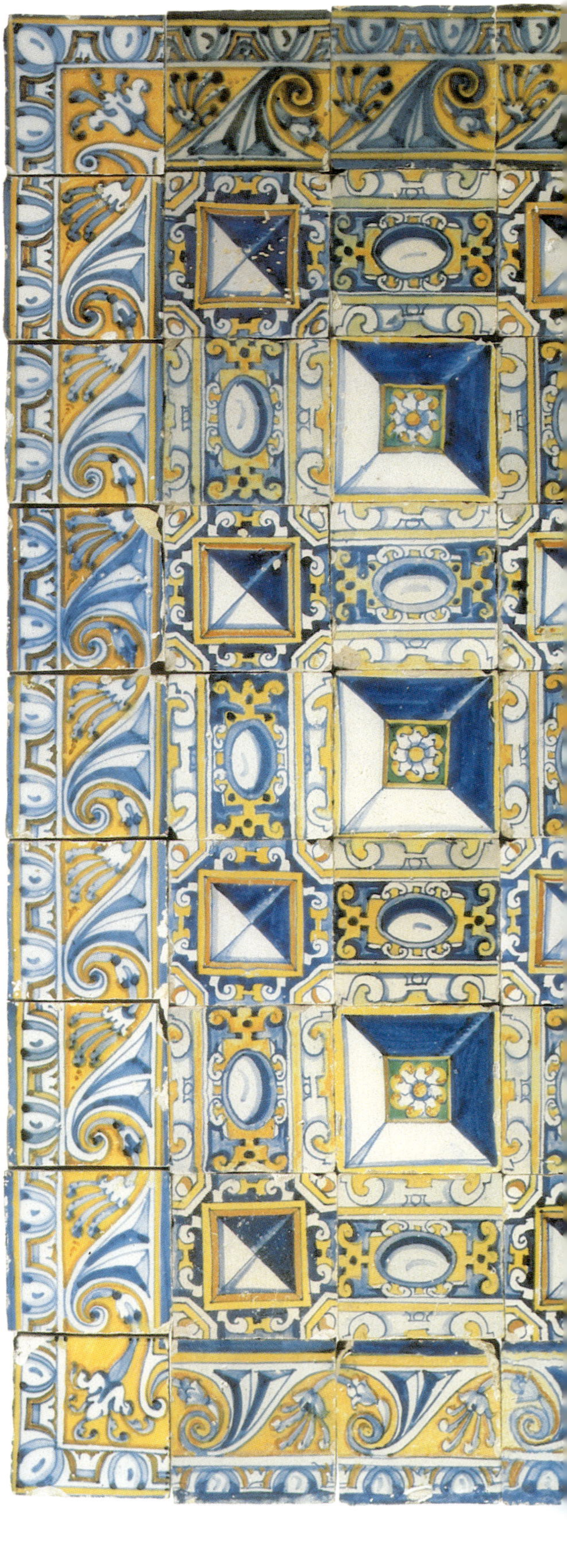

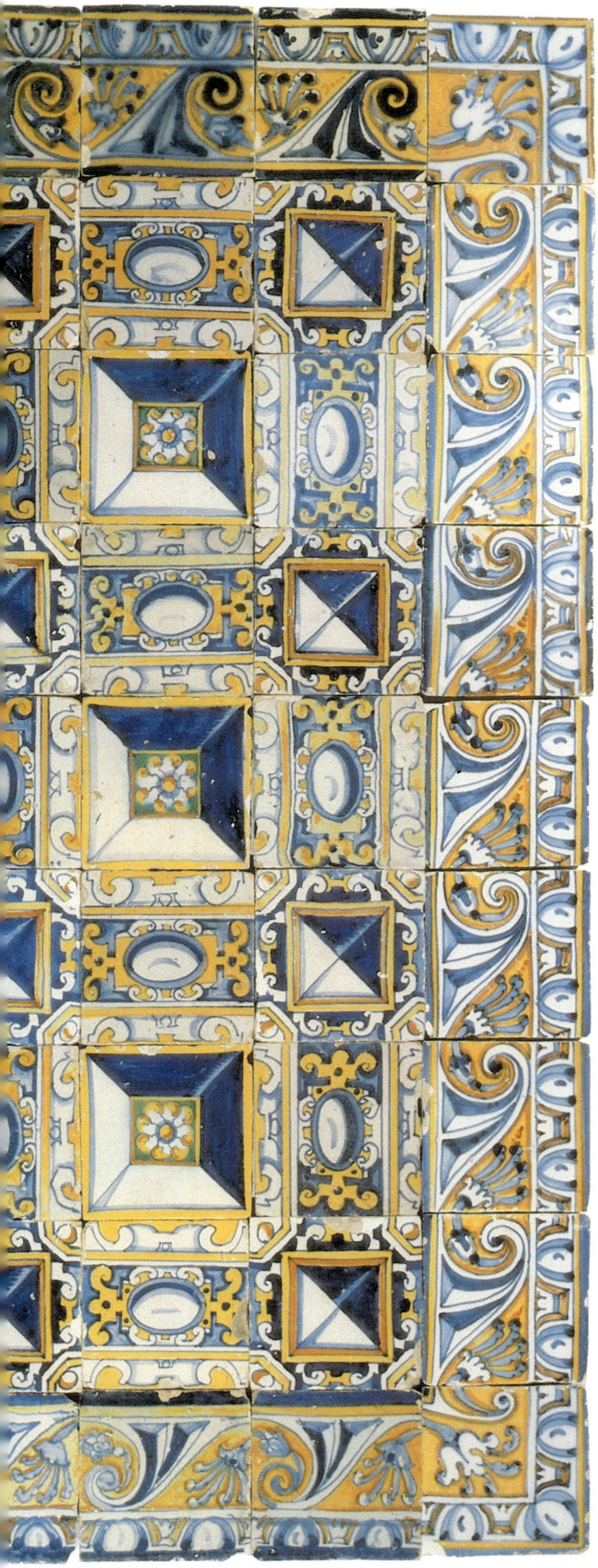

learned in Faenza, with Spain's traditional use of tiles for large expanses of architectural decoration, a tradition derived from the Islamic world.

Niculoso died in 1529 and, for the next 30 years or so, the Spanish potters of Seville worked only in the *cuenca* tradition. It was not until the 1560s and the arrival of the first of a new wave of immigrant craftsmen — this time from the Low Countries as well as Italy — that maiolica painting was revived in Spain.

Among the arrivals was the Antwerp tile-master Jan Floris who settled in Plasencia, south-west of Madrid, where he carried out tile commissions for Philip II and spawned a whole school of Italo-Flemish tile-painters. Another was Frans Andries (son of Guido), who went to Seville. He re-introduced the art of maiolica painting there and greatly influenced the tile-makers of the later 16th century. Parallel with this form of decoration was the purely ornamental style long favoured in Spain, but now executed in the maiolica technique and in a combination of Italian Renaissance and Flemish motifs. Later, in the 1570s, came another group of Italian tile-painters who introduced the maiolica styles of Genoa and Albisola to Seville. Native Spanish tile-makers also moved about and undertook tile schemes in Mallorca, Valencia and Barcelona, taking all these influences with them.

Portugal's tradition of tiled decoration is even more vigorous than that of Spain, although its industries were rather later in developing. From the 15th century onward, tiles from Seville and Valencia were imported into Portugal and used in such prestigious buildings as the old Cathedral of Coimbra and the Royal Palace of Sintra. Other imports came from Antwerp, and, eventually, during the mid-16th century, the production of maiolica tiles began in Lisbon itself under the inevitable Italo-Flemish influence. Portuguese enthusiasm for *azulejos* in both religious and secular buildings was to become more wholehearted than that of practically any other country. Colourful tiles still adorn the majority of buildings there and in further-flung areas of Portuguese influence such as the Azores, Madeira and Brazil.

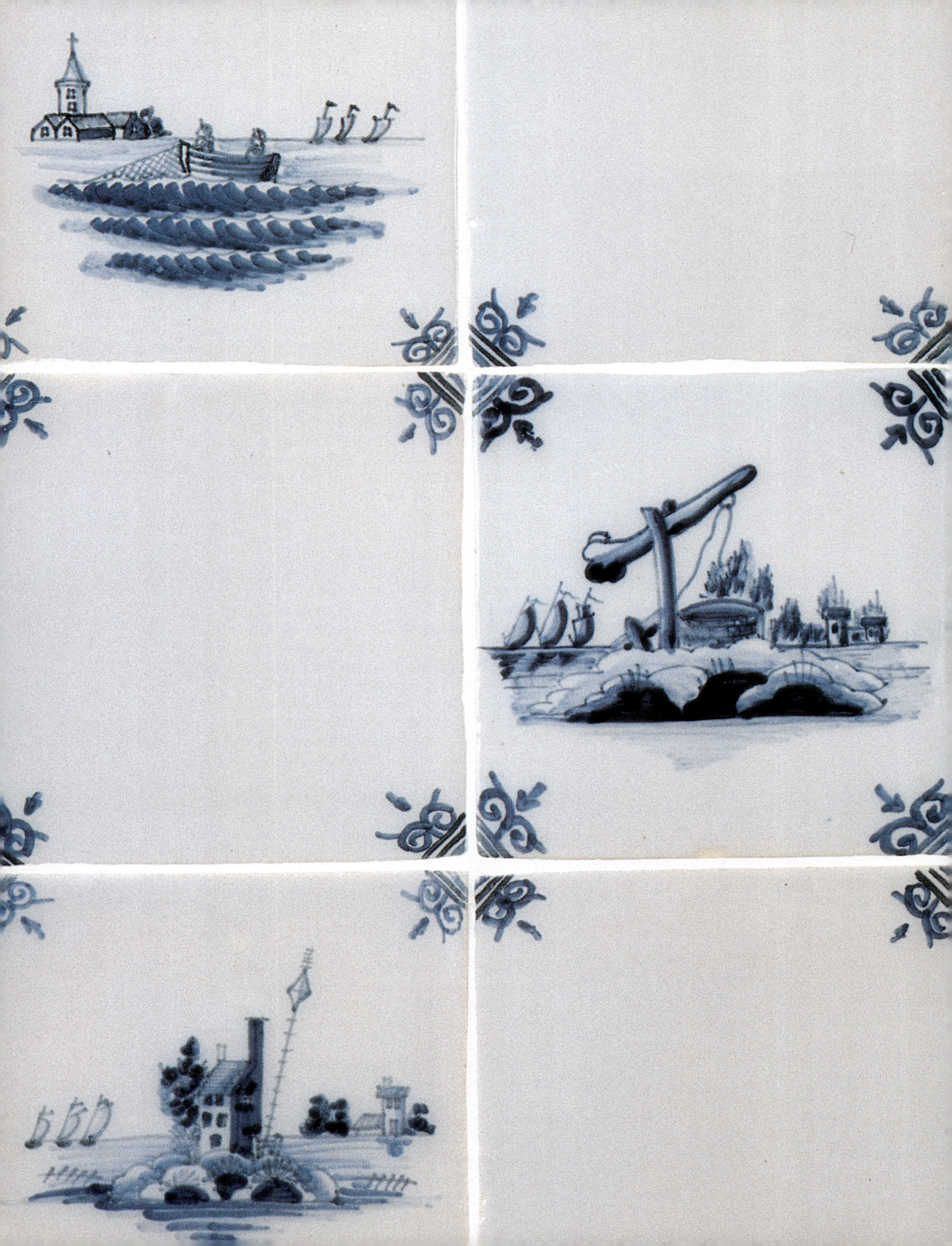

CHAPTER SIX

DUTCH TILES

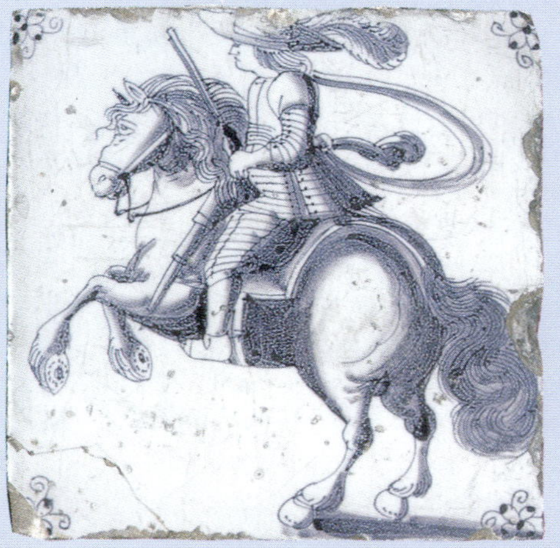

*P*OTTERY OF *a maiolica type is thought to have been produced in Bruges as well as Antwerp in the late 15th century, but by the beginning of the 16th, Antwerp was the more important of the two towns. Furthermore it was from Antwerp that a number of pottery craftsmen, notably members of the Andries and Floris families, emigrated to other parts of Europe — Spain, Germany and England — taking their maiolica expertise with them. Most significantly for the future development of tile-making, many Antwerp craftsmen moved to the northern Netherlands and helped to establish a strong maiolica industry there.*

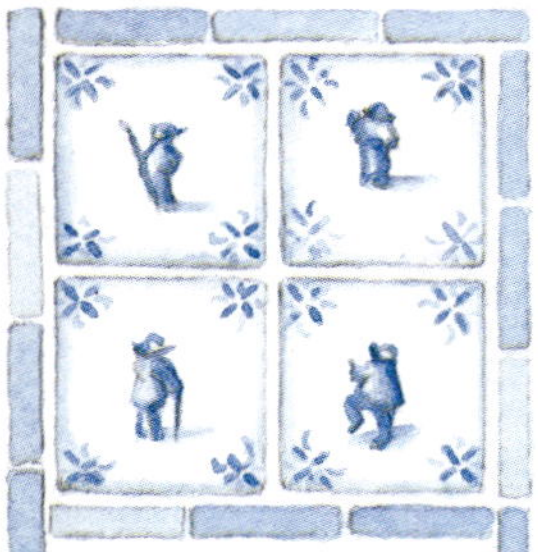

TILE ART

•

OVERLEAF (BACKGROUND) *A selection of modern tiles, based on traditional designs, made by the Royal Makkum Factory, the Netherlands.*

OVERLEAF (INSET) *Dutch tile, second half of the 17th century.*

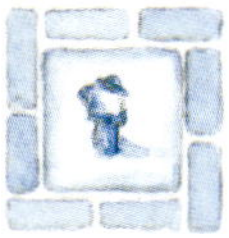

MAIOLICA was becoming increasingly known in the northern Netherlands during the second half of the 16th century, and a version was soon being produced there, though rather crude in contrast with the products of the south. Trade relations between the provinces provided a growing influence from south to north Netherlands, but religious strife in the Catholic south — and finally the sack of Antwerp by the Spaniards in 1585 — precipitated both a mass migration of Flemish potters northward and the consequent establishment of more potteries producing high-quality tin-glazed earthenwares.

While pottery production in the old centres of Bruges and Antwerp had almost completely faded out by the beginning of the 17th century, it was burgeoning in the Dutch towns of Rotterdam, Haarlem, Delft, Gouda, Amsterdam, Utrecht and Hoorn. Other towns, such as Makkum and Harlingen in Friesland, established their potteries later. Traditional links between certain towns and factories further enhanced their commercial strength. Of them all, Rotterdam was at the forefront of tile-making and its development in the Netherlands, while the quality of the wares produced at Delft ensured its dominance in maiolica production generally.

During the late 16th and early 17th centuries, polychrome tiles in the characteristic shades of blue, yellow, orange and green were predominant, and while blue-and-white tiles became increasingly important as the 17th century progressed, both types continued to be produced. The usual size of a tile was 5 in (13 cm) square.

The use of tiles in northern Europe underwent predictable changes in the 16th and 17th centuries. While the earliest maiolica tiles made in Antwerp, like the majority of Italian examples, had been for pavements, the close links between Spain and the Low Countries led to the influence of the Spanish habit of tiling walls. Outside wall panels and, later, single- and composite-tiled house signs were also popular. From the 17th century onward in the Netherlands, tiles were used to cover the walls of kitchens, dairies, halls and cellars, and composite pictorial arrangements were used as decoration in place of paintings; single rows of tiles were customarily used as skirtings around stone-floored rooms. Later, decorative tiles were used on and around fireplaces. In the Zaan district north of Amsterdam the tiled chimney-piece took a specific form and was known as a *smuiger*.

The range of designs was wide and included portraits, human and animal figures, military subjects, fruit, flowers and abstract patterns in the Hispano-Moresque style. These were the designs most obviously derived from the Mediterranean maiolica wares that in turn drew their influences from the East, but like all the others, they developed a distinctively Dutch form. Interlacing lines, circles, diagonals, stars, leaves and arabesques were painted or outlined in white reserves and the patterns were arranged to match the corners of others so that when four, or multiples of four, tiles were placed together, they formed larger patterns, ideal for wall decoration.

This reserve decoration in the corners of Dutch tiles persisted long after the Hispano-Moresque style had been superseded by more characteristically Dutch motifs. For example, the corners of portrait, animal and flower tiles commonly had rosette or petal motifs in reserves on dark blue in the corners, which made larger composite patterns of flowers or arabesques in lozenge shapes over the assembled fours. Later, these corner motifs, no longer in reserves, became more varied, but were still used as link patterns between tiles placed in groups.

Besides petals and fleurs-de-lis, later 17th-century corner motifs included spiders, ox-heads, sprigs and oak leaves (*c* 1650), with carnations making their appearance in the early 18th century. A Chinese motif, known as the meander, or maze, pattern and introduced *c* 1630, was based on designs on Wan Li porcelain, which was imported in the early 17th century. As well as corner motifs, some tiles have a half-baluster shape along the sides; when two tiles were placed alongside each other, they formed a complete column. These balustrade tiles, most often with fleur-de-lis

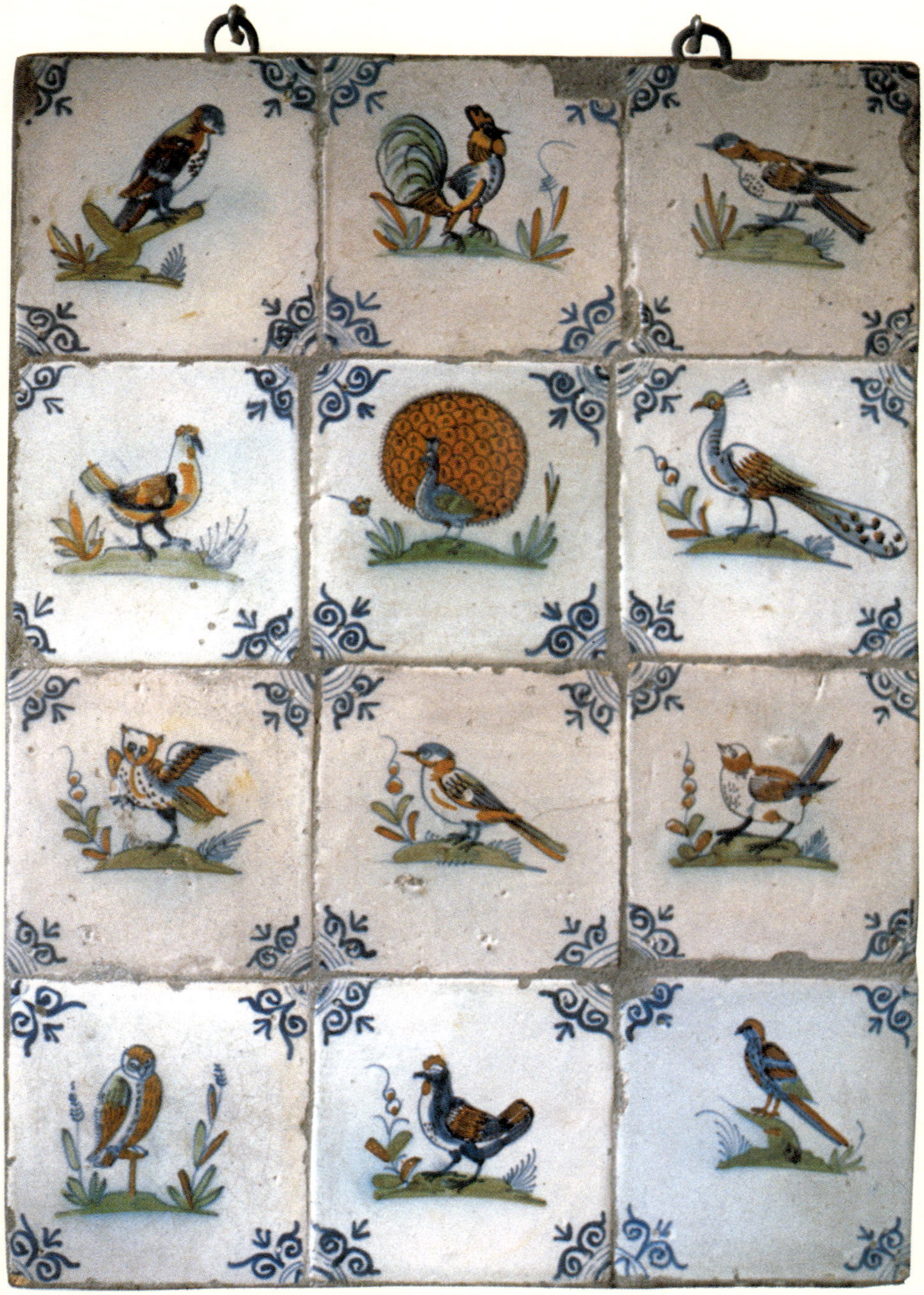

CHAPTER SIX

•

LEFT *A series of mid-17th-century Dutch tiles depicting a variety of birds painted in polychrome, with blue ox-head corner motifs forming a secondary pattern linking the tiles.*

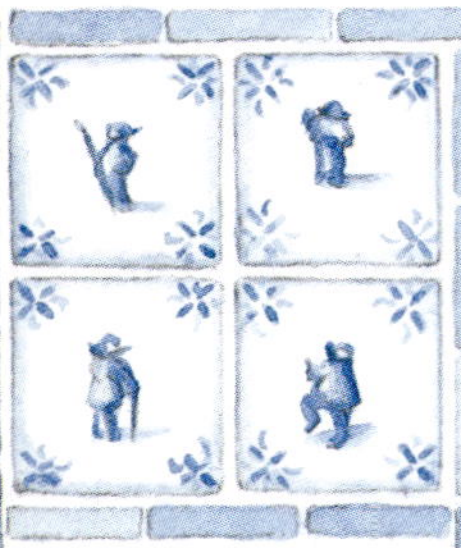

RIGHT *Dutch tile showing a camel, with corner motifs in reserves, early 17th century.*

corners, are thought to date from the second quarter of the 17th century onward.

Portraits of persons both famous and anonymous, archaic and contemporary, were among the earliest polychrome tiles made by Flemish potters under Italian influence, but in the compositions of fruit, particularly pomegranates and grapes — again designed to form larger repeating patterns in groups of four tiles — the Mediterranean influence is also evident. But it is in the wonderful array of animals, birds, sportsmen, soldiers and flowers, generally shown in central round, lobed or lozenge-shaped medallions, that the instantly recognizable Dutch style emerges. Many were undoubtedly copied from the books of engravings of flowers, exotic animals and other subjects that proliferated during the 17th century.

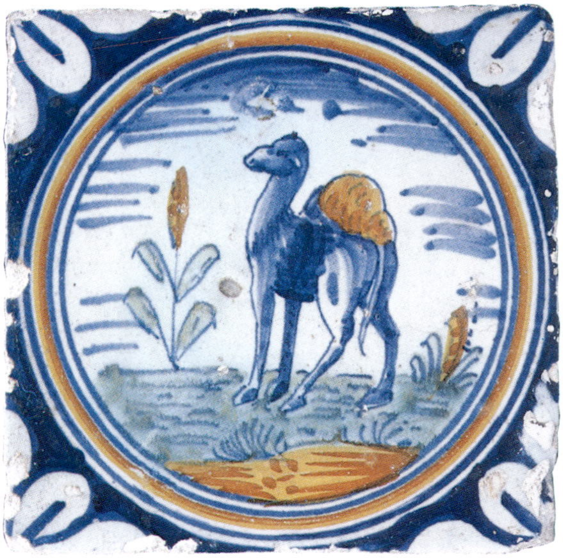

The designs were often translated from the engravings by means of pouncing: the outline of a picture was pricked out on a tile-sized piece of paper and powdered pumice, or pounce, was rubbed through the holes onto the tile. This outline was then painted in with a fine brush and the other tints, whether colours or shades of blue, were added. The preservation of many of these pounces, mostly from the late 17th and 18th centuries, has enabled ceramic historians to trace the origins of certain tile designs more accurately than would otherwise have been possible.

Flower tiles are perhaps those that best typify the polychrome period of tile production. Stylized flowers — sometimes said to be marigolds and marshmallows — in two-handled Renaissance-style vases with reserve decoration in the corners were the earliest type. From early in the 17th century onward came the realistically portrayed blooms — tulips, carnations, lilies, fritillaries, violets, poppies, irises and many others — sometimes set in round, lozenge-shaped or scalloped medallions, sometimes growing out of a patch of earth toward a cloudy sky suggested by a stylized pattern of sparse squiggles. They were copied, more or less accurately, from herbals and *florilegia* such as the *Hortus Floridus* of Crispin van de Passex, published in 1614, or from the tulip books of the 1630s, on which some of the great flower painters of the period collaborated. Many flower tiles had their central subjects painted in polychrome, while the surrounding medallions and corner motifs were in blue.

Certain types of decoration were associated with particular places: for instance, Rotterdam with tiles depicting fabulous sea creatures and with those portraying Turkish soldiers, or Saracens; Harlingen and Makkum with ship tiles; and Haarlem with a series of medallion designs of leaf-encircled cherubs, based on Italian maiolica ware, and with feathery circular medallions enclosing animals or birds in light blue, with sprigs or spider motifs in the corners. From Gouda came a celebrated series of polychrome birds perched on nails, and from Utrecht so-called shepherd tiles: all these are known to have been made — and were very expensive — in the 17th century, but 18th-century examples are the only ones seen now.

However, most designs cannot definitely be ascribed to any particular artist, pottery or town, and while some designs are associated with individual locations, nearly all were copied and imitated elsewhere, especially in the 18th century. A number of potteries, especially in Rotterdam, specialized in tiles, and some combined tile-making with other wares. Even so, more than 80 specific tile-works were eventually established throughout the Netherlands. Although since about 1900 the term 'Delft' has often been attached indiscriminately to all Netherlandish maiolica, this solecism probably arose because of both the consistently high quality of all the wares, including tiles, produced there, and the unquestioned dominance of Delft in the tin-glazed earthenware industry between *c* 1630 and 1750.

The Chinese porcelain that began to arrive in the Netherlands by the shipload from the early 17th century onward made an immense impact on the Dutch pottery industry. The potters now had large quantities of these highly prized blue-and-white wares to copy and they incorporated Chinese designs into the traditional Dutch repertoire of patterns and also made more purely imitative Chinese-style wares. Above all, the Dutch pottery itself became finer, especially at Delft. The thick reddish-bodied tiles of the early 17th century had, by mid-century, become much thinner and of a pale buff body colour.

The development of blue tiles was influenced by Chinese porcelain rather than Italian maiolica and therefore took a discernibly different course, but the use of medallions — round, lobed or lozenge-shaped — to frame the central design of a tile was similar at first. Biblical scenes in roundels became especially popular in the northern provinces. It was not until the second quarter of the 17th century that these frames around the central subject began to be dropped. Corner decoration, at first in reserves, also persisted on most tiles throughout the 17th century, and although the motifs grew smaller and more isolated from the central subjects, they nonetheless became more varied. Some tiles, particularly those depicting animals and flowers, dispensed with corner motifs altogether in favour of earth below and clouds above; both were drawn in such a stylized manner that they still formed corresponding patterns with juxtaposed tiles.

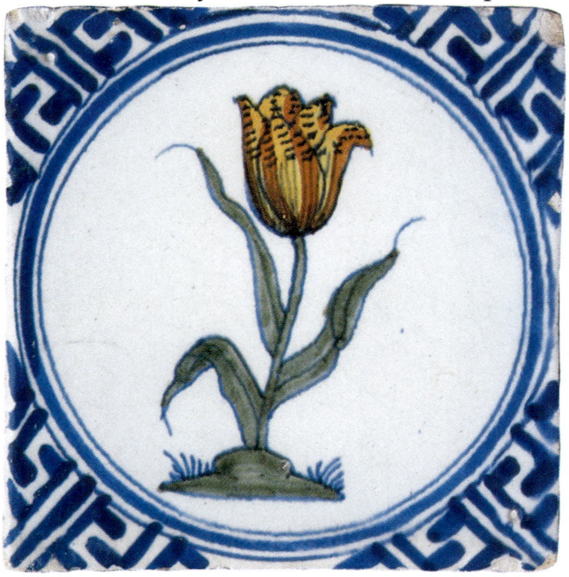

As in polychrome tiles, portraits were produced in blue from an early period, but they soon reached much higher levels of accuracy: most were copied from engravings of famous personages like Prince William of Orange, King Philip II or the Duke of Alva, and portraits of the Dutch royalty, many after prints by Cornelis Visscher, were popular up to the 18th century. A group of portraits of scholars and theologians who preached in the Reformed Church at Delft, and made there about 1660, are regarded as supreme examples of this type of tile.

Delft produced some of the best examples of tiles depicting soldiers and horsemen, a type made on a widespread scale. A vast tiled floor at the Château of Beauregard, near Blois in France, is known as *toute une armée en marche*. It consists of more than 6,000 tiles representing cavalry and foot-soldiers, which were dispatched from Delftshaven to Nantes and are recorded as being paid for in 1627. The soldiers depicted are based on Jacob de Gheiyn's illustrations from Prince Maurice's book on *The Handling of Firelocks, Muskets and Pikes* (1608). As well as soldiers, many other kinds of figures — merchants, craftsmen, traders, ordinary citizens and peasants — were painted on blue tiles, giving a fascinating glimpse of life in 17th-century Netherlands.

Animal tiles, and particularly those of elephants, were just as popular in blue and white as in polychrome and great numbers were made from about 1625 onward. Most of the designs were taken from prints in the animal books that in turn had been stimulated by

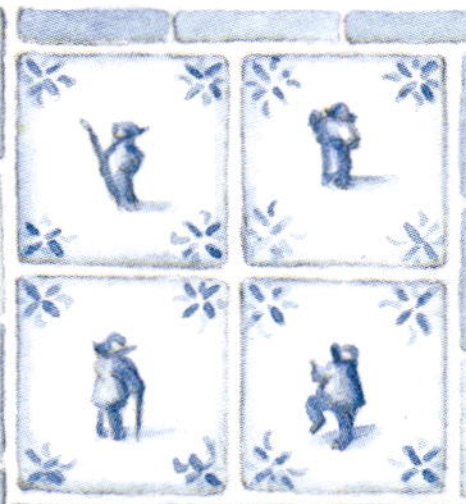

CHAPTER SIX

•

LEFT *Tile depicting a tulip with so-called Wan Li corner motifs, early 17th century.*

LEISURELY PURSUITS

BELOW *Dutch figure tile with spider's head corner motifs, 18th century.*

BOTTOM *Dutch tile depicting boys playing with a crossbow, the second half of the 17th century.*

RIGHT *Dutch tile with two boys, one dressed as a jester as part of a Shrove Tuesday ritual, second half of the 17th century.*

BELOW RIGHT *Tile with two boys playing a game of* kelf *(later to become golf), second half of the 17th century.*

BOTTOM RIGHT *Depicting children's games on tiles remained popular throughout the 17th, 18th and 19th centuries; here a late 19th-century Dutch tile made by the Utrecht firm of Revesteyn shows two boys playing a game of whip-top.*

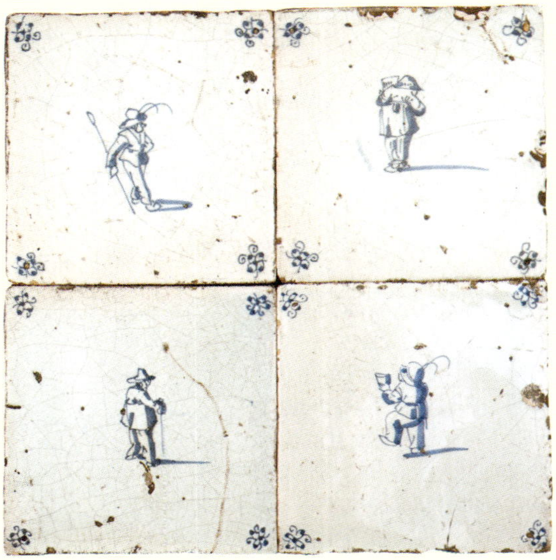

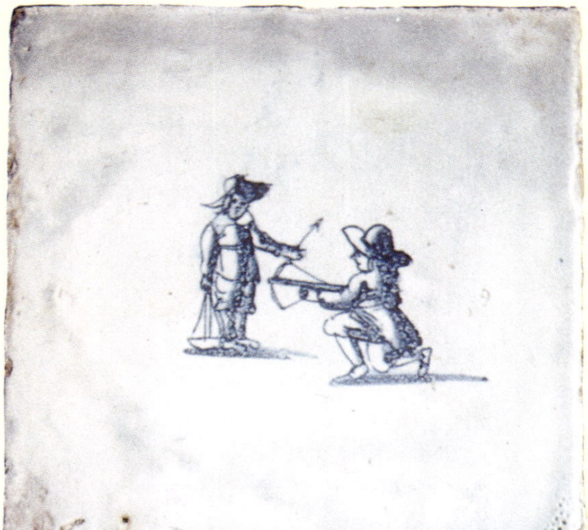

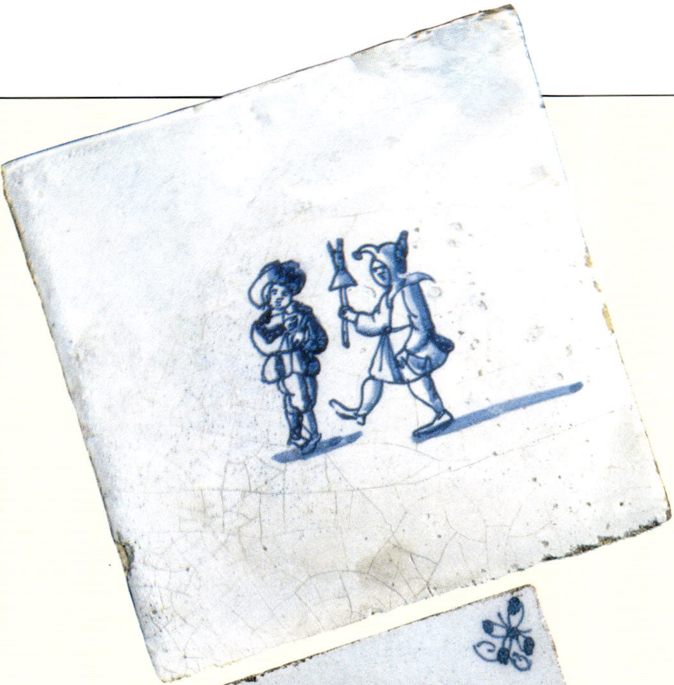

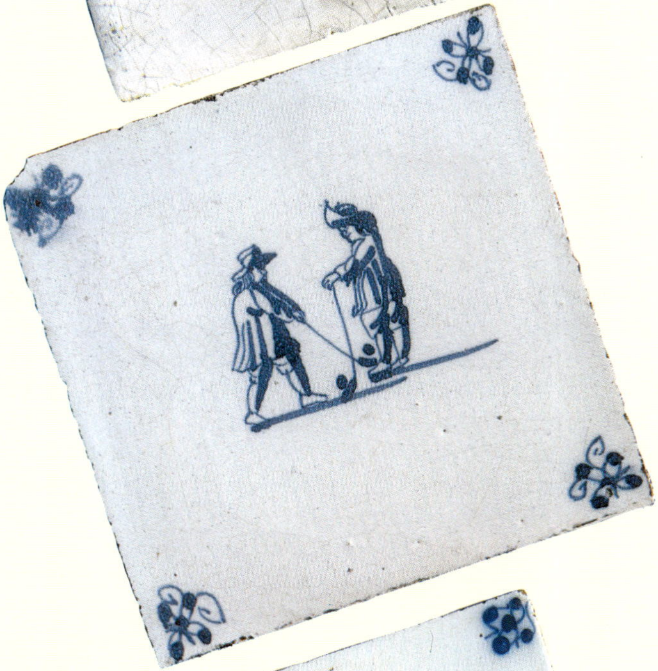

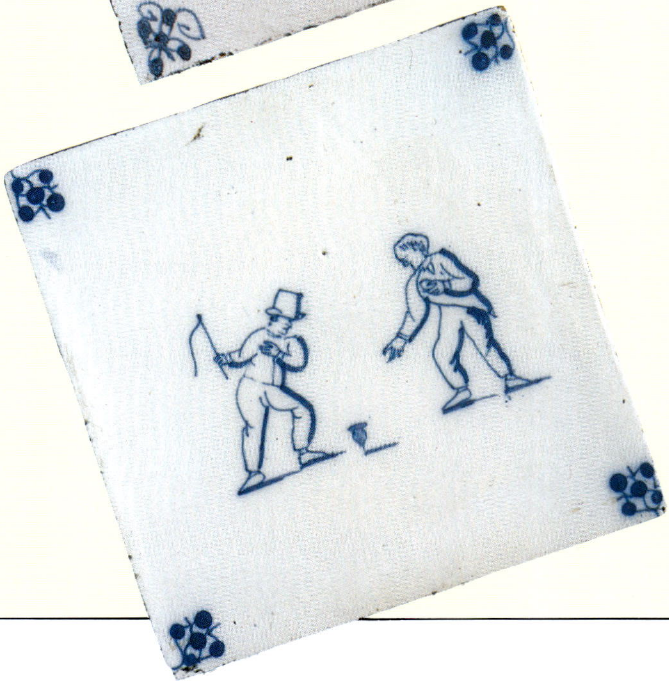

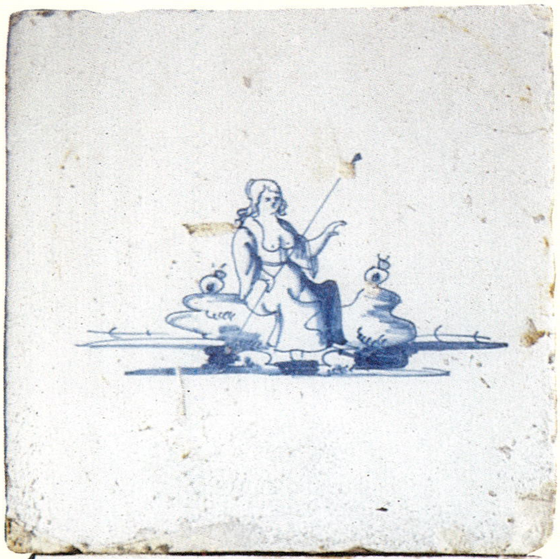

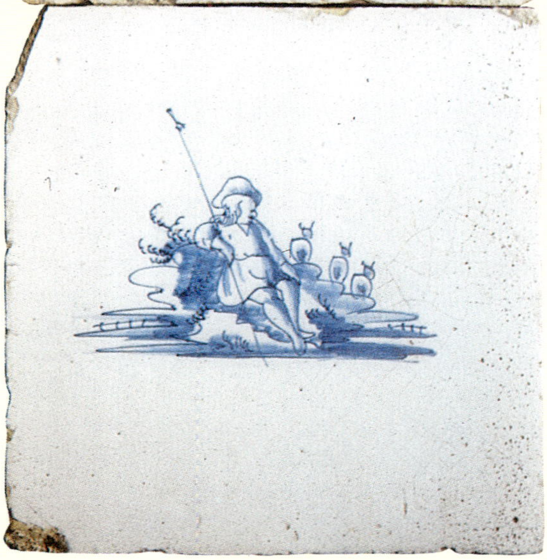

FIGURES AND PORTRAITS

ABOVE *Two Dutch tiles depicting a shepherd and a shepherdess, 18th century.*

TOP RIGHT *Dutch tile with a portrait of a woman in 17th-century Dutch costume and headdress, early 17th century. The corner motifs are a variation of the ox-head.*

ABOVE RIGHT *Tile depicting a soldier, with leaf and tendril motifs in the corners, early 17th century.*

RIGHT *Dutch tile with a knight on horseback and spider's-head corner motifs, second half of the 17th century.*

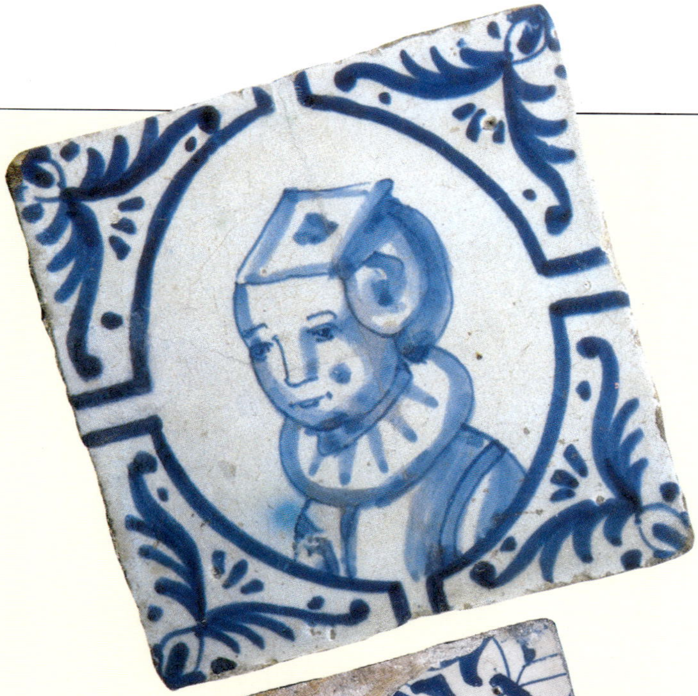

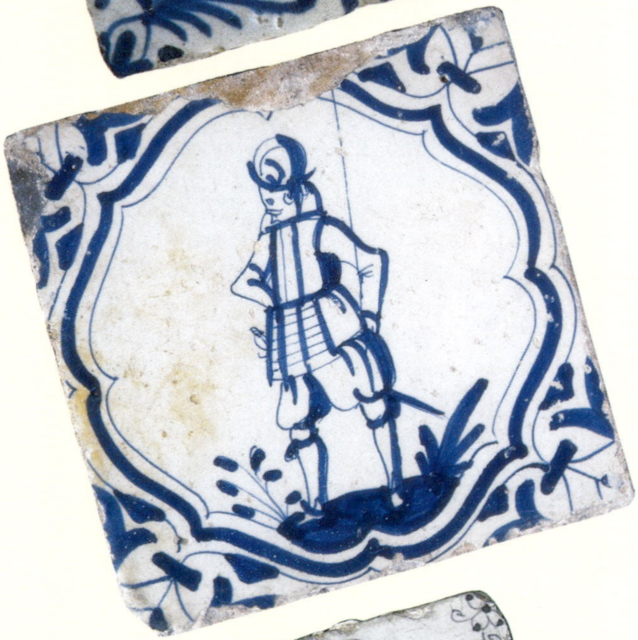

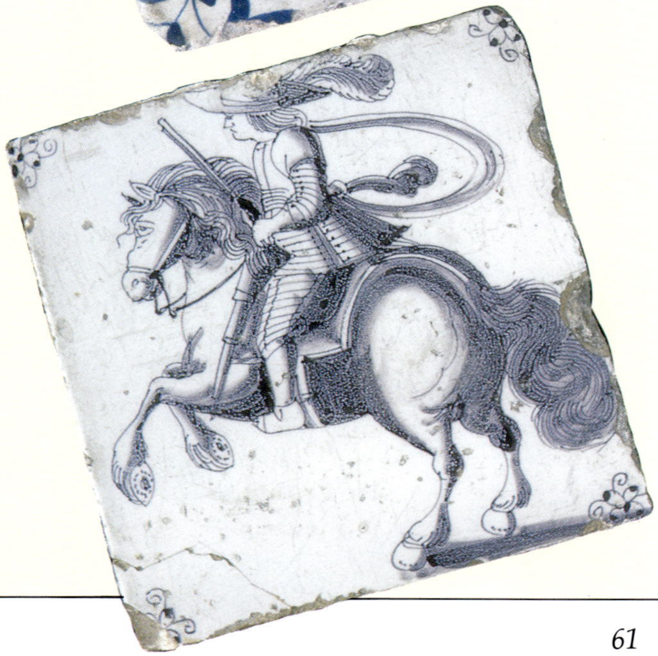

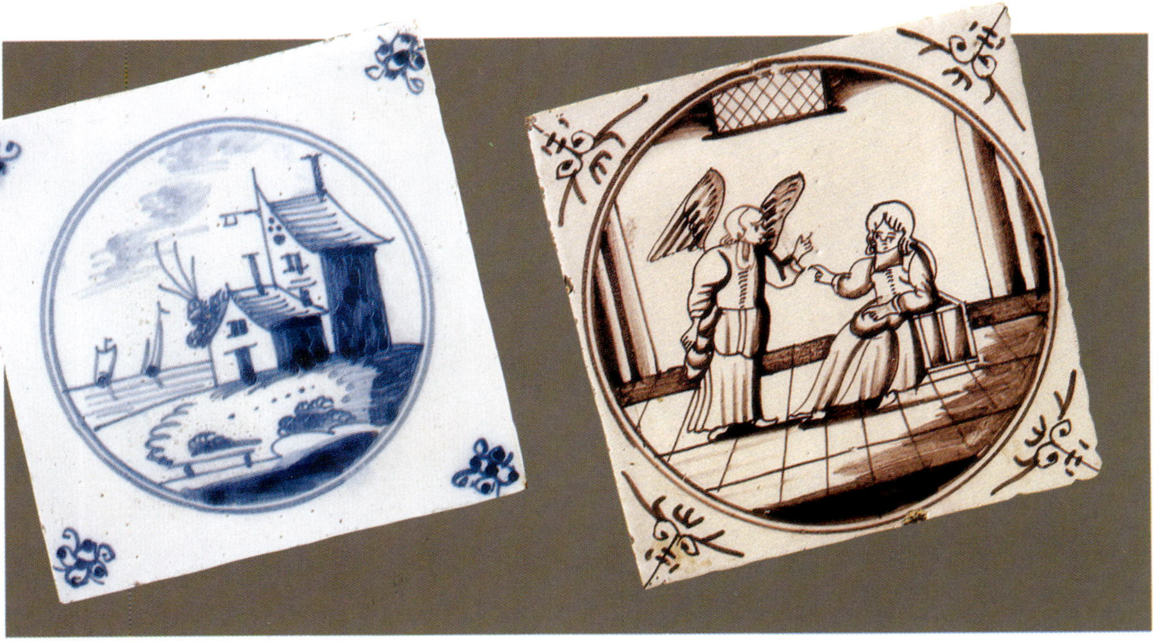

RIGHT *Landscape tile with a coastal scene and spider's-head corners, 18th century.*

FAR RIGHT *Dutch biblical tile depicting the Annunciation, with ox-head corners, 18th century.*

the exploration of the Americas and the Indies.

After about 1630, blue tiles developed a vast range of themes, independent of the polychrome tradition. These included landscapes, biblical subjects, ships and children's games. The landscapes, like the human subjects, provided an evocative view of the Netherlands, with windmills, canals, isolated farmhouses, churches and castles. Some include figures — fishing, skating or just walking in the flat countryside with its sparse trees and broad horizon. The early versions of these landscapes were often enclosed in roundels or set off, rather incongruously, by balusters at the sides and large fleurs-de-lis at the corners. Later in the 17th century the corner motifs faded to delicate florets or disappeared altogether and a sense of almost eternal distance remained — a consummate achievement on tiles no bigger than 5 in (13 cm) square. Landscape tiles without corner motifs were referred to in old inventories as 'open-air work'.

A quite different and much rarer type of landscape tile was a form of miniature landscape painting: stories from the Bible, historic battles and genre scenes were copied in the finest detail from the paintings of such artists as Jan van Goyen, Jacob van Mosscher, Nicolaes Berchem and Jan Martsen the Younger. In this idiom, the late 17th-century tile-painter Frederik van Frijtom of Delft is celebrated for his beautifully executed riverside and other landscape scenes.

Biblical stories with their often complicated figure groupings were especially demanding for tile-painters, who were mostly folk artists with little or no formal artistic training. Toward the end of the 17th century some used manganese purple instead of cobalt blue, which was easier to apply with clarity, and most of the scenes were given a biblical reference. Although these tiles may not have reached the artistic standards of some other types, in their own day they were more highly priced than most because of the labour involved in drawing them. Over 460 different scenes have been identified. Biblical tiles were used as decoration on whole walls as well as fireplaces, particularly in the most northerly districts of the Netherlands, and they were exported to Germany and Denmark in large quantities. Religious tiles with identifiably Catholic subjects, such as scenes from the Life of the Virgin, were also produced, many of them undoubtedly for export to Spain and Portugal, where they were used, along with the universally popular Bible scenes, in churches and cloisters.

Besides the ships that appeared in Dutch landscape and seascape tiles, portraits of individual vessels were produced from the

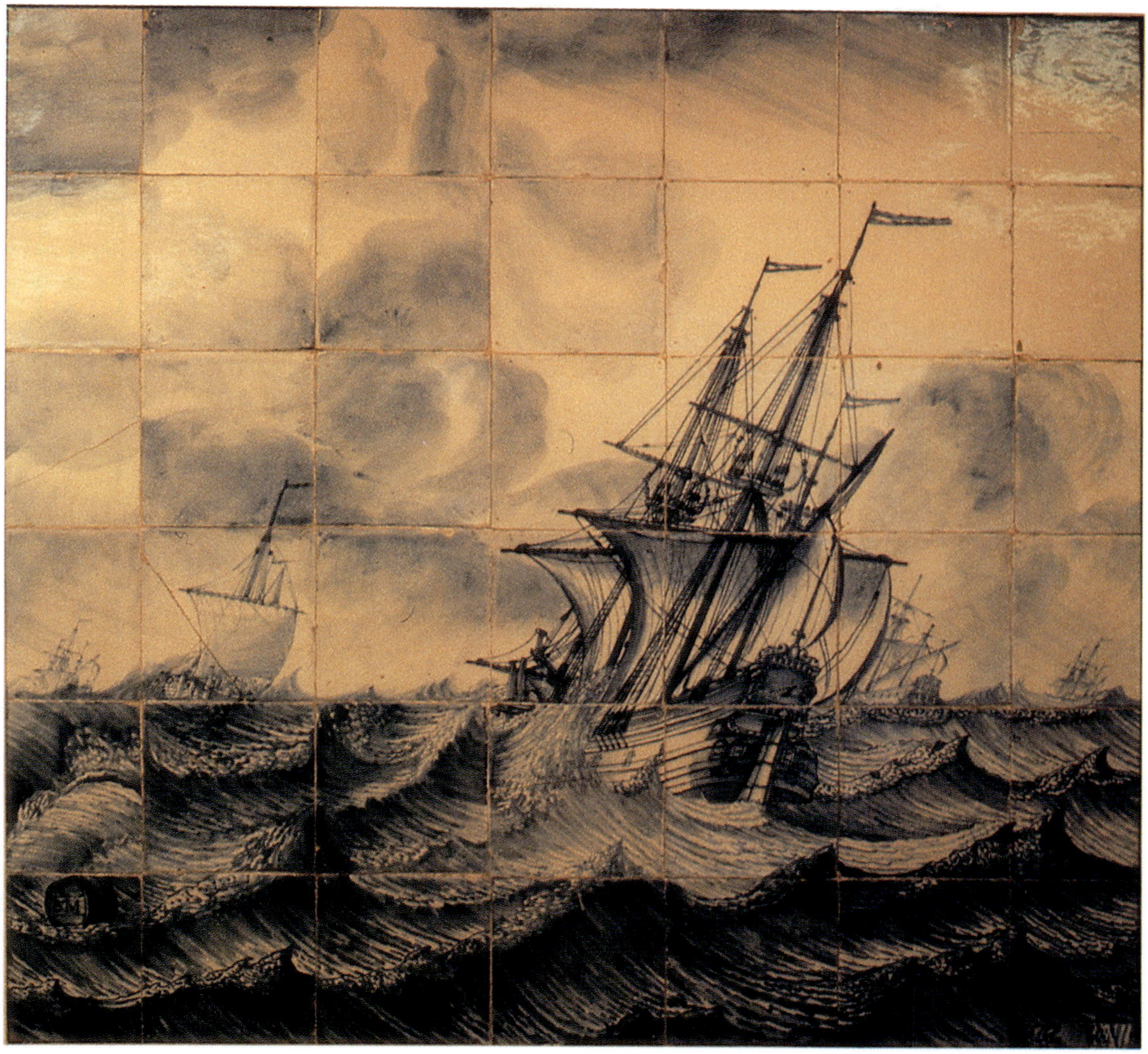

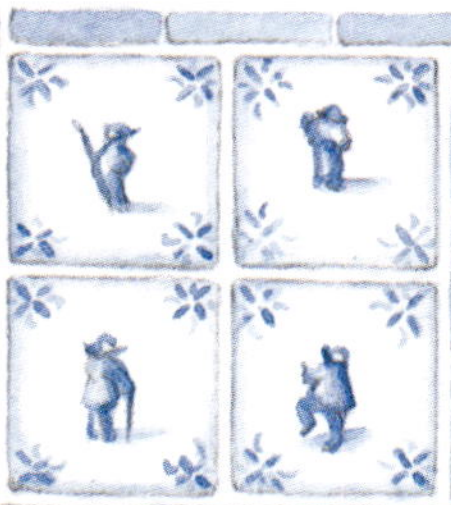

LEFT *Tile panel with a seascape by the Rotterdam tile-painter Cornelis Boumeester, c. 1700.*

1630s until the 18th century. From the later 17th century onward large tile pictures of maritime subjects such as sea battles, the embarkation of Prince William III for England in 1688, whaling scenes and general seascapes were made, predominantly in the potteries of Harlingen and Makkum. The tile-painters copied drawings and prints and, by doing so, translated the work of Dutch sea painters such as Reinier Nooms, Aert van Antum and Willem van de Velde the Elder into ceramic form. The most famous painter of these tiled shipping scenes was Cornelis Boumeester (1652–1733), who was chief tile-maker at one of the Rotterdam factories from 1676.

Of all Dutch tiles, those depicting children's games have been the most consistently popular, and were made from the mid-17th century until well into the 19th. Small figures of children, playing with bat and ball, hoops, tops or knucklebones, walking on stilts, playing leap-frog or skipping, appear in the middle of the tiles, often with spider motifs in the corners. Chinamen occupied in various pursuits were depicted in a similar style.

Many of the 17th-century tile designs were continued during the 18th century, and after 1700 it is almost impossible to attribute any of them to particular towns, as they all copied each other's designs, no matter where they originated. But despite the traditional nature of much tile production, there were changes in the industry.

Around the middle of the 17th century demand for polychrome tiles had declined, while the blue-tile industry grew from

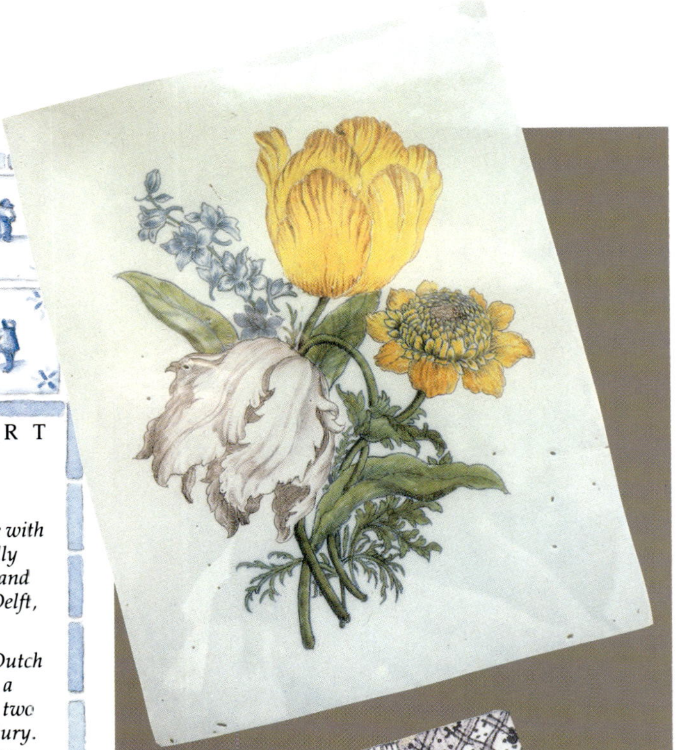

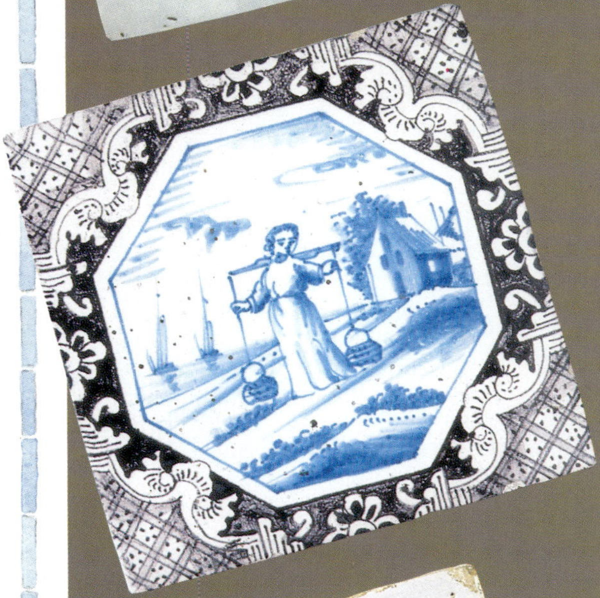

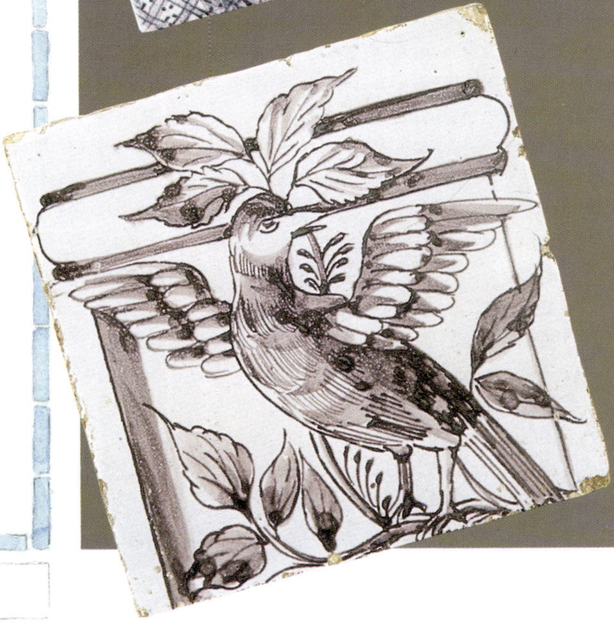

RIGHT *Dutch tile with naturalistically painted tulips and other flowers, Delft, c. 1700.*

CENTRE RIGHT *Dutch tile showing a milkmaid with two pails, 18th century. The tile has an elaborate Louis XIV border with trellis corners.*

BELOW RIGHT *Dutch tile with a bird seen against the top of a column, 18th century.*

strength to strength. It was not until the beginning of the 18th century that the polychrome market picked up again, with an increasing demand for wall pictures of flowers, landscapes and other scenes. Japanese Imari ware, produced by the muffle-kiln process, had been imported by the Dutch and a few of the Delft potteries — always among the most enterprising as regards experimentation — managed to procure the necessary kilns for making a similar ware with red and gold decoration. Although this had a considerable impact on most 18th-century Delftwares, it was rarely used for tiles and then only for major commissions such as the chinoiserie tiles for the Amalienburg Pavilion at Nymphenburg, near Munich.

As well as being characterized by a renewed interest in polychrome decoration, particularly on flower pieces, early 18th-century tiles were decorated in a combination of blue and manganese purple. Some were painted in the two pigments, while in other examples the central subject was painted in blue in a frame or medallion while the background was covered in powdered manganese, giving a stippled effect.

More and more, tiles replaced paintings as wall decoration, and as well as large tile pictures of flowers in vases, landscapes and seascapes were turned out; many had decorative frames painted on the surrounding row of tiles. These pictures were sometimes used as overdoors and for embellishing chimney-pieces, or they might be incorporated into large-scale decoration of the walls of rooms.

Tiled fireplaces, or *smuigers,* which curved inward toward the ceiling, were traditional to the Zaan district, but the habit of tiling fireplaces as well as large wall areas had spread to other parts of the Netherlands long before the end of the 17th century. During the 18th century tiles sometimes covered the hearth pillars supporting the mantel shelves of fireplaces, and even doorposts in important buildings. In each case this pillar decoration was carefully tailored to the function, taking the form of decorated architectural columns, elongated flower garlands or vines. Most commonly, the back of the fireplace itself was decorated with a tiled tableau of flowers in a vase, and these flower pieces, whether of polychrome or blue tiles, grew more and more elaborate with the development of the rococo style. During this period the tiled decoration of rooms sometimes included a rococo clock.

A tiled vase of flowers was customarily set into the wall behind the cooking range in Friesland, and it was in this area of the Netherlands that most of the fully tiled rooms originated, although the tiles themselves came from Rotterdam as often as from Harlingen and Makkum, the potteries whose tiles took on a distinctively Friesian style during the 18th century.

A further division began to exist between the folk-art tiles produced in such centres as Rotterdam, Amsterdam, Harlingen and Makkum, and the high-quality products of the Delft and Rotterdam potteries. While great quantities of the traditional blue tiles were exported all over Europe — and as far afield as Brazil — these factories made faïence for the luxury market, and this included important tile-picture schemes for palaces in England, France and Germany.

When William and Mary came from the Netherlands in 1688 to be the new joint monarchs of England, they already had a well-developed taste for Delft faïence, and the Het Loo Palace, their country seat and hunting lodge at Appeldoorn, was already under reconstruction according to plans by the architect Daniel Marot. The scheme included a remarkable tiled cellar, and as it is known that Marot made designs for the tile-works known as The Greek A in Delft, it is thought that the tiles used at Het Loo, which included vases of flowers, landscapes, geometrical figures and marbled effects, were probably made there.

Soon after their accession in England, William and Mary engaged Sir Christopher Wren to reconstruct Hampton Court as a more comfortable and convenient palace than Henry VIII's original. Among the many architects and artists employed there, Daniel Marot was entrusted with the tiled decoration of a 'dairy with all conveniences, in which Her Majesty took great delight'. These unusually large tiles were also made

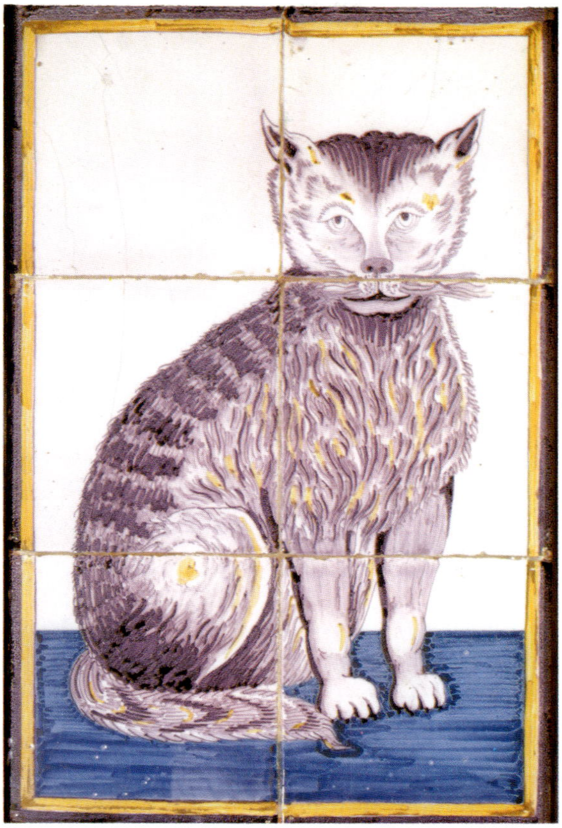

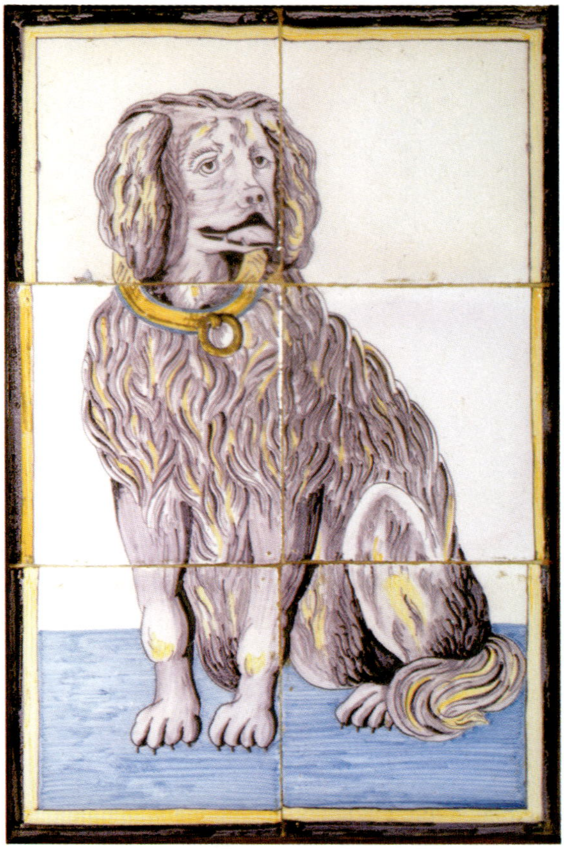

LEFT *A pair of Dutch tile pictures of a dog and a cat, 18th century.*

RIGHT *Queen Mary's kitchen cellar decorated with blue and manganese tiles, c. 1686.*

BELOW RIGHT *The Hindeloopen Room in the Fries Museum. The wall tiles were made at the Royal Makkum Factory, the Netherlands, 17th century.*

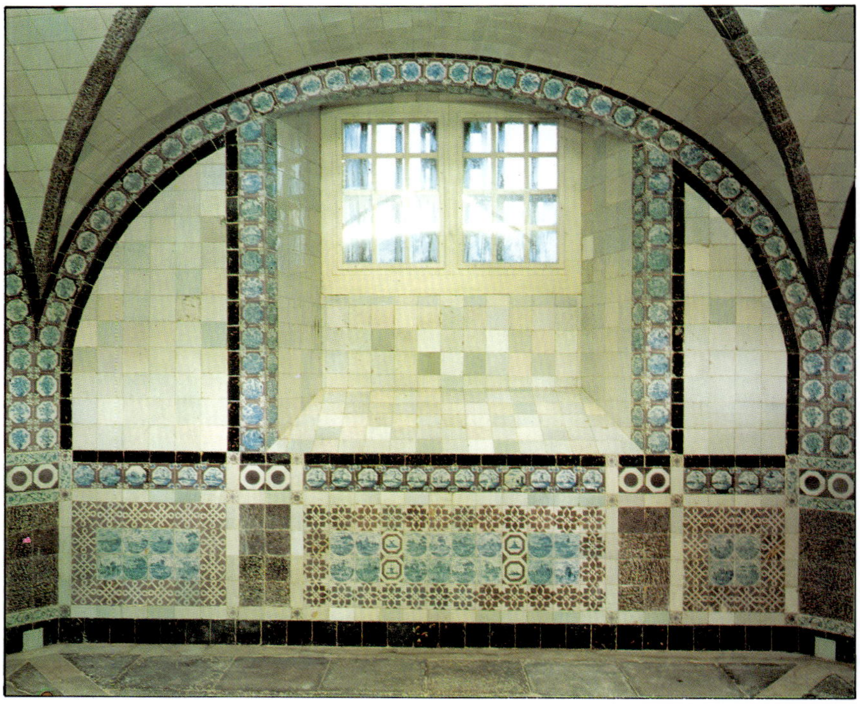

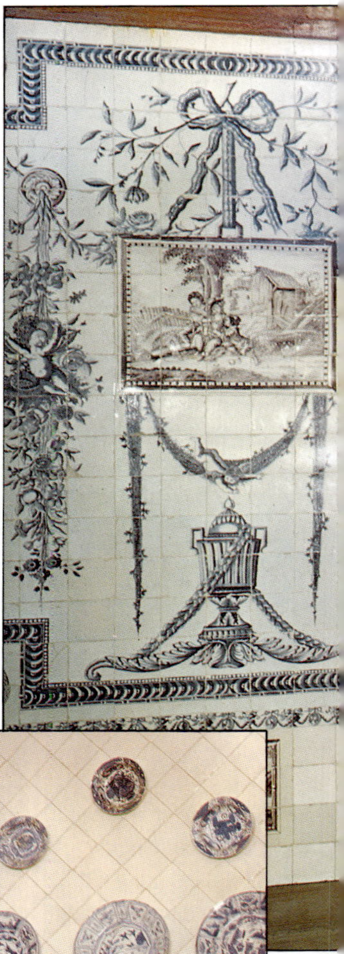

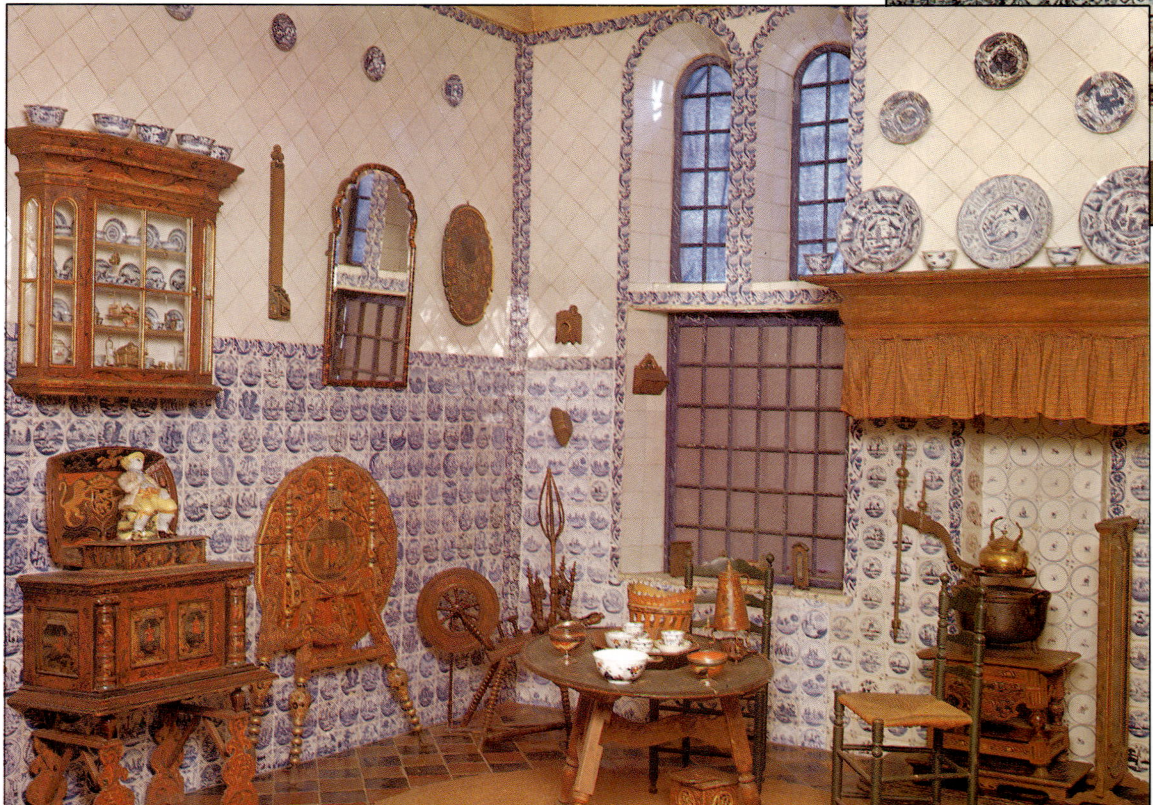

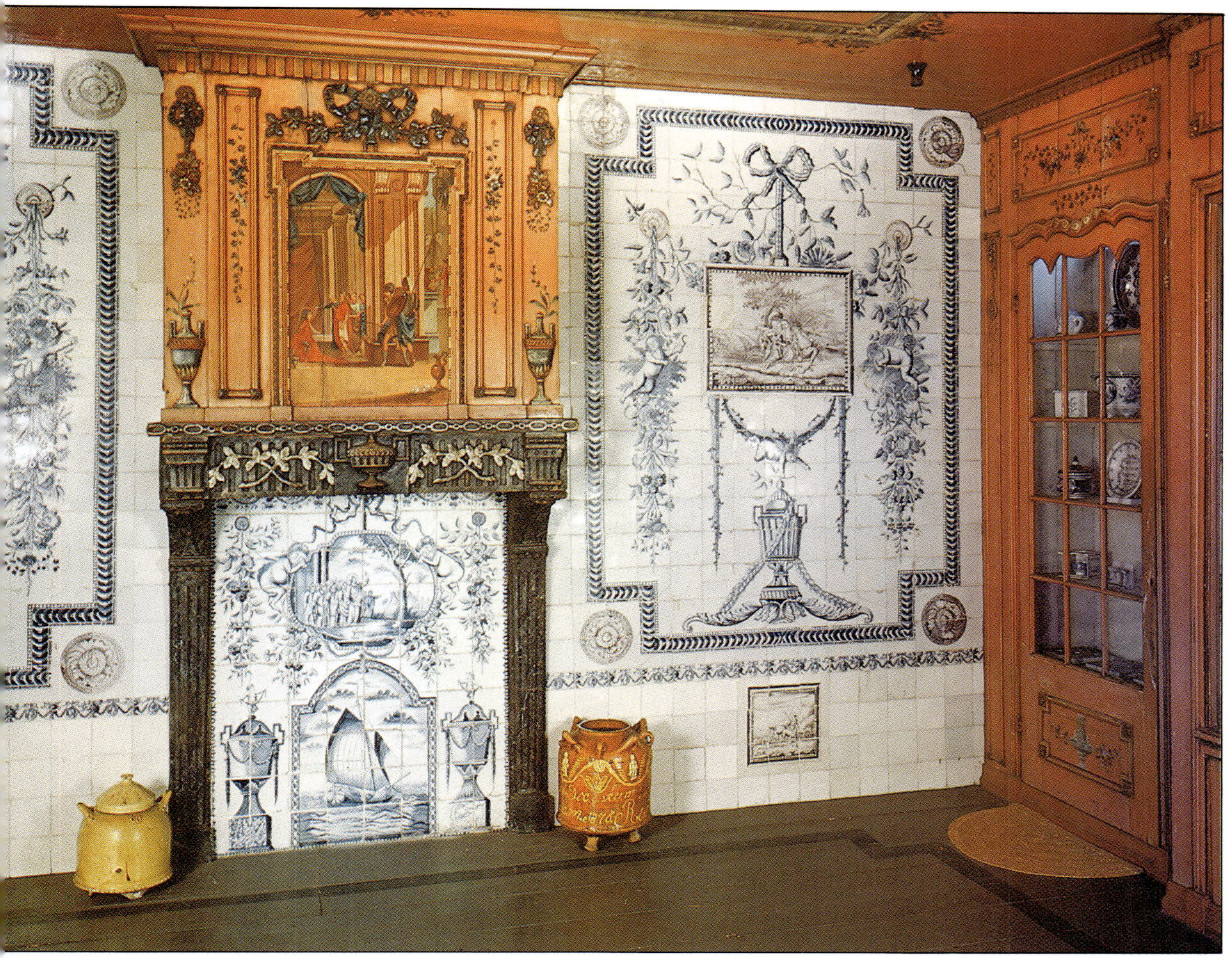

LEFT *This tiled tableau, representing the seasons, was handpainted by A G Sijbet and manufactured at the Royal Makkum Factory,* c. 1797.

at The Greek A tile-works of Delft. Unfortunately no more than a few tiles from this exotic decorative scheme have survived: the King had the dairy destroyed in 1698, some years after Queen Mary's death from smallpox.

Exports to France during the second half of the 17th century not only included faïence and tiles from Delft, but some of the potters themselves, who worked at various French establishments to produce Delftware. The French royal accounts record the purchase of blue and manganese tiles from Rouen, Nevers and Lisieux as well as Rotterdam, the latter of whose tiles were used at Versailles as early as 1670.

Some time later, between 1715 and 1730, the Comte de Toulouse carried out a modernization programme at his seat, the Château of Rambouillet, which included a tiled summer dining room. As befitted an *Amiral de France* with a passion for the sea and ships, the scheme at Rambouillet included composite shipping and harbour scenes in blue tiles, as well as landscapes and flower pieces in polychrome.

French influence was strong in Germany, where a plethora of princes (both ecclesiastical and secular) employed French architects and decorators in their many residences and follies. One of the most extravagant of these was the Chinese pagoda at the Nymphenburg Palace near Munich, dating from 1716–19, the entire ground floor of which was tiled. There were landscape, figurative and biblical tiles, as well as composite tableaux in blue and white. All 2,000 of the tiles used came from The Flowerpot works in Rotterdam. The owner of Nymphenburg, the Elector Maximilian Emmanuel of Bavaria, was a former Governor of the Spanish Netherlands, and his period of residence in Brussels must have stimulated his strong liking for tiles.

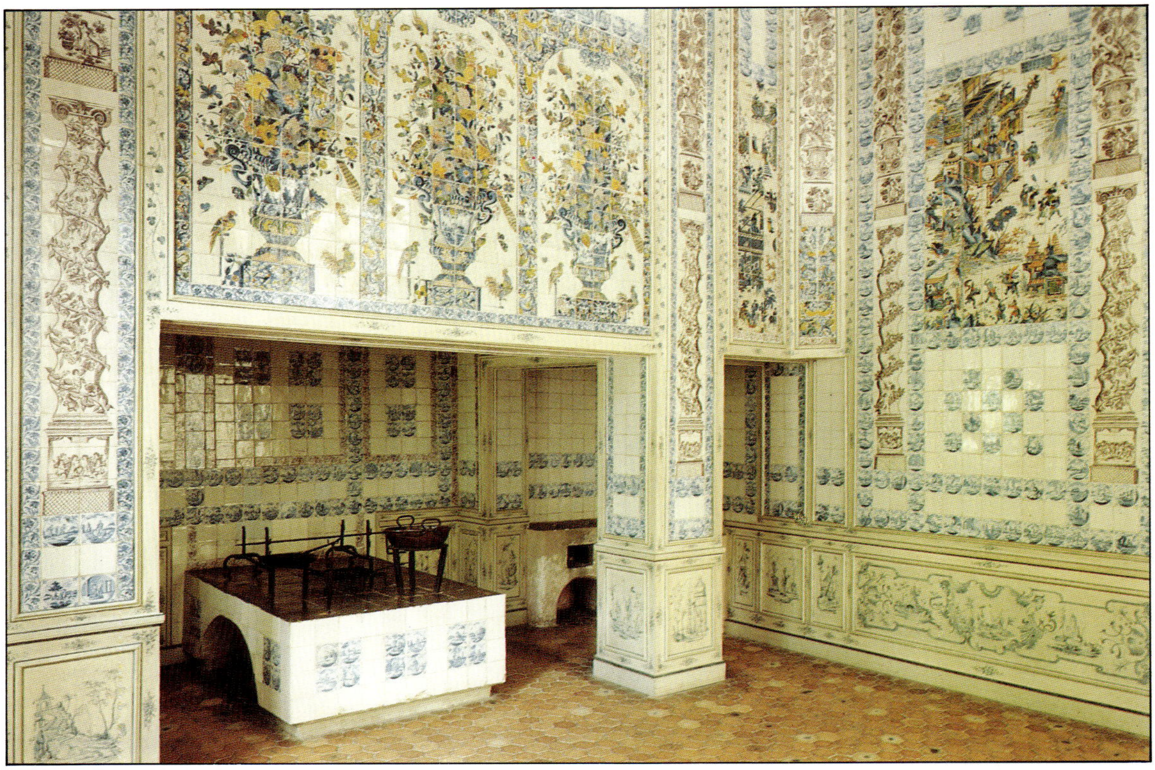

RIGHT *The tiled kitchen in the Amalienburg, Nymphenburg Gardens, Bavaria.*

Even before the 'Pagodenburg' was finished he had caused work to be started on a bathing pavilion that included whole walls of Dutch tiling. Between 1734 and 1739, he had a hunting lodge, the exotic Amalienburg Pavilion, installed at Schloss Nymphenburg. Its outstanding feature was a combined kitchen-dining room for indoor picnics, whose walls were covered in tiles. The tiled tableaux of the Amalienburg rank among the great achievements of the tile-maker's art, and include a series of Chinese scenes in polychrome with added black, and three massive vases of flowers surrounded by birds and butterflies. All were the products of Delft factories.

French architects were employed at the Augustusburg Palace at Brühl, near Bonn, where Maximilian Emmanuel's son, Clemens August, Elector of Cologne, installed a number of tiled rooms between 1740 and 1748. There were two anterooms, the audience chamber, a bedroom and bathroom decorated with a restrained and light-enhancing arrangement of blue geometric tiles, and a summer dining room with tile pictures based on paintings by David Teniers, Harlequin and Pulcinella figures, and flower bouquets in vases. Clemens August's Falkenlust hunting lodge at Brühl, with its decoration of tiles relating to hawking, was built in the 1730s. The tiles themselves, like so many of these grandiose arrangements for German princes, came from The Flowerpot factory in Rotterdam, and some of the pounces for them have been preserved.

Other palatial schemes in Germany and Poland were supplied with Dutch tiles during the 18th century, and a vast export of both polychrome and blue-and-white tiles was made to southern Europe, and particularly Portugal, during the second half of the 17th century and the first half of the 18th. After about 1760 these exports dwindled, mainly owing to historical circumstances in other parts of Europe. The demands of the home market diminished, so much so that by the early 19th century the large numbers of tile factories once scattered all over the Netherlands had been reduced to a mere sprinkling. Through a series of factory mergers, tiles were produced in Rotterdam until 1873; only one factory each in Utrecht, Harlingen and Delft survived through the 19th century, and

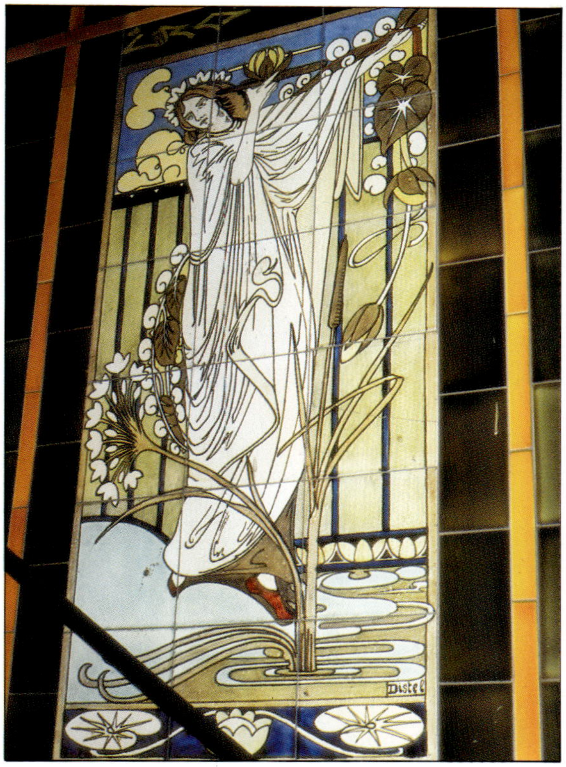

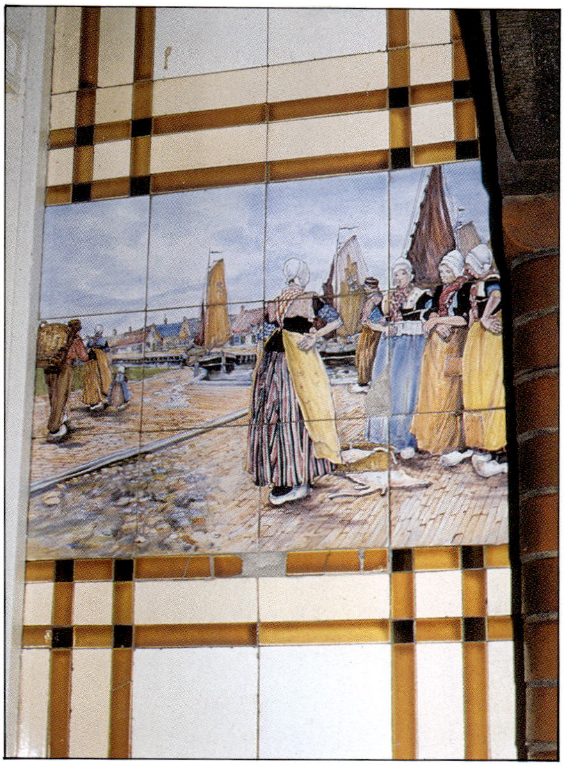

CHAPTER SIX

•

FAR LEFT *Art Nouveau panel depicting a young woman in a long flowing dress among waterlilies, probably symbolizing Spring; signed at the bottom right with the name of the manufacturer de Distel, c. 1905. This splendid panel can be found in the porch of 168 Ferdinand Bolstraat, Amsterdam.*

LEFT *One of two panels depicting Dutch scenes based on designs by the painter H Cassiers and made by the Utrecht firm of Westraven, c. 1908. They can be seen in the entrance porch of 68 Admiraal de Ruyterweg, Amsterdam.*

only the Tichelaar family firm in Makkum continued in Friesland.

Toward the end of the 19th century, however, tile-making in the Netherlands enjoyed a spectacular revival. Dutch Art Nouveau tiles, usually in composite pictorial groupings on the outsides of buildings, provide some of the best examples of fin-de-siècle decoration. Some of the finest can be seen in Amsterdam.

The Dutch were strongly influenced by English Arts and Crafts designers such as William Morris, Walter Crane, C F A Voysey and Lewis Day, by the Belgian Henri van de Velde, and by artistic ideas from the East — Japan, Java and Bali in particular. Several Dutch tile-works still made their wares by the traditional plastic method, by which designs were stencilled or painted onto the tin-glazed surface; in this they were closer to Arts and Crafts ideals than their English counterparts with the exception of William De Morgan. Some of these tiles were of the old-style 5-in (13-cm) size, instead of the 6-in (15-cm) squares typical of most 19th-century tiles.

The new factories that started up in response to the 19th-century demand for tiles used the dust-pressing method, like most of those in England, but they also favoured hand-painting or stencilled decoration rather than transfer-printing or relief-pressing. At De Porcelayne Fles in Delft, a new technique known as *sectiel* developed; in this the tiles were cut into shapes following the lines of the design and then coloured appropriately, in the manner of stained glass. De Porcelayne Fles was one of the few tile-making firms to have survived since the 17th century; others were van Hulst of Harlingen and Tichelaar of Makkum, while among the new arrivals on the late 19th-century scene were Holland of Utrecht; de Distel and Lotus, both of Amsterdam, and Rozenburg in The Hague.

The flowering was short-lived, however, and nearly all the tile factories closed after a few years. For most of the present century, production of Dutch decorative tiles rested on a handful of factories, the Royal Delft Porcelain factory (De Porcelayne Fles) and Tichelaar's Royal Makkum Pottery and Tile-works being the most important. More recently, however, there has been an upsurge of interest in tiles and considerable investment in new production.

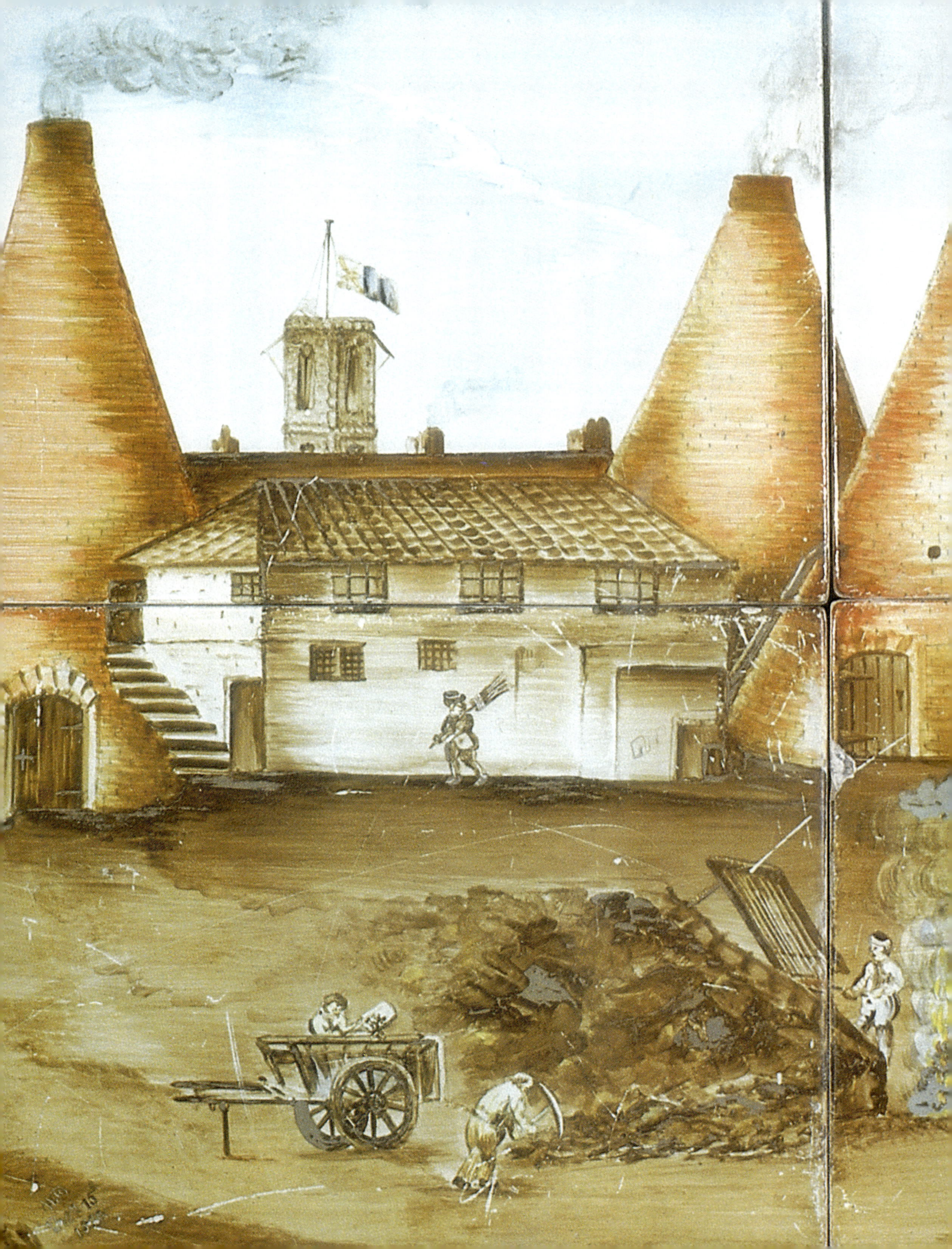

CHAPTER SEVEN

ENGLISH DELFTWARE

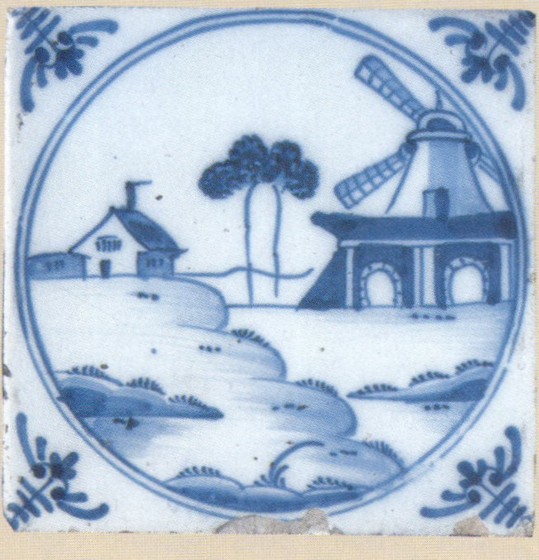

SOME TIME in the 1560s, Jasper Andries, one of the sons of Guido Andries of Antwerp, emigrated to Norwich with another potter, Jacob Jansen. They were the first of a steady stream of Netherlandish potters who settled and worked in England, at first in East Anglia and Kent, but very soon in London, establishing a delftware industry which, while it never reached the sheer volume of the Dutch, was nevertheless of enormous importance in the 17th and 18th centuries.

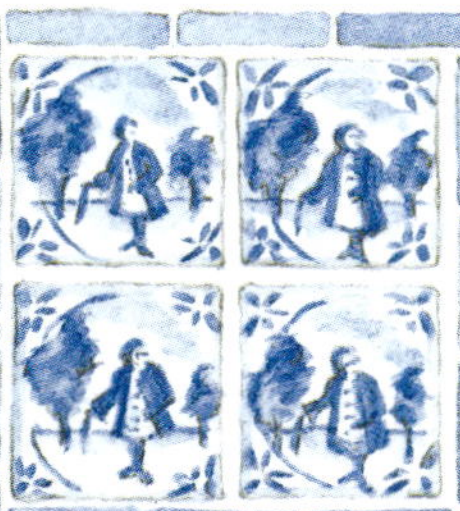

OVERLEAF (BACKGROUND) *A pearlware tile picture of Bristol Pottery painted by William Fifield, signed and dated* WF/Feb 15 1820.

OVERLEAF (INSET) *English delftware tile showing a windmill, with barred ox-head corners, Bristol, 1755-70.*

JACOB JANSEN came to London and in 1570 petitioned Elizabeth I for a patent to make tin-glazed earthenware, or 'galliware' as it was called, and 'Galley pavinge tyles'. Although his petition was not granted, he apparently set up a pottery in Aldgate, and anglicized his name to Jacob Johnson. It is likely that he employed other Flemish immigrant craftsmen: several were living in the same parish in the 1570s.

In 1613 two London merchants were granted a patent to make 'all paving tiles of all Sises dishes of all sises . . . after such manner as used at Fiansa [Faenza] and other parte beyond the Seas . . .' in Southwark, where another Fleming, Christian Wilhelm, had already established a pottery making paving tiles and other wares.

It is likely that wall tiles were also being made in London by the 1620s and 1630s. Many fragments have been found on old factory sites, but there is a great deal of uncertainty surrounding them: many were almost certainly imports from the Netherlands, while some may have been close copies — made from imported Dutch clays by Dutch immigrants — of the tiles from their native land, which were by this time growing in popularity among the English.

In 1676 a Delft potter, Jan Ariens van Hamme, was granted a patent to make 'Tiles and Porcelain and other earthen wares after the way practised in Holland' and although his factory in Vauxhall probably closed with his death three years later, there appear to have been several other potteries producing tiles in the Dutch style in the second half of the 17th century. At the same time, despite prohibitions in 1672 and 1676 on the importation of 'any earthenware painted with white, blue or any other colours', which were obviously designed to protect the English delftware pottery industry, it is clear that many of the potters and other merchants kept stocks of genuine 'Holland tile' with which to supply the ever-growing market. Difficulties in obtaining the right clays and in firing the tiles satisfactorily, meant that home production of tin-glazed wares was somewhat erratic in this period in England, while the Dutch industry, by now established on a huge

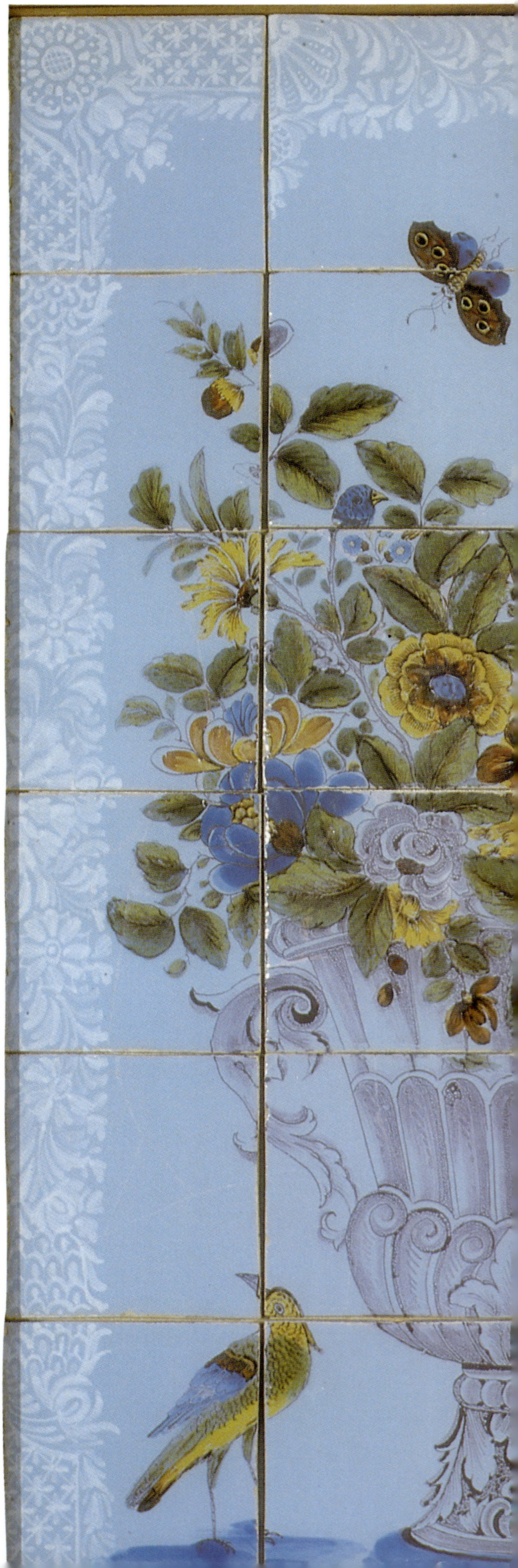

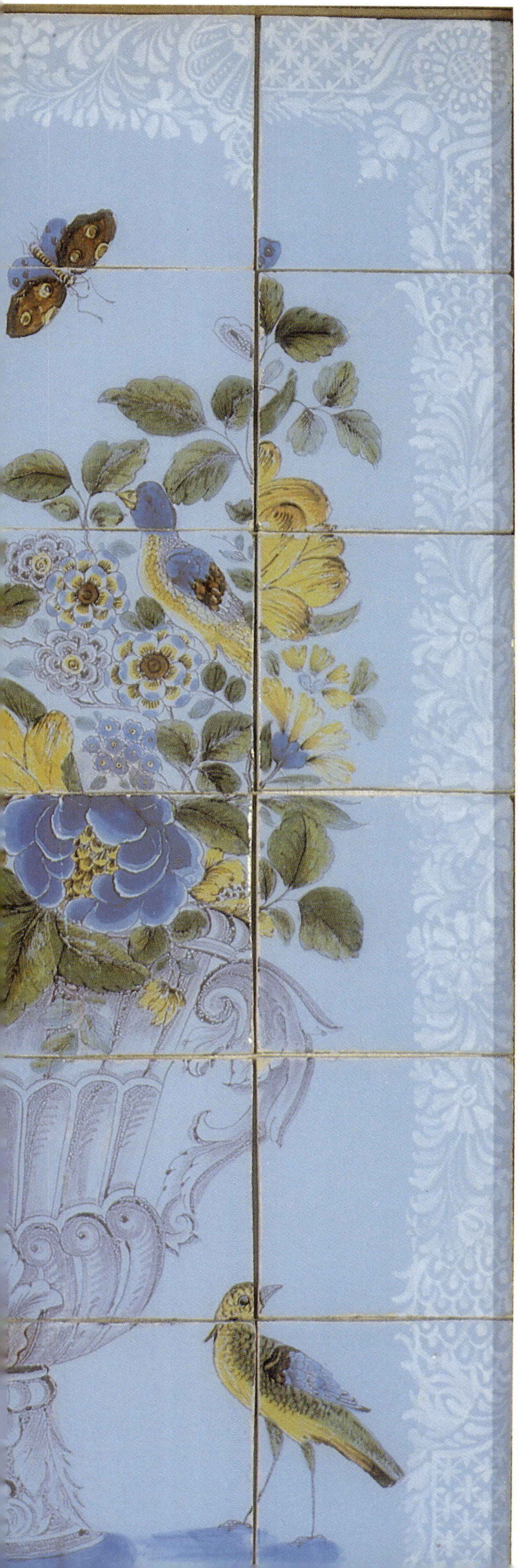

scale, had overcome such problems long before.

Even with the accession of the Dutch King William and his consort Queen Mary in 1688 and the consequently enhanced popularity of Dutch wares, the import ban was not lifted, and the fact that the demand for delftware could not be met by the English potters stimulated a broadside from the Company of Glass Sellers in 1695, against 'the Bill for Prohibiting Earthwares'. In it they point out that 'a great part of the trade consists in selling white and Painted tiles for Chimnies . . .' and because the English industry could not keep up the supply in sufficient quantity, many merchants risked going out of business unless they were allowed to sell imported Dutch wares. The struggling industry was still further threatened in 1696 by a tax levied on the production of all kinds of earthenware to pay for the French wars. Fortunately the potters' protests were heeded, and the tax was soon abolished.

The production of English tin-glazed tiles improved both in quantity and quality during the early 18th century, and although some critics continued to argue that the Dutch wares were technically superior, there is no doubt that the English were overcoming their initial difficulties and were producing a refreshingly wide range of designs. The inventory of just one London potter's stock in 1726 lists more than 10,000 fired tiles, a certain indication of the growth of the English tile industry.

The main domestic use of tiles in both England and America during the 18th century was for fireplaces. Other purposes included dairies and the 'Sides of Cold Baths'. Bathrooms as they are known today were not a normal domestic fitting in this period; cold plunges were taken for medicinal reasons and some grand houses had plunge baths — more like indoor swimming pools — built on their grounds and set with plain and/or decorated tiles. Tile pictures were much rarer in England than in the Netherlands, but a few have survived to show that they must have been used both indoors, to brighten up a dull wall, and out, as shop signs. In the Bristol area a small number of tiled wash-basin recesses have

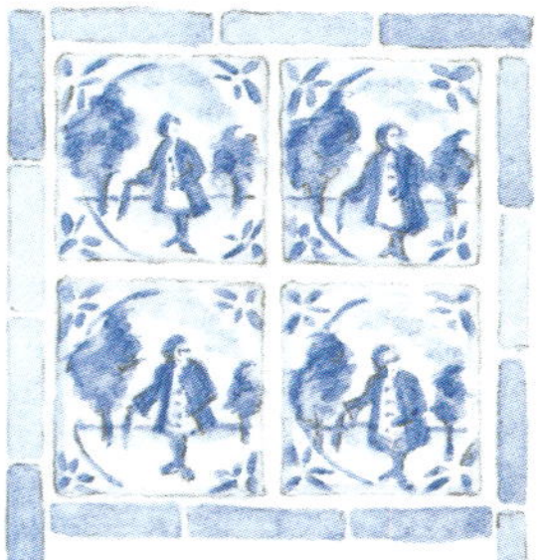

LEFT *A tiled flower-vase panel with* bianco sopra bianco *borders, Bristol,* c. *1765.*

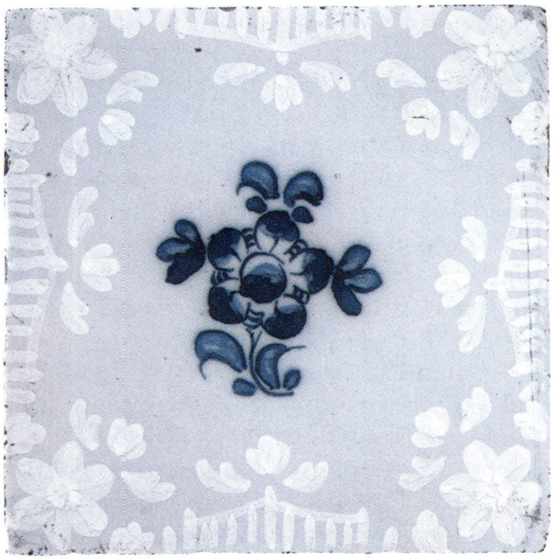

RIGHT *English delftware tile depicting a flower with a* bianco sopra bianco *border, Bristol, 1760-70.*

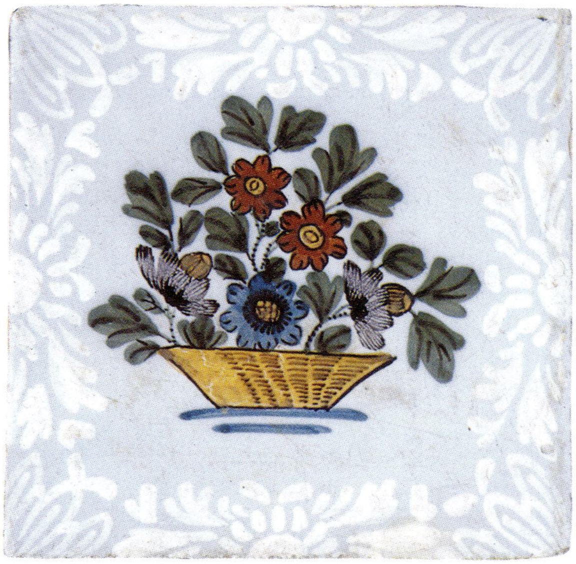

BELOW RIGHT *Polychrome painted flower basket with a* bianco sopra bianco *border, Bristol, 1760-70.*

survived, suggesting that they may have been an architectural feature of the district.

The making of delftware spread beyond London during the 17th century. Although tin-glazed earthenware manufacture had been established at Brislington, near Bristol, by two potters from Southwark in about 1640, no tiles have been definitely attributed to Brislington and it was not until 1683 that a tile-producing delftware factory was set up in Bristol itself. This was the Temple Back pottery, which survived until the 1770s. Other Bristol potteries included Limekiln Lane, started in 1692 and probably a producer of tiles from about 1720 until 1746 (when the factory closed), and Redcliff Back pottery, operating first under Thomas Frank and later his son Richard from 1706 until the 1770s, among whose notable achievements was the production of tiles and other wares with *bianco sopra bianco*, or white-on-white, borders.

The *bianco sopra bianco* technique involved painting the bluish- or greyish-white tin-glazed surface with a mixture made much whiter and more viscous by adding a higher proportion of tin oxide. This 'super-white' decoration stood out in slight relief against the not-quite-white background whose glaze was often tinged with cobalt to enhance the contrast.

The *bianco sopra bianco* technique was first developed by Italian maiolica painters in the late 15th century, and was practiced at the Rörstrand faïence factory in Sweden from about 1745. It was from here that it is thought to have been introduced, first to Lambeth and later to Bristol. A Swedish potter, Magnus Lundberg, formerly of Rörstrand, came to England in the late 1740s and worked at the Frank factory in Bristol between about 1757 and 1767, and it was during this period that *bianco sopra bianco* tiles were produced there.

The city of Liverpool, well placed for exporting to America and the West Indies, became the most prolific centre of delftware tile production during the 18th century. The first factory was set up in Lord Street in 1710 by Richard Holt, with workmen from Southwark. A contemporary newspaper announcement affirmed its intention to produce 'all sorts of fine and painted pots and other vessels and tiles in imitation of China both for Inland and Outland trade . . .', which makes it clear that tiles were produced at the outset and that export was a major consideration. Several other factories were set up in Liverpool during the 18th century, many of them producing tiles, although detailed evidence is scanty.

Among the best recorded was the factory of Zachariah Barnes in the Old Haymarket pottery, established *c* 1765–70. His output included both painted tiles and plain white ones, or 'blanks', many of which were supplied to the printer John Sadler. Apart from the sheer volume of tiles emanating

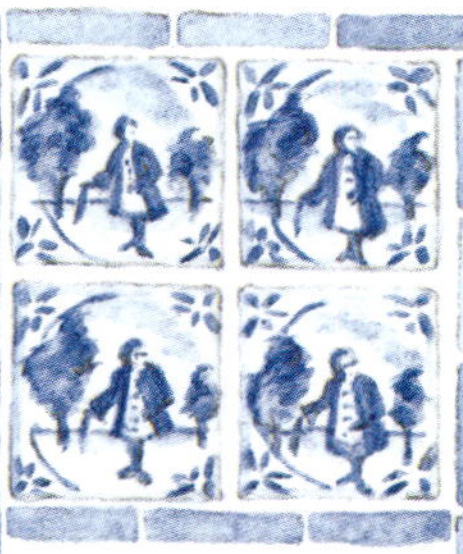

CHAPTER SEVEN

•

from the Liverpool factories during the third quarter of the 18th century, the range of designs and the bright polychrome palette used there, as well as the traditional 'Dutch' blue and white, make them the most varied of all.

Tiles were also produced at the Delftfield pottery in Glasgow, established in 1748, and at Wednesbury in Staffordshire during the third quarter of the 18th century, but their products have so far not been identified with certainty. At Wincanton in Somerset, tiles of a similar type as those made at nearby Bristol were probably produced in the 1730s and 1740s.

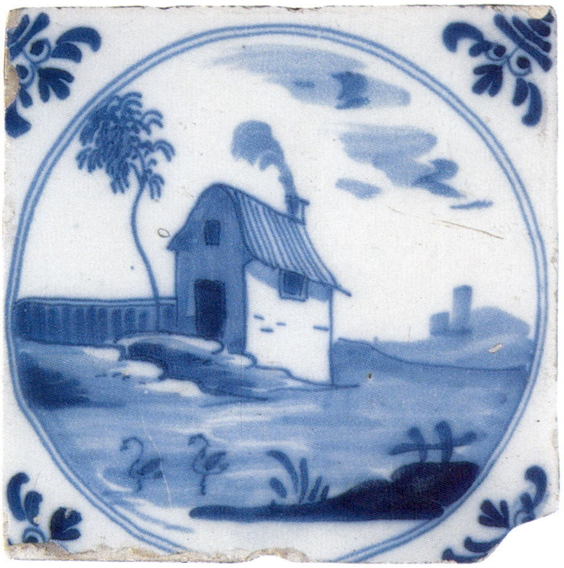

LEFT *English delftware tile showing a small cottage with a smoking chimney and barred ox-head corner motifs, Bristol, 1755-70.*

As the English delftware industry was established by Dutch potters, and because, later on, one of its objectives was to imitate the popular Dutch wares as accurately and as cheaply as possible, it is hardly surprising that there are so many similarities between Dutch and English tiles, regarding both methods of production and design. This is especially true until the mid-18th century, by which time English tiles had developed their own styles and identity. It must be remembered that throughout the period of English tile production, that is, until the last quarter of the 18th century, the traditional Dutch blue-and-white tiles continued to be copied as closely as possible, as much to undercut the Dutch export market as to supply popular demand at home, so a steady stream of 'Dutch' designs with only slight differences is discernible. Some of these were painted freehand, but engraved sources were common and the outlines of the designs on many English tiles appear to have been drawn onto tiles by pounces or pricked transfers, in much the same way as they were in the Netherlands. Pattern books were probably used fairly widely by the English, as by the Dutch. In addition, and unlike Dutch practice at this period, stencils appear to have been used at Liverpool for some flower, bird and leaf designs.

Engraved designs came from many sources. Among the earliest identifiable examples is the series of tiles illustrating the Popish Plot, probably made *c* 1680 in the factory of Jan Ariens van Hamme, whose designs were copied from a pack of playing cards. Bookplates may have been the origin of the rare portraits and coats of arms on tiles, and the engraved designs of figures in landscapes in contemporary song books relate to some of those on tiles. Naturally enough, Continental — and particularly Dutch and Flemish — engravings were used extensively for biblical tiles, many of whose illustrations can be directly traced to 17th- and early 18th-century Bibles.

During the 1750–70 period tile-makers in Liverpool, and possibly also in Bristol, made extensive use of a series of engravings of animals by the Dutch artist Nicolaes Berchem (1620–83). Most popular, and exclusively English, were the tiles produced after illustrations in a drawing book published by John Bowles in 1756–7, and after the French Rococo painter Jean-Baptiste Pillement's plates for Robert Sayer's *The Ladies' Amusement* (1759 or 1760), whose animals, birds, figures and chinoiserie designs were universally copied.

English delftware tile borders and corner motifs were as varied as the Dutch, and often provide clues to the origin of tiles decorated with traditional Dutch designs. The ox-head motif, for example, which appeared in many forms in the corners of both Dutch and English tiles, frequently took a barred form with lines across the corners in England. The flower-head corner and the studded border were also peculiarly

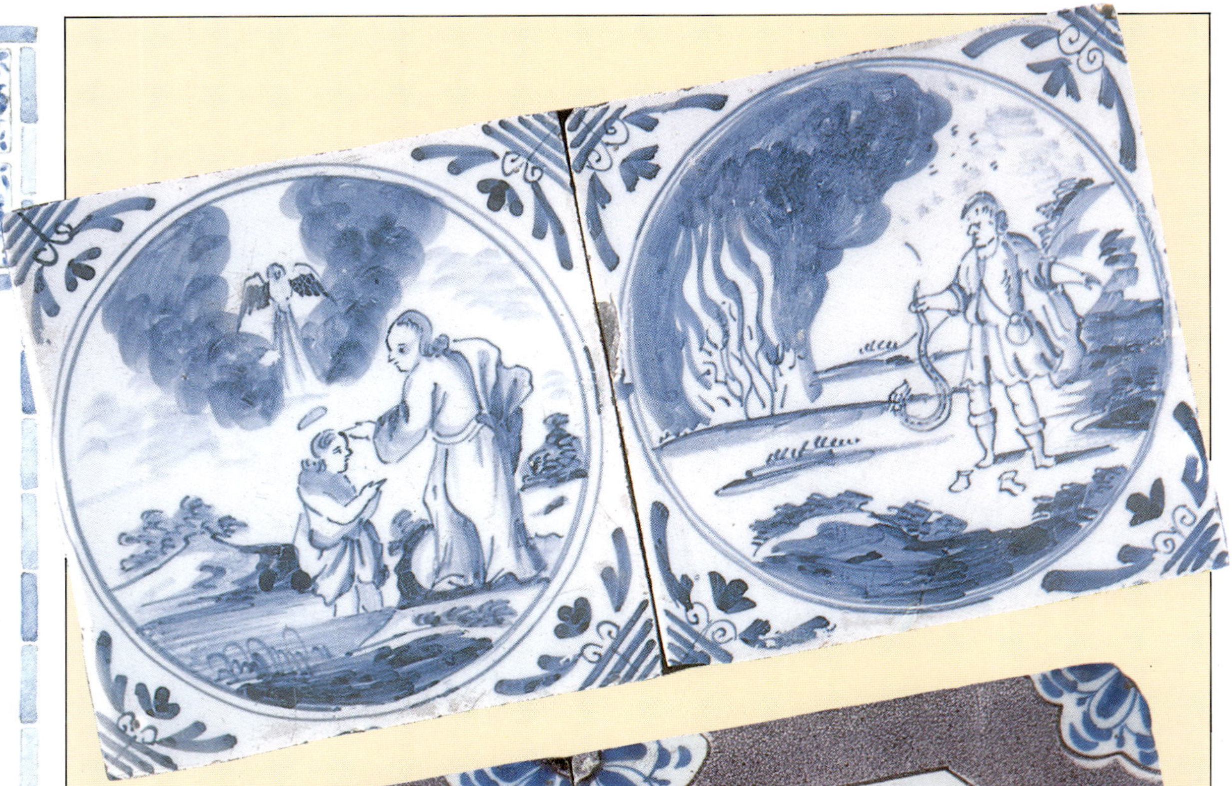

RIGHT *Two English biblical tiles with barred ox-head corners: St John the Baptist baptizing Christ in the River Jordan, and Moses in front of the Burning Bush, holding the staff that God changed into a snake; both London, 1725-50.*

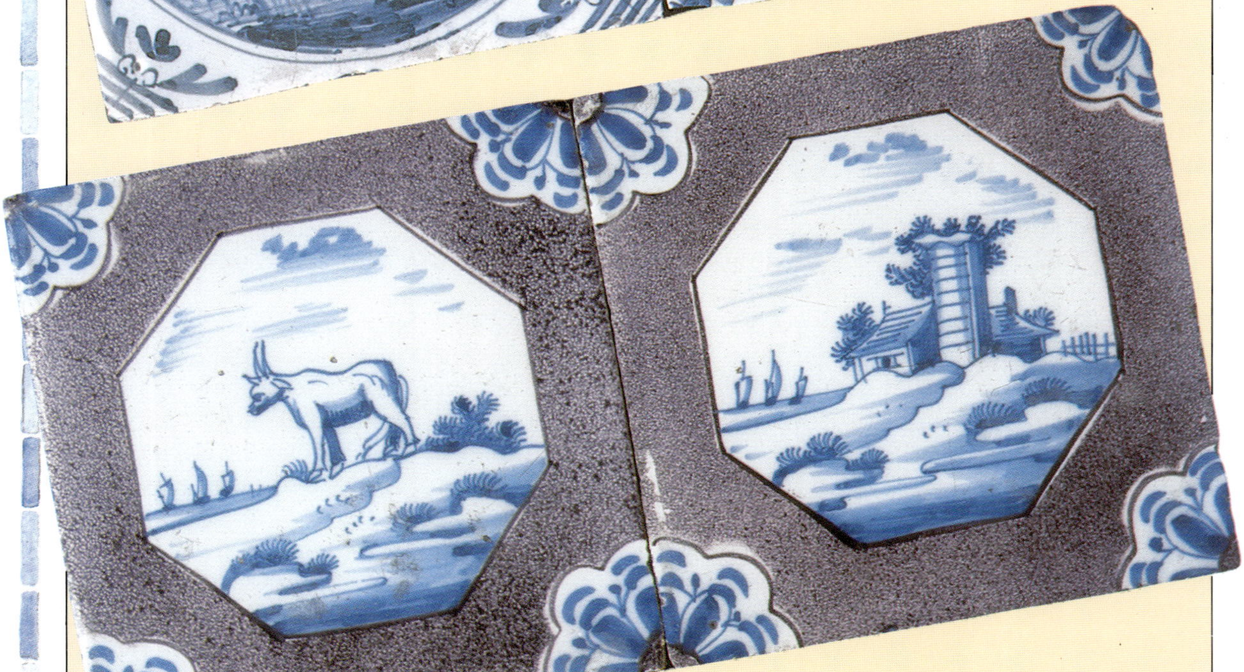

BELOW RIGHT *Two delftware tiles with coastal scenes within octagonal manganese-powdered grounds and Chinese-style quarter rosette corners, Bristol, 1725-50.*

English; so were cherub heads, dandelions, diaper corners and chain borders. Tiles with blue, red or green grounds were also made in England but not, apparently, in the Netherlands. English tiles tend to be very slightly larger than the customary 5-in (13-cm) squares of the Dutch.

While many of the designs and types were produced in London, Bristol and Liverpool, certain characteristics have come to be associated with particular regions. Most London tiles, for example, were decorated in blue or manganese or both, with only a few examples, such as flower-vase tiles, in polychrome. The blues were typically dark and inky, and the manganese dark and brownish. London most commonly copied Dutch tile designs, which is not surprising since such a high proportion of the London pottery craftsmen were themselves of Dutch or Flemish origin. A noted characteristic of Bristol tiles was the appearance of small nail holes in the corners of the backs. These were probably due to a different method of cutting the tile blanks than that of other centres both in England and the Netherlands, which resulted in nail holes appearing on the fronts of the tiles, as least until *c* 1750. Bristol tiles were usually slightly larger than other English tiles, thinner in body and sometimes slightly convex in shape, and with very smooth backs. A pale manganese ground may also point to a Bristol origin, and *bianco sopra bianco* borders were associated with the Frank factory. Bristol tiles from the early period were usually of blue and/or manganese, with designs after the Dutch, but from the 1750s onward a great variety of decoration appeared, including rococo-figure subjects based on engravings and executed in rather muddy polychrome colours.

Liverpool seems to have conquered the technical problems of tile production more successfully than London or Bristol, with the result that Liverpool tiles tend to be more perfectly flat and even than others. Liverpool tiles are characterized by a particularly bright blue, and by the use of polychrome in the 'Fazackerly colours' — red, blue, yellow, mauve and green — named after a pair of mugs traditionally made for Thomas and Catherine Fazackerly in 1757–8 (destroyed by bomb damage to the Liverpool Museum during World War II). A number from 1 to 13 fired on the back of a tile generally denotes a Liverpool origin, and was probably a batch number.

As well as far greater quantities of tiles, Liverpool produced a wider range of designs and motifs than any other centre. While many were similar to those of London, Bristol and the Dutch factories, some were peculiar to Liverpool. Among these were leaf, buttercup and Michaelmas daisy corners; fish-roe, trellis, daisy-chain and barbed medallion borders, and a series of rococo-patterned grounds around circular or octagonal shapes.

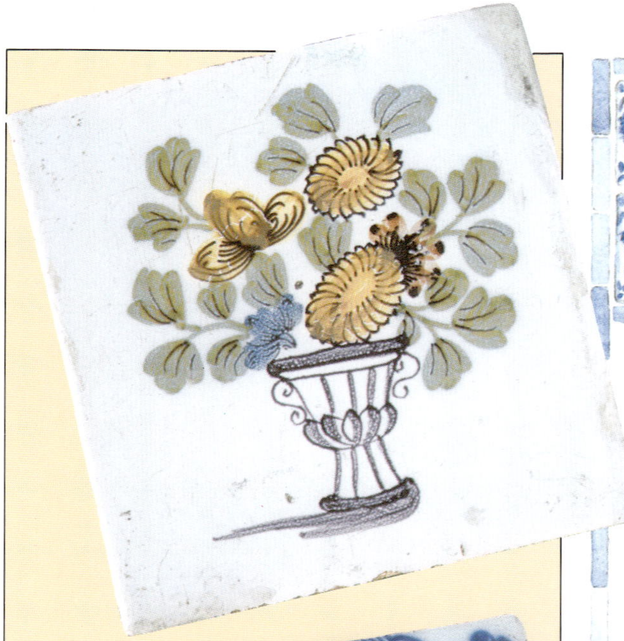

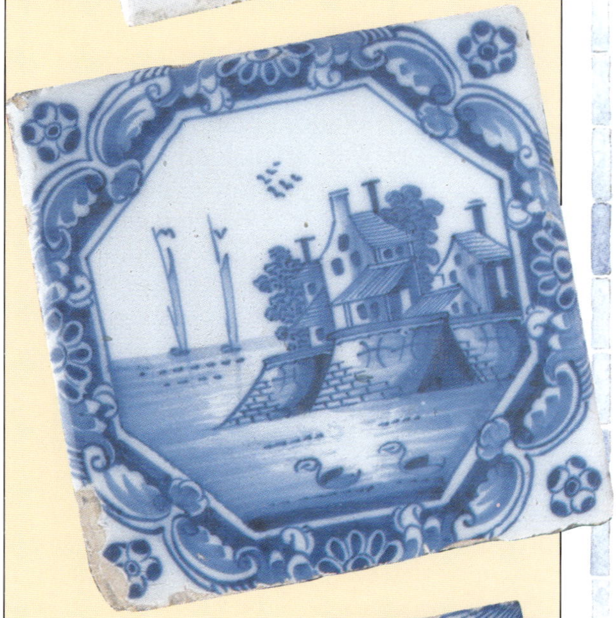

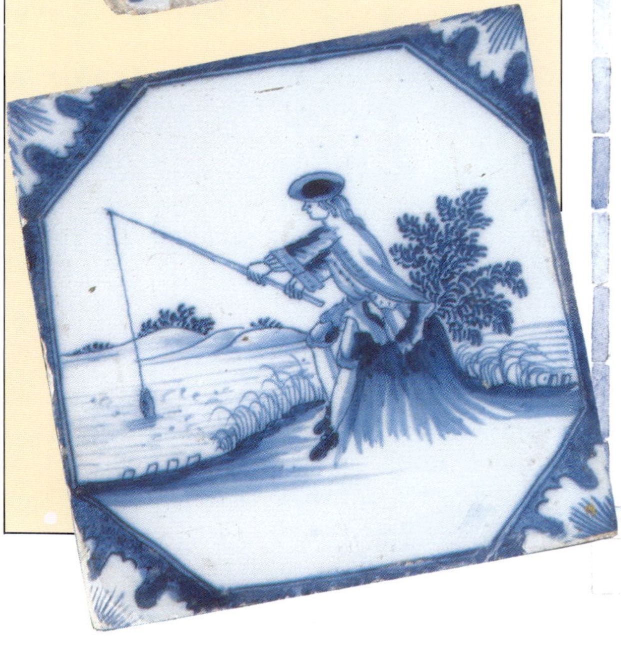

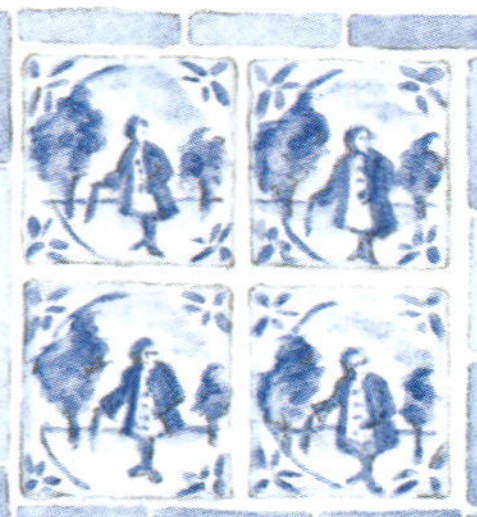

LEFT *Tile painted with a vase of flowers in 'Fazackerly' colours, Liverpool, c. 1760.*

CENTRE LEFT *Tile painted with coastal scene within octagonal Louis XV border with buttercup corner motifs, Liverpool, 1740-75.*

BELOW LEFT *Tile depicting a gentleman fishing within an octagonal border with ragged flower corners, Liverpool, 1750-1770.*

SADLER AND GREEN

Around 1756 in Liverpool a new method of decorating tiles was introduced that was to have a great impact not just on the tile industry, but on ceramics generally. In August 1756 two Liverpool printers, John Sadler and Guy Green, signed an affidavit in which they affirmed that they 'did within the space of six hours . . . print upwards of twelve hundred earthenware tiles of different patterns . . . which . . . were more in number, and better, and neater than one hundred skilful pot painters could have painted in the like space of time in the common and usual way of painting with a pencil . . .' Their claim was supported by a certificate signed by two witnesses, Alderman Shaw and Samuel Goodbody, both potters, who also swore 'That we have since burnt [fired] the above tiles, and that they are considerably neater than any we have seen pencilled, and may be sold at little more than half the price. We are also assured that the said John Sadler and Guy Green have been several years in bringing the art of printing on earthenware to perfection . . . .'

It is unlikely that Sadler and Green actually invented the technique of transfer-printing on pottery: another claimant (who may in fact only have been the developer rather than the originator of the idea) was an Irish engraver, John Brooks, who came to London in 1746 and five years later applied for a patent for his method 'of printing, impressing, and reversing upon enamel and china from engraved, etched and *mezzotinto* plates, and from cuttings on wood and mettel, impressions

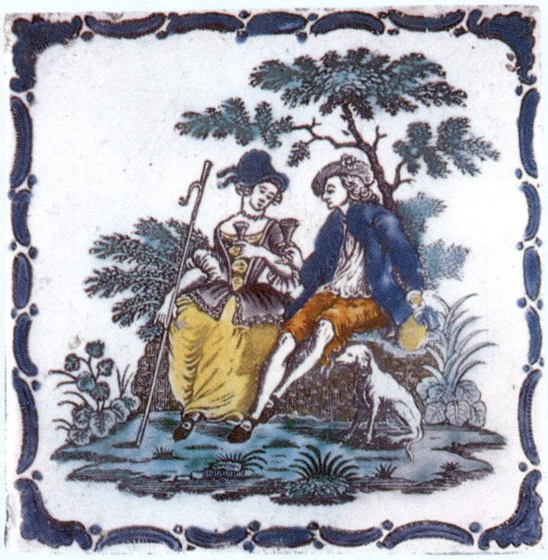

of History, Portraits, Landskips, Foliages, Coats of Arms, Cyphers, Letters and other Devices.' This petition, and two later ones, were not granted, but he was a partner in the Battersea enamel factory from 1753 to 1756, and transfer prints were applied to enamels both at Battersea and Birmingham, and to porcelain at Bow and Worcester. Sadler, however, seems to have been the only person to produce transfer-printed tiles in this period. There was virtually no competition, even though he did not bother to apply, for a patent.

The fact that tiles could be decorated so much more speedily by printing than by painting gave Sadler the advantage over the Dutch, whose tiles were still being imported into Liverpool on a large scale. His concern seems to have been to undercut the Dutch rather than to damage the trade in Liverpool painted tiles, which apparently continued to flourish at the same time. Both painted and printed tiles from Liverpool were shipped across the Atlantic in large quantities and were used to decorate the fireplaces of well-to-do New Englanders.

Sadler's earliest tiles, produced between 1756 and 1757, were printed with wood blocks, mainly in purple or blue monochrome; occasionally a design would be black and coloured in polychrome enamels. Designs were mostly figurative, and many of them, like their borders, were similar to those of painted tiles. These early woodblock tiles seem to have met with little enthusiasm from the English, and a high proportion were exported to the Americans.

It was not until Sadler realized the advantages of transfer-printing using copperplates, in 1757, that his success was assured. It is likely that he employed a number of engravers to produce designs for the tiles, many of which bear Sadler's signature. These designs are nearly always in the figurative rococo style with various forms of scrolling borders that grow less elaborate toward the mid-1760s, when a standardized form, incorporating a figure 8 on each side, known as an '88' border, seems to have been adopted.

Subjects were often taken from Pillement's *The Ladies' Amusement*, Bowles's drawing book, and engravings after Watteau, Boucher,

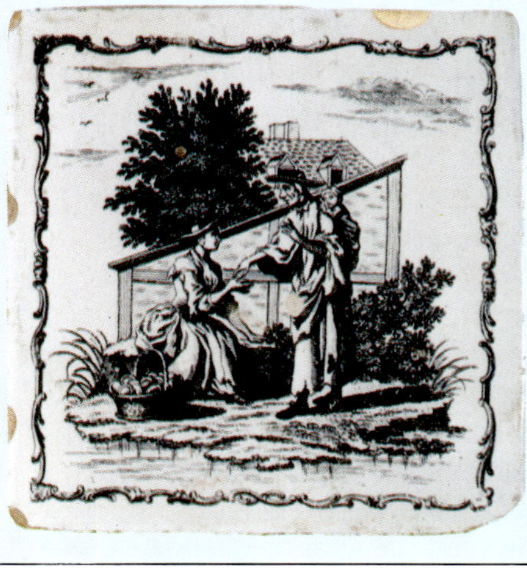

Lancret, Chardin and other rococo painters. Except in rare instances when polychrome was used — perhaps for a special order, or experimentally — these tiles were printed in monochrome: the colours used included black, iron-red, lilac, sepia and (rarely) green, the palette narrowing to black, red, red-brown and sepia later on, with plum and green used occasionally.

Sadler did not make the tiles he decorated, but was supplied with blanks by a number of local potters, including Zachariah Barnes. Considerable variations in both clay body and glaze were discernible: the early printed tiles tended to be heavier than the later ones, which, like Liverpool painted tiles of the 1760s and 1770s, were generally of a thin, light body.

In 1761 Sadler began an association with Josiah Wedgwood that involved applying transfer prints to his creamware and led to an expansion of the business. In order to cope with the extra work resulting from both creamware and tile decoration, Sadler took into partnership Guy Green, who had worked with him for some time previously and who had also signed the famous affidavit. Although the creamware side of the business apparently prospered, the decorating of tiles positively rampaged, and Sadler was hard pressed to meet the overwhelming demand, especially from London. Sadler retired in 1770, and the tile-decorating business was continued by Guy Green until about 1780, when it apparently ceased to specialize in tiles and became a china factory of a more general nature. However, Green continued to print tiles for Wedgwood until

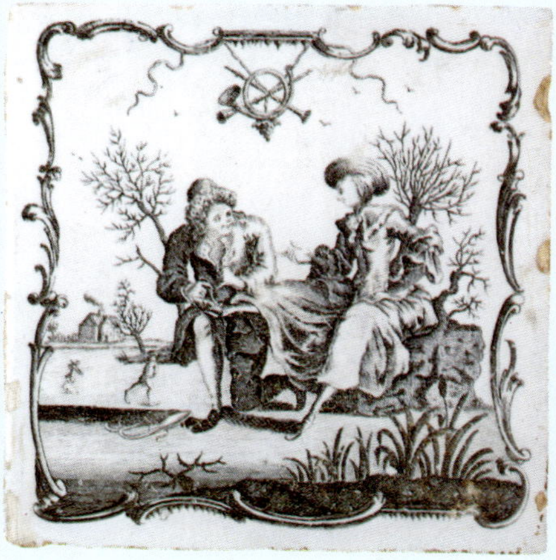

about 1784. While Green went on using the earlier designs, he also commissioned new ones, many of them based on contemporary prints. The 'Green' period is particularly associated with three distinct types: fable-inspired, neo-classical and theatrical tiles.

In 1773 a former apprentice of Sadler and subsequent employee of Green, Richard Abbey, advertised 'his shop at No. 11 in Cleveland Square [Liverpool] where he manufactures and sells all sorts of Queen's Ware printed in the neatest manner and in a Variety of Colours'. Tiles were among the wares he advertised but very few can be attributed to him with certainty; it is likely, however, that he made engraved designs, notably of fables, for Green to print. Illustrations of Aesop's Fables were especially popular at this time.

As well as commissioning Sadler and Green to print large quantities of tiles in his cream-coloured earthenware, or Queen's Ware, for which he supplied the blanks, Josiah Wedgwood produced tiles with painted decoration. Most of these were used, like the printed tiles, in conjunction with plain tiles, for 'Dairys, Baths, Summer Houses, Temples etc.' — but particularly dairies — during the 1770s and 1780s. A well-preserved example is the dairy at Althorp, built for Lavinia, Lady Spencer in 1786. For this, Wedgwood not only supplied ivy-decorated and plain tiles for the walls, but vases, pans and dairy dishes to match.

It was the development of new ceramic bodies by Wedgwood and others in the late 18th century that effectively killed the delftware industry. However colourful and attractive the tin-glazed earthenwares were, they were neither as cheap nor, with their tendency to chip, as durable as the highly serviceable new creamwares. Hence the production of English delftware virtually ceased by 1790.

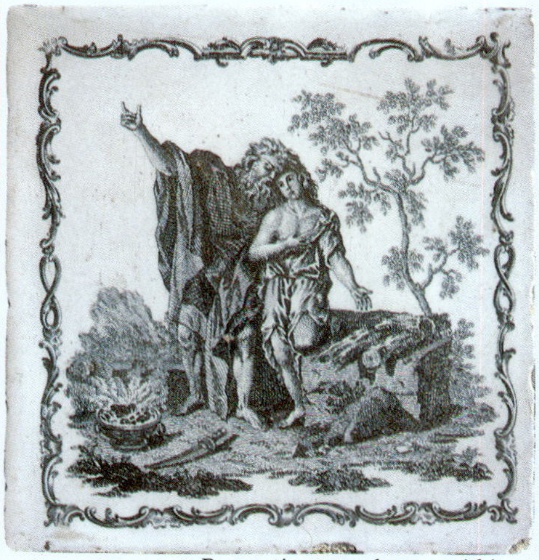

OPPOSITE ABOVE *Romantic pastoral scene within a rococo border, printed from a wood block with on-glaze coloured enamels by John Sadler, Liverpool, 1756-67.*

OPPOSITE BELOW *'The Fortune Teller', transfer-printed in black (from copperplates) by John Sadler, Liverpool, c. 1760.*

ABOVE LEFT *A country-scene tile, transfer-printed in black by John Sadler, Liverpool. The elaborate rococo border is typical of the 1757-61 period.*

ABOVE *A transfer-printed tile showing the Sacrifice of Isaac within '88' borders by John Sadler, Liverpool, 1761-70.*

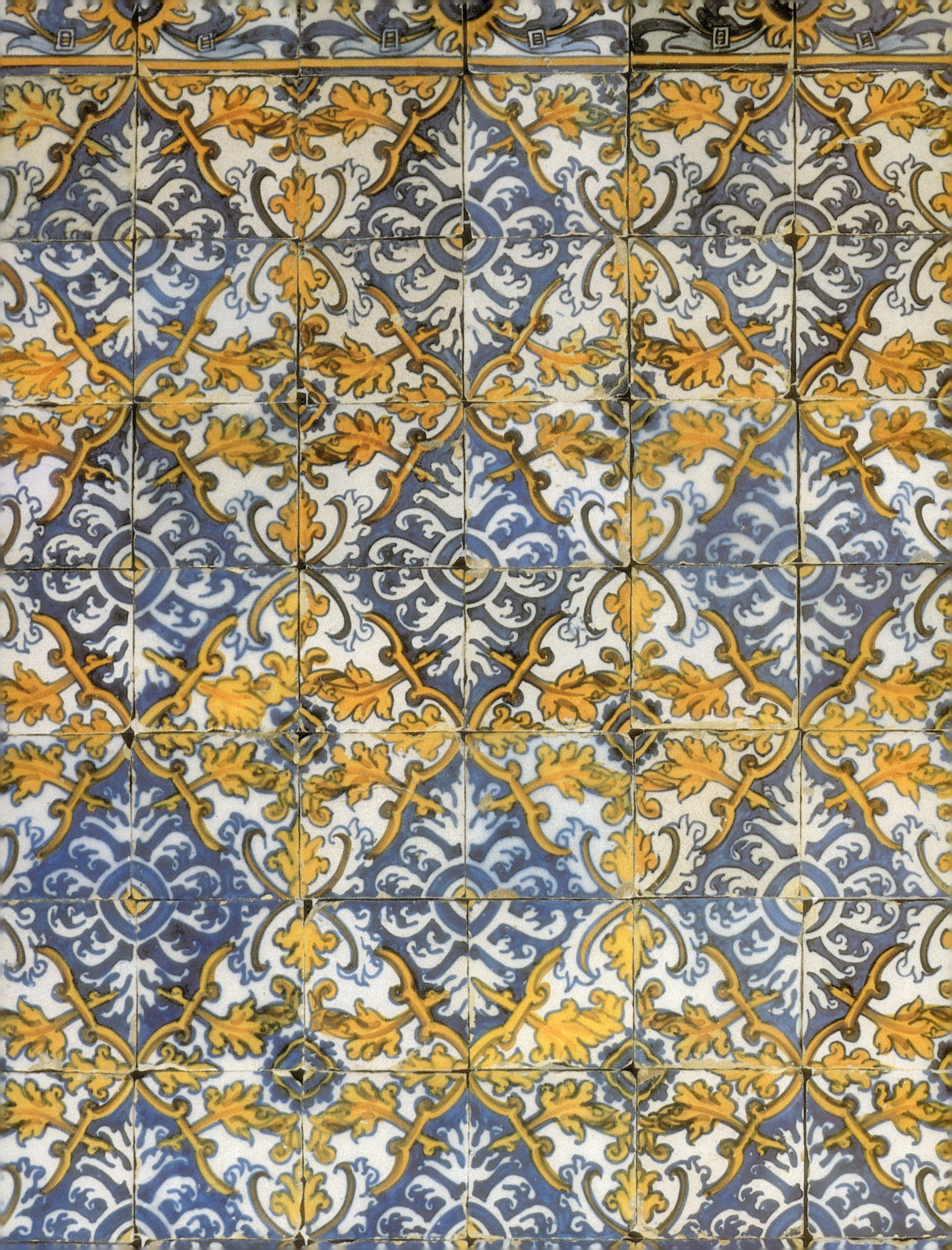

CHAPTER EIGHT

LATER TIN GLAZING IN EUROPE AND AMERICA

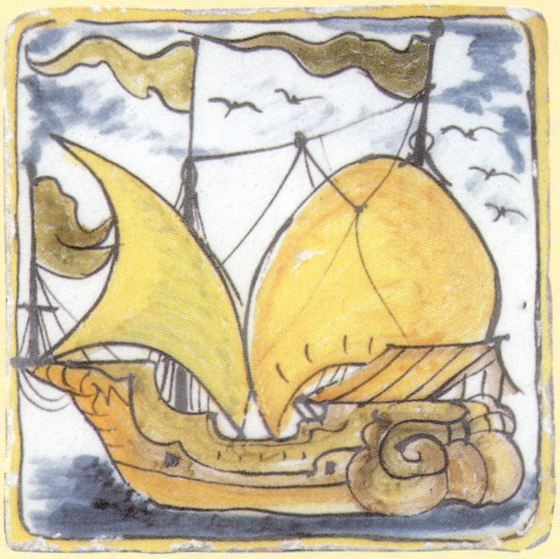

WHILE THE tin-glazed tile industries of the Netherlands and England were at the forefront for the sheer volume of their output, and because their exports brought them world-wide fame during the 17th and 18th centuries, other countries continued the tile-making traditions already established, mainly to provide both internal and external decoration for buildings. The fact that these tiles were made predominantly for home markets meant that they are often unfamiliar outside their countries of origin, but they should not be dismissed as insignificant. In many parts of Europe, and later America, tiles were an important aspect of ceramic production, reflecting both the artistic styles and the furnishing and decorating habits of different periods and places.

OVERLEAF (BACKGROUND) *Portuguese tile pattern, first half of the 17th century.*

OVERLEAF (INSET) *Spanish painted tile depicting a ship, Catalonia,* c. *1800.*

RIGHT *French faïence tile from the Beauvais region, second half of the 19th century.*

CENTRE RIGHT *A tiled panel of Adam and Eve in Our Lady of El Prado, Talavera.*

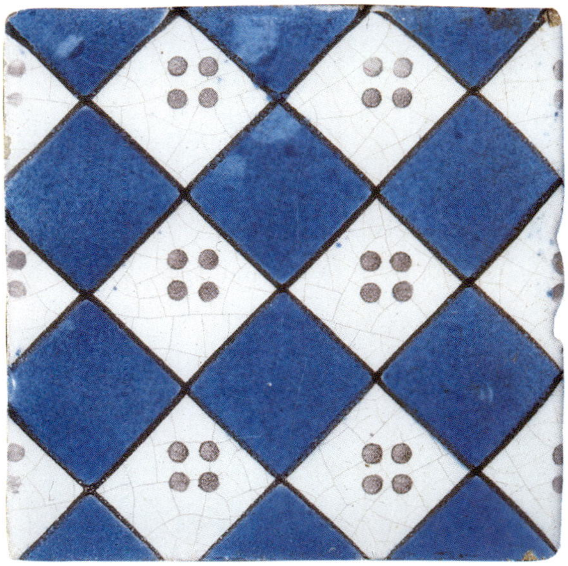

BY THE middle of the 17th century the dominating influence on ceramics was switching from Italian maiolica to Chinese porcelain, and although more than 50 years were to elapse before true hard-paste porcelain was successfully made in Europe, the tin-glaze potters imitated as closely as possible the fineness of the body and the decorative styles of the Oriental blue-and-white wares that became a craze among well-to-do Europeans. Thanks to the Dutch, cobalt blue was the dominant colour in the ceramic palette from the early 17th century.

The leading French faïence pottery of the early 17th century was that of the Italian-born Conrade brothers at Nevers, which enjoyed royal privilege for at least three decades. Later, other potteries were set up in the same place and in other French towns, but there was little competition for Nevers until the second half of the 17th century, when Rouen emerged as a leading pottery centre. Whereas Italian and Persian traditions had inspired production at Nevers, Dutch influence was more in evidence at Rouen (it is known that Delft potters worked there). By the last quarter of the 17th century, Moustiers and Marseilles were the dominant pottery centres in the south of France, while Montpellier had a long-established tile industry.

The 'Trianon de Porcelaine', built *c* 1670 by Louis XIV for Madame de Montespan at

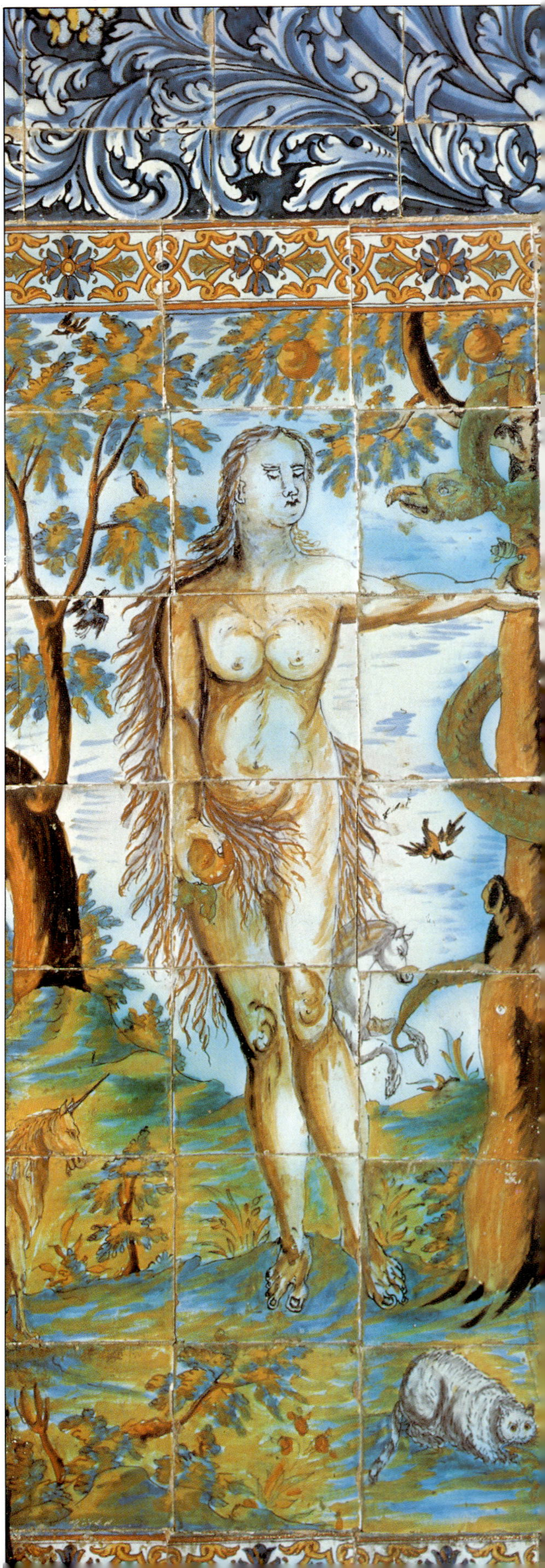

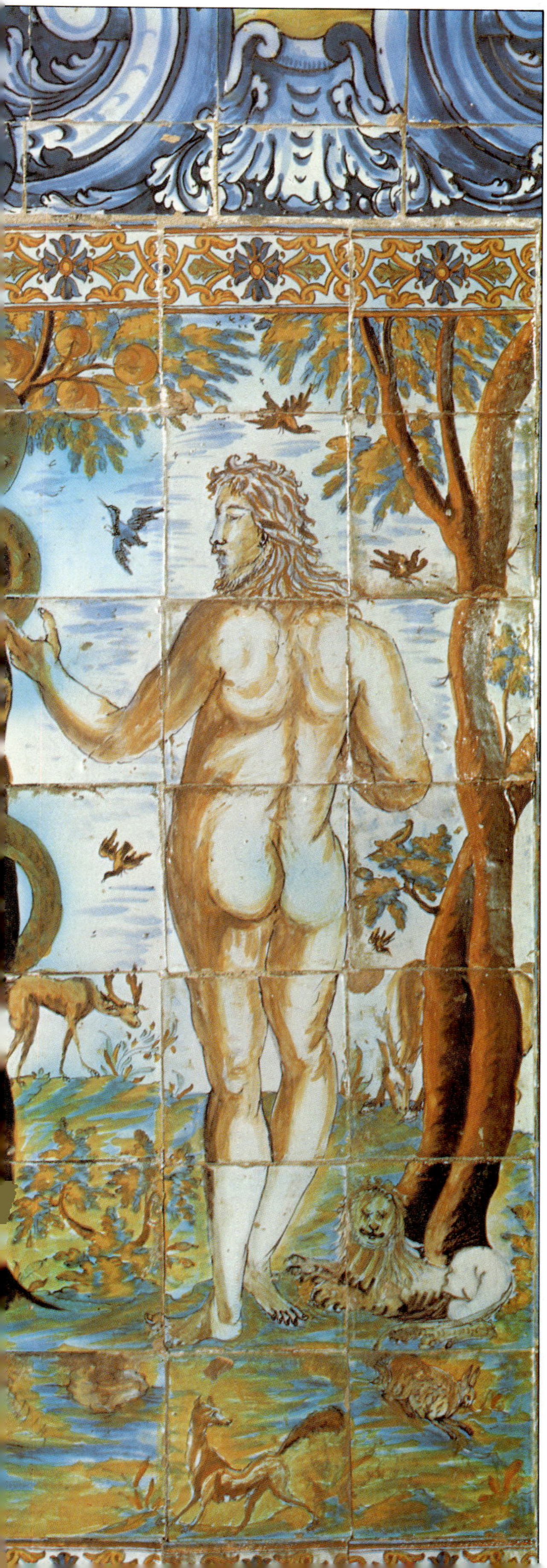

Versailles, was decorated both inside and out with blue and manganese tiles supplied at enormous cost by Rotterdam, Rouen, Nevers and Lisieux. Unfortunately the façade tiles were damaged by frost within a few years and the Trianon was pulled down in 1687. Among the 18th-century French pottery centres Strasbourg, Moustiers, Marseilles and Rouen were the most important, but many other concerns flourished in provincial towns all over the country. Among those where tiles were produced were several factories in Marseilles, Lille, Lisieux (where *cuerda seca* tiles were made) and the small factory at Vron, operating from 1770 to 1845, which specialized in them.

By the close of the 18th century the French faïence factories were on a downward swing. The French Revolution reduced the demand for expensive wares, which in any case was being fulfilled by hard-paste porcelains, while the everyday needs of the bourgeoisie were being met by the much cheaper English white earthenwares that were imported in large quantities after the Free Trade agreement of 1786. Tiles were affected as much as other wares, and few were made in France until the great 19th-century revival.

While Seville had dominated tile production in 16th-century Spain, Talavera became the leading producer of pottery, including tiles, during the 17th. Ironically, this was largely due to long-standing collaboration

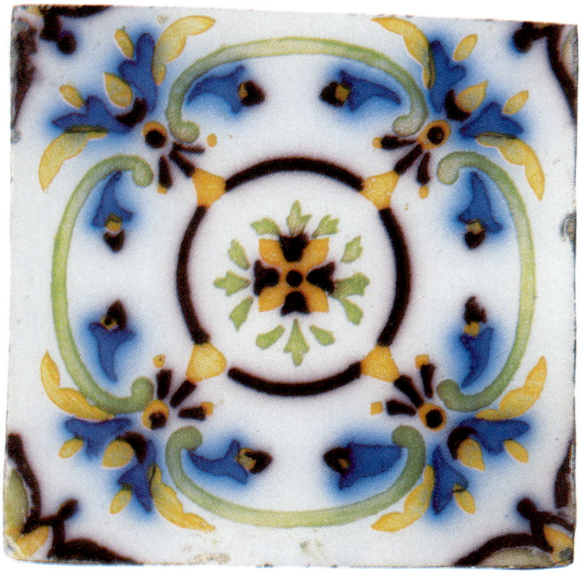

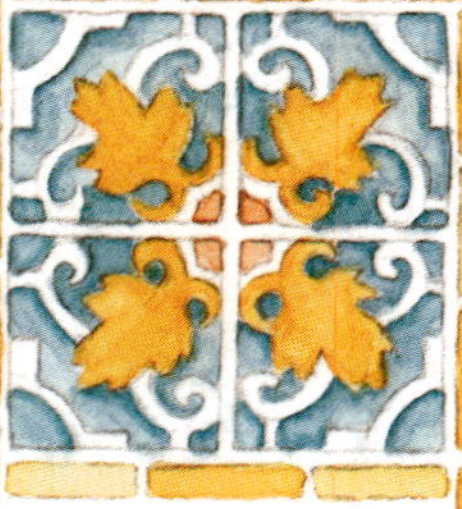

BELOW LEFT *French faïence tile by Fourmaintraux of Desvres, second half of the 19th century.*

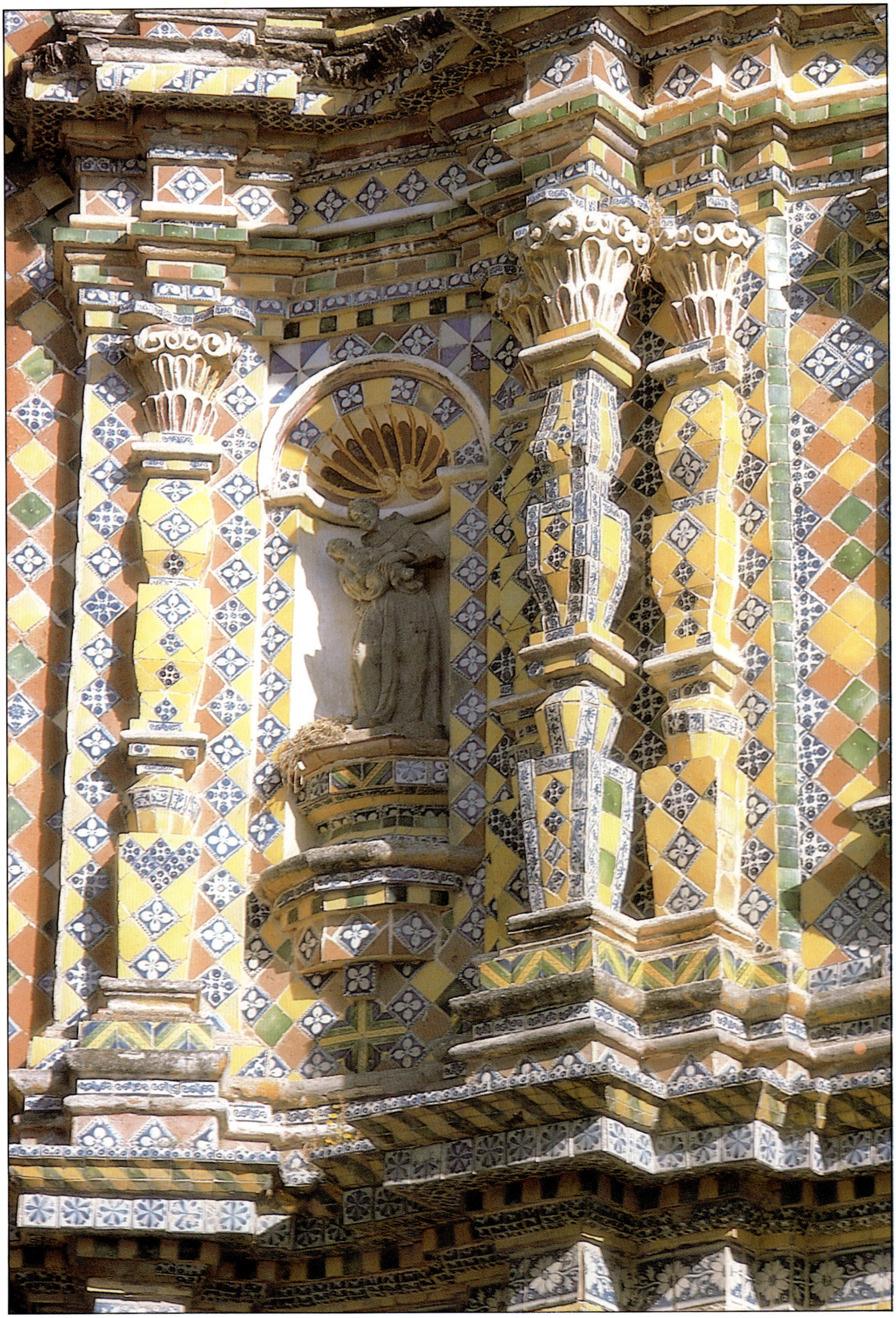

RIGHT *The tiled façade of the church of San Francisco, Acatepec, Mexico.*

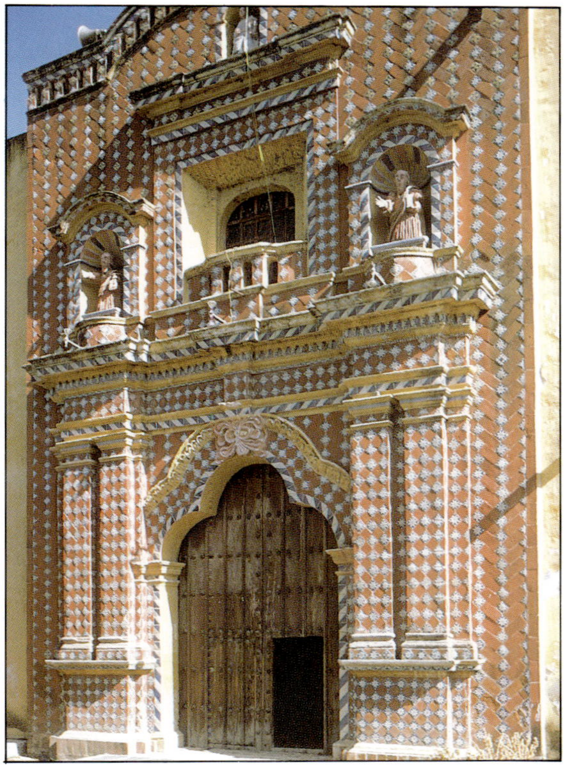

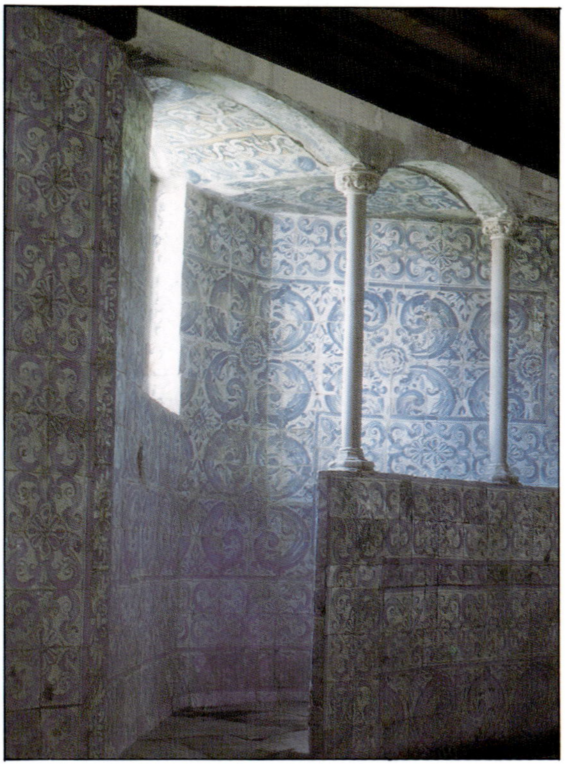

CHAPTER EIGHT

FAR LEFT *The tiled front of the church of Santa Maria, Tonantzintla, Mexico.*

LEFT *Tiled walls and lectern in the refectory of the Convent of Jesus, Aveiro, Portugal.*

between the two towns, whereby the potters of Talavera had been helped by Sevillian experts to improve the quality of their products. Eventually, Seville was to look toward Talavera for inspiration. Hunting and bullfighting scenes were among the most popular subjects on pottery, and a series of battles is depicted on tile panels in the City Hall of Toledo (dating from 1696). Churches, of course, were tiled with religious themes. In Our Lady of El Prado at Talavera developments from the 16th to the 18th century can be followed. Migrant craftsmen from Seville and Talavera travelled as far as Mexico in the second half of the 17th century, and maiolica tiles, along with other wares, in the lively style known as *puebla*, were made. Influences from both Europe and the Orient were interpreted in a naively vivid fashion, mostly in blue and white and polychrome. Tiles were still made in Catalonia as well as Seville and Talavera in Spain, and those of Barcelona were most popular in the 18th century. They were produced in rich profusion for civic and domestic purposes, as well as for churches and other religious buildings.

The largest tile panels seem to have been used in Portugal. Whereas in Spain tiled decoration was mainly concentrated on the insides, and only to a limited extent used on the outsides of ecclesiastical buildings, in Portugal tiles adorned both the interiors and exteriors of churches, monasteries, schools, factories, public buildings, palaces and ordinary houses. By the early 18th century they were an integral feature of architecture as they were in no other country. While tile production had been established in Lisbon since the mid-16th century, it was not until the end of the century that Portuguese tiles, known as *azulejos* (from the Arab word for ceramic mosaic), developed their own characteristics. By now they were produced by artisans in small workshops who took their design influences from many quarters, including the textiles imported from India at the time. During the 17th and 18th centuries tiles were made by the thousands, mostly in Lisbon, Oporto and Coimbra, and many were exported.

From the mid-17th century the Portuguese tile industry was gravely threatened by the massive influx of tiles from the Netherlands. These were banned from 1687 to 1698, but Dutch styles were enormously popular and widely imitated. From the early 18th century onward it is virtually impossible to distinguish Dutch from Portuguese tiles, although few Dutch tiles were imported into Portugal after about 1730. As in Spain, panels of tiles painted with religious subjects had been used to decorate the altars and walls of churches from the 16th century onward, but their use for secular purposes grew from the end of the 17th century. Blue-and-white inevitably gained preference over polychrome at this time, and, starting in the early 18th century, sumptuous figurative scenes — both religious and secular — were appearing on tiles painted by artists such as Antonio Pereira, Manuel dos Santos and Antonio de Olivera Bernades.

The opulence of the 18th century, when gold and other rich imports were flowing into Portugal from Brazil and India, was expressed in large-scale tile schemes of luxurious theatricality. Mythological and allegorical stories, landscapes and architectural fantasies and *fêtes galantes* are typical of this period, but purely decorative panels of flowers and swirling rococo ornament in polychrome also appeared from mid-century. Tiles were used not only in the grandiose schemes of the nobility, who used them copiously on both the interior and exterior walls of their villas and palaces, but also by the merchant and professional classes. During the second half of the 18th century, when polychrome was once more favoured, large sections of pictorial wall panelling began to give way to small, often shaped tile pictures.

After the Lisbon earthquake of 1755 a more disciplined form of tile decoration, often in repetitive but colourful patterns of flowers, was used to complement the rather severe architecture of the reconstructed city, and by the 1790s tile decoration had been absorbed into the newly fashionable neo-classical style. Like many other European tile industries, that of Portugal deteriorated and eventually ceased to exist in the early years of the 19th century. It was carried on in Brazil with great vigour, however, and it was mainly through the efforts of Brazilians who resettled in Portugal in the 1860s and

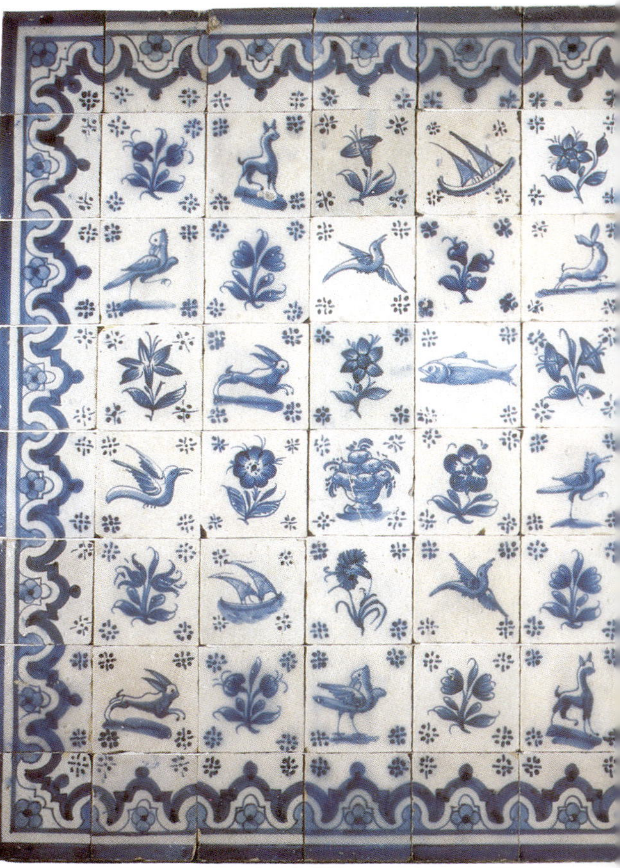

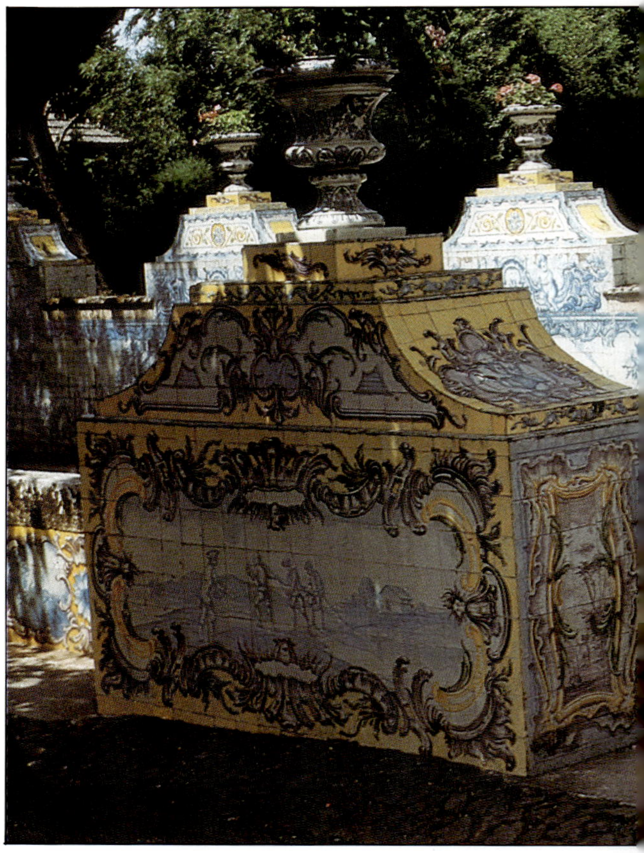

RIGHT *Panel of decorative blue-and-white tiles, Portugal, late 17th century.*

BELOW RIGHT *Canal-side* azulejos *in the Palace Gardens at Queluz, Portugal.*

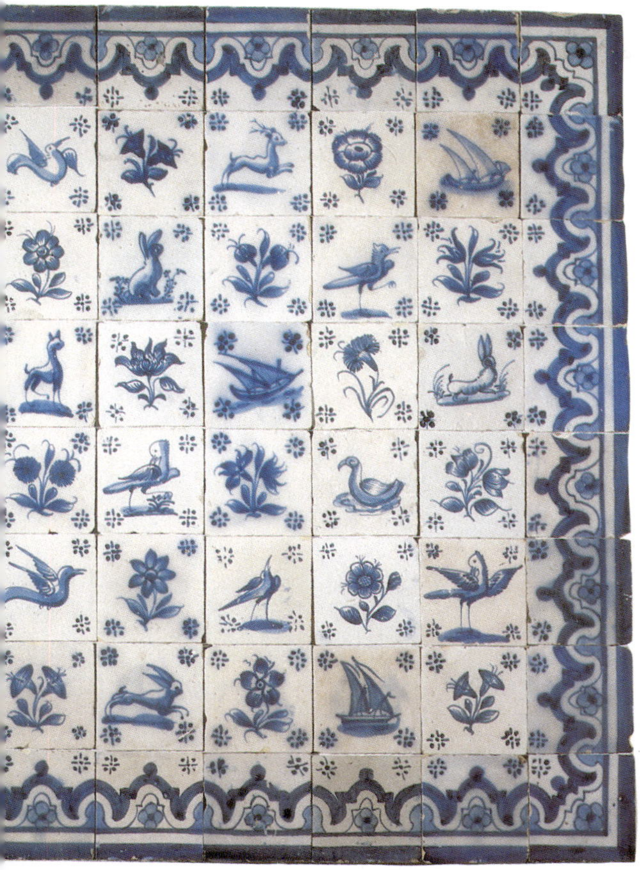

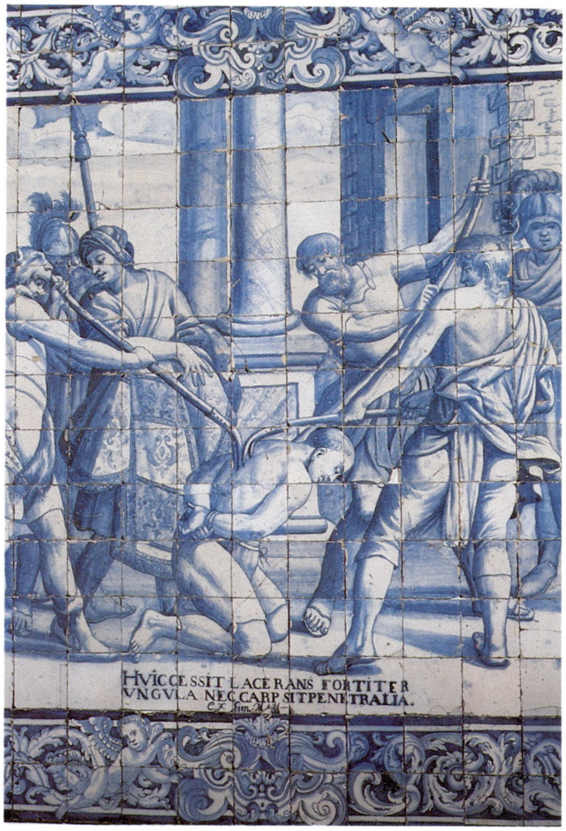

CHAPTER EIGHT

LEFT *Scene from the Martyrdom of St Lawrence by Policarpo de Oliveira Bernardes*, c. 1730.

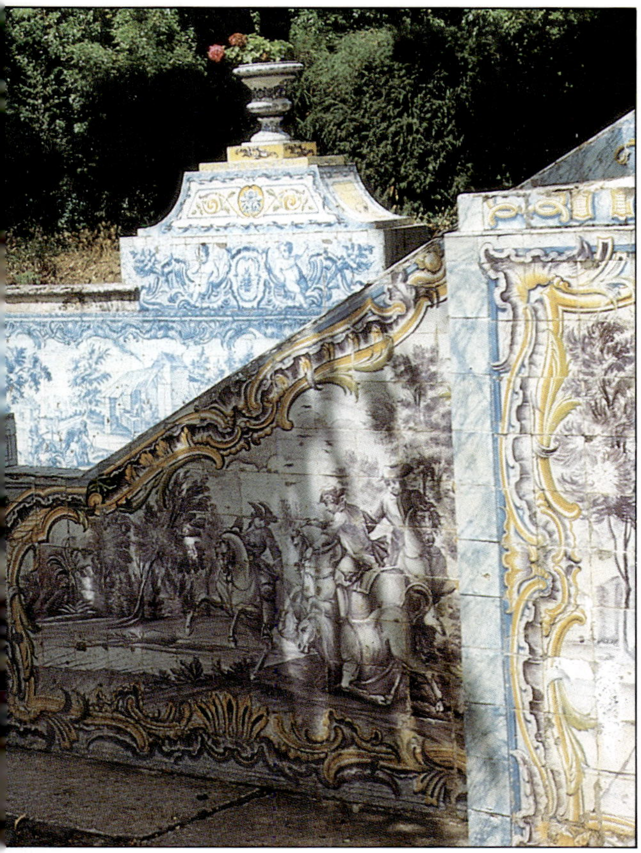

1870s that the Portuguese tile industry underwent a renaissance similar to that of northern Europe. From the late 19th century, industrially produced tiles were used to adorn domestic buildings of all kinds; the tradition continues to this day, and Portuguese-made tiles are widely exported.

In 17th-century Italy, the use of maiolica tiles continued on the floors of churches, particularly in the Naples area, where a vigorous industry flourished at this time. In Liguria, too, the well-established tradition of *laggioni* continued. Together with most European countries, Italy enjoyed a tile-making revival during the 19th century.

Tin-glazed tiles in Germany were strongly influenced by Dutch styles, even when, during the second half of the 18th century, the importation of Dutch tiles declined in favour of native German manufacture, at least at the top end of the market. The proliferation of German princely porcelain factories led to the home production of tiles for the luxurious interior decoration of palaces and mansions, as well as for the homes of the well-to-do. As in

RIGHT *Ceramic tablet in relief depicting the metamorphosis of the head of a woman and a snail by Querubim Lapa, made in the factory of Viuva Lamego, Lisbon, 1985.*

England, Dutch or Dutch-trained potters were employed in the German faïence factories. Whereas few of these were specialist tile producers as they were in the Netherlands, their number was considerable from the late 17th century onward. However, none succeeded in rivalling the Dutch, whose tiles were still imported in large quantities. Among the German factories that produced Dutch-style tiles were those at Frankfurt, Berlin, Brunswick, Nuremberg, Erfurt, Zerbst, Magdeburg, Rheinsberg and, most prolifically, Kellinghusen in Schleswig-Holstein. Some of these produced tiles almost indistinguishable from the Dutch originals while others, notably Ansbach, made tiles of a more distinctively German flavour. Despite attempts to prohibit the import of Dutch tiles, especially in the Schleswig-Holstein area at the end of the 18th century, it continued on a large scale, and tile use there was as widespread among the middle classes — farmers, sea captains, merchants and other professionals — as it was in the Netherlands.

Parallel with the production of tiles in the Dutch style, the tradition of peasant tile-making continued in Germany and Eastern Europe during the 17th and 18th centuries. Lead- and salt-glazed tiles, as well as tin-glazed ones, were made in different areas, and many were used for floors and stoves as well as for walls. A rather folksy interpretation of Dutch tiles was taken to America by emigrants from the Black Forest region of Germany. These people, who became known, rather misleadingly, as Pennsylvania Dutch (from *Deutsch,* meaning German), took many crafts with them, including furniture-making and pottery. Porcelain tiles were also produced at Meissen and other factories for special commissions, usually for the palaces of the princes who owned them.

A similar situation existed in Denmark: high-quality Dutch tiles were sent to decorate Danish palaces from the 17th century onward and later, during the 18th century, huge quantities were imported from the Friesland potteries for use in the houses of the upper classes. While some of the Danish faïence factories, notably Copenhagen, produced their own tiles in the 18th century, these also fell under the Dutch spell and were mostly copies of Dutch designs. At the same time, they were unable to compete commercially with the vast scale of Dutch mass-production, and imports from the Netherlands continued. In remote areas, a folk tradition of tile-making was less influenced by the Dutch. Small local museums in both northern Germany and in Denmark are often the best places to see such tiles.

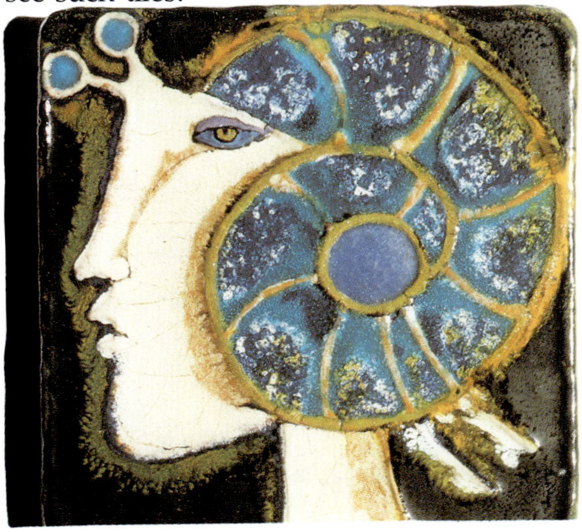

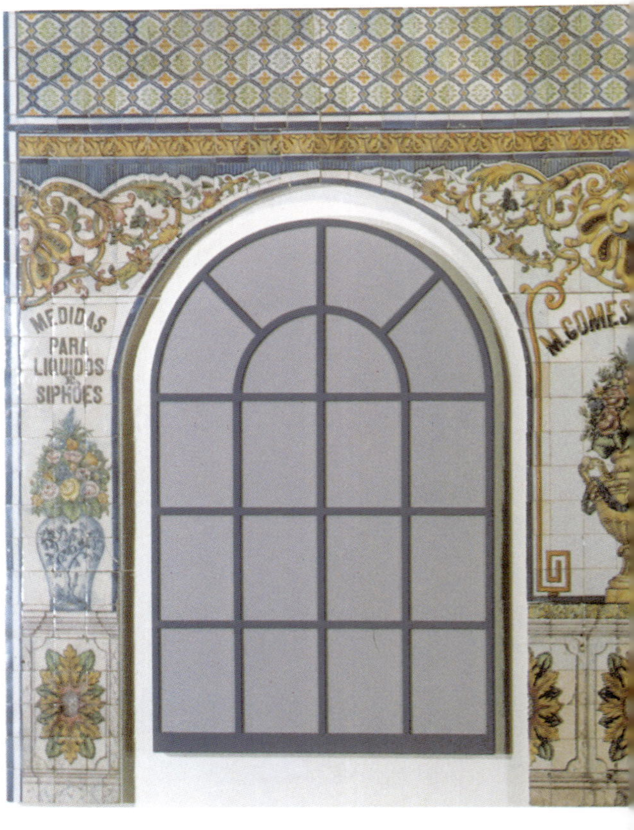

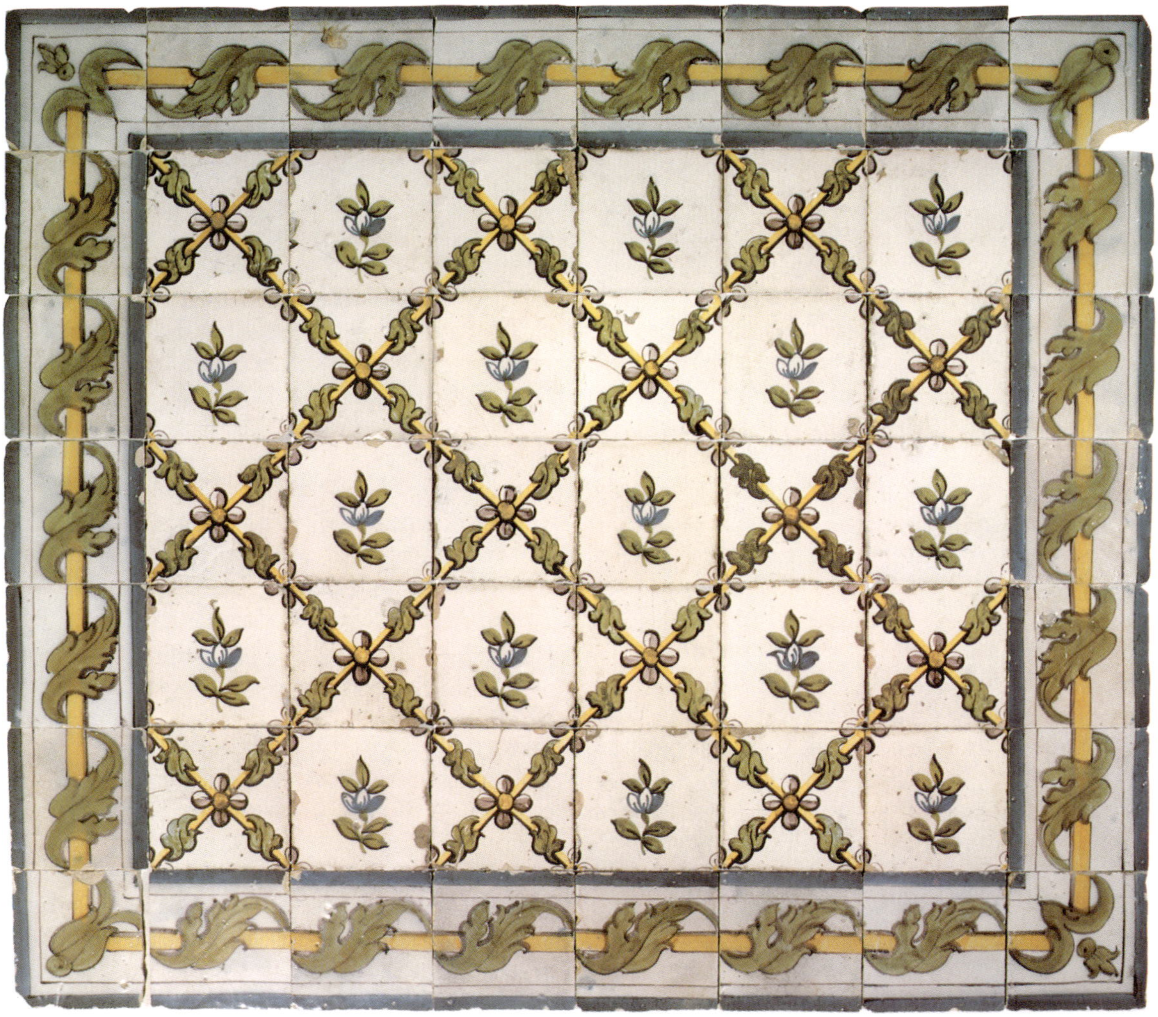

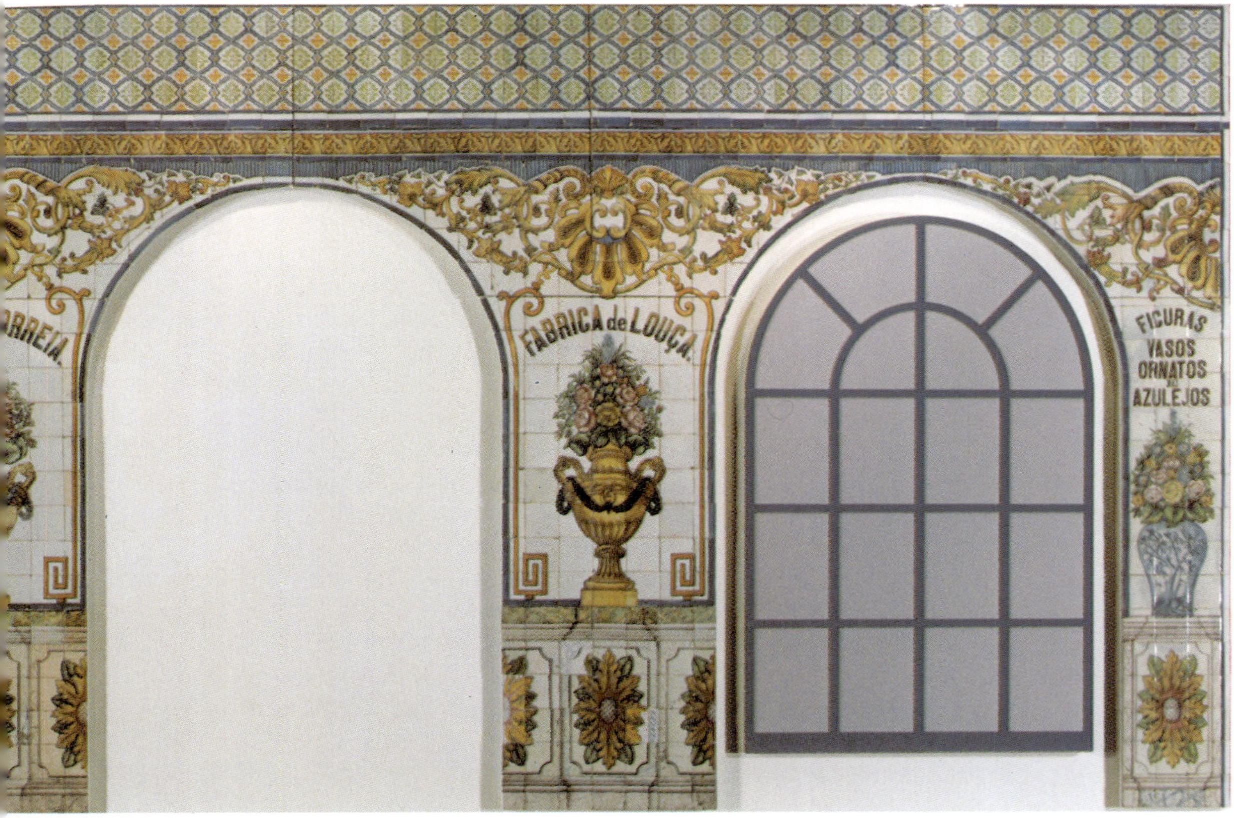

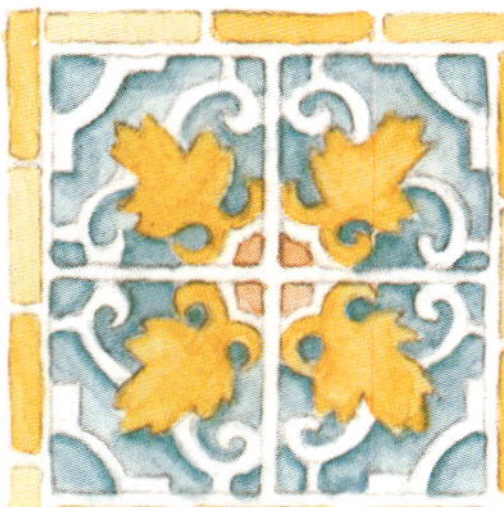

CHAPTER EIGHT

•

LEFT *Portuguese Pombaline-style pattern, c. 1760-80.*

BELOW LEFT *The shop façade of a ceramics factory by José da Silva, c. 1871.*

STOVE TILES

THE PICTURESQUE, tower-shaped stoves covered with tiles that appear in the corners of rooms in illustrations of all kinds, from medieval manuscripts to the domestic interiors of the 20th-century Swedish artist Carl Larsson, were in widespread use in certain parts of Europe — mostly mountainous regions — for centuries. Their long-standing popularity was undoubtedly due as much to their decorative properties as to their efficiency in providing heat.

From the medieval period these tile-enclosed stoves began to replace open fires in many parts, and it is likely that they originated in potters' workshops. In any case, the making of stove tiles became a distinct industry in certain areas, particularly in Germany and Switzerland, from an early period. First developments probably took place, not surprisingly, in the Alps and in Germany during the late 13th and 14th centuries. The earliest stove tiles were simply bowls set into the clay sides of the stove to increase its radiated heat. Interestingly, the German word for tile, *Kachel*, is derived from the old High German word, *Cachala*, meaning bowl. Soon the outer surfaces of the bowls were being coated with lead glaze to maximize their radiation, and almost inevitably the curved bowl shapes began to give way to relief-moulded tiles that admirably combined practical and aesthetic considerations.

By the 15th century the making of stove tiles in relief had become an autonomous craft that assumed increasing importance as the century progressed. In 16th-century Germany the whole ceramics industry was influenced by stove-making: moulded high-relief tiles, most often covered in green but also in black or yellow lead glazes, were made in profusion. During the 15th century they were generally decorated with religious subjects such as saints and allegories and set into architectural surrounds, but by the early 16th century both religious and secular subjects were used.

Nuremberg, at that time under the strong influence of Italian maiolica, was an important centre of production, and some of the most splendid stove tiles were made there. Dating from the middle decades of the 16th century is a set of 12 cylindrical relief tiles that is thought to have been made originally for a stove in Nuremberg Castle. They are unusually large (28½ in/72 cm high) and consist of fashionably dressed figures — probably royal personages — set into niches and decorated in blue, green, yellow and brown lead glazes enhanced with white tin glaze.

Polychrome was increasingly favoured by the stove-tile makers, who nevertheless — and for obvious practical reasons — continued to mould their tiles in relief, and Nuremberg remained the most important centre of production well into the 17th century. Those made by the Leupold family, with their fine modelling and black glazes sometimes heightened with gold, are considered some of the most accomplished.

It was a small and logical step from making tiles with a combination of lead- and tin-glaze to making fully tin-glazed stove tiles, and potters in Nuremberg and the South Tyrol began to produce maiolica stove tiles, as well as floor and wall tiles, from the early 16th century. One of the few known painters of figure-decorated stove tiles was Bartholomaus Dill. A former pupil of Dürer, he was a painter of easel pictures and wall paintings as well as stove tiles, and he worked in Bozen from 1526. He painted figurative subjects such as scenes from the lives of Hercules, Samson, and Jason based on designs by Hans Burgkmair and other German engravers.

By the end of the 16th century Swiss stove-makers, notably at Winterthur, were also producing maiolica painted and relief-moulded stove tiles. Ludwig Pfau the Elder and his son Ludwig Pfau the Younger are among the few identifiable artists, and they produced dishes and jugs as well as tiles decorated with plants, scrolls, fruit, figures, landscapes and coats of arms. Their Winterthur workshop continued for two centuries. Hans Weckerly, working at Zug, is also known to have painted stove tiles.

While stove-making was by this time a specialized craft, set apart from the production of other ceramic wares, some workshops — and that of the Pfau family must be included — undoubtedly made vessels as a sideline. An example of this was almost certainly the Swiss owl jug, a lidded pot in the form of the bird, usually with moulded decoration of figures or a coat of arms on the front of the belly. Similar relief-moulded designs have been found on stove tiles, and these jugs are therefore thought to have emanated from

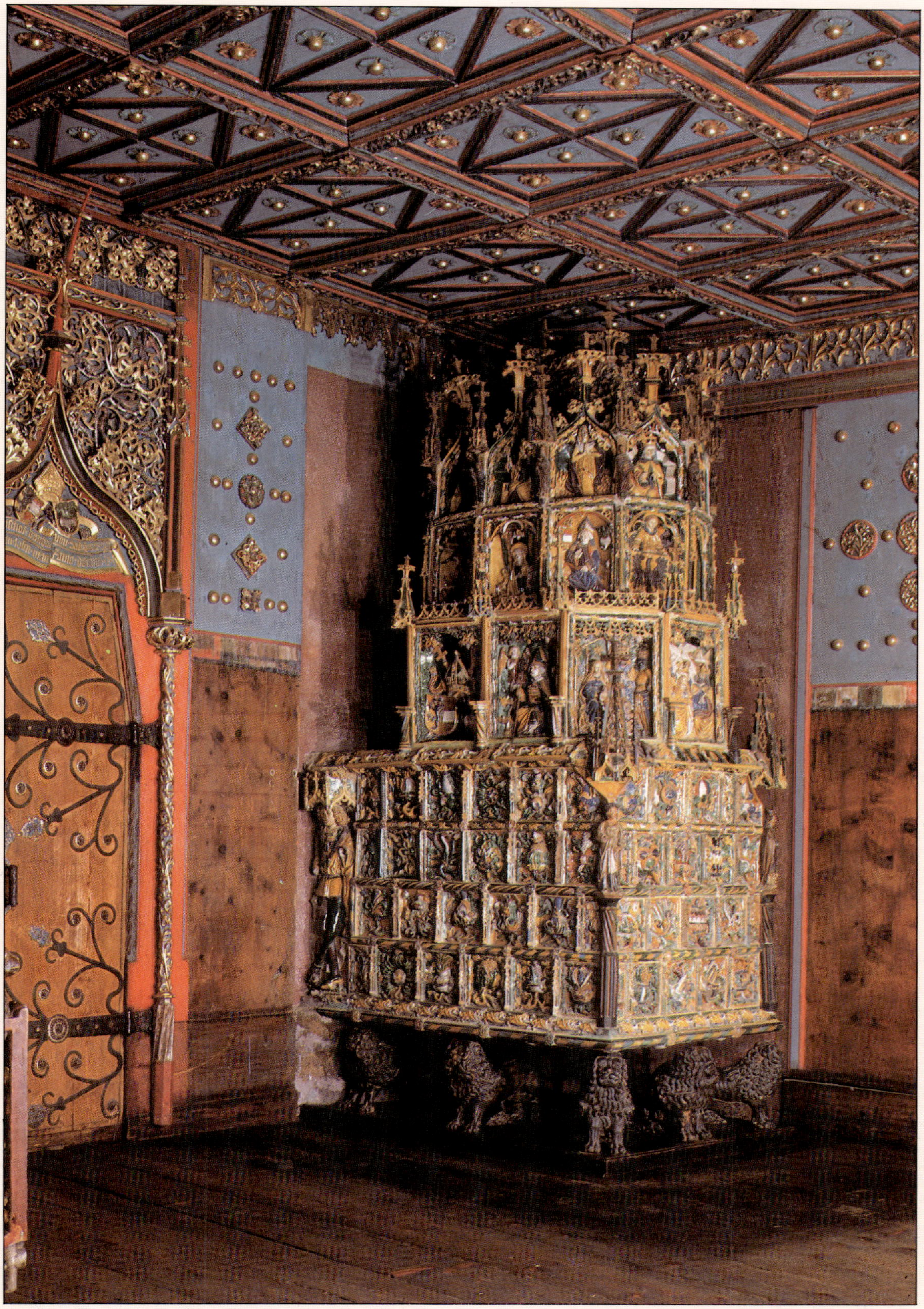

LEFT *A late medieval ceramic stove from the Golden Room in Hohensalsburg, Austria.*

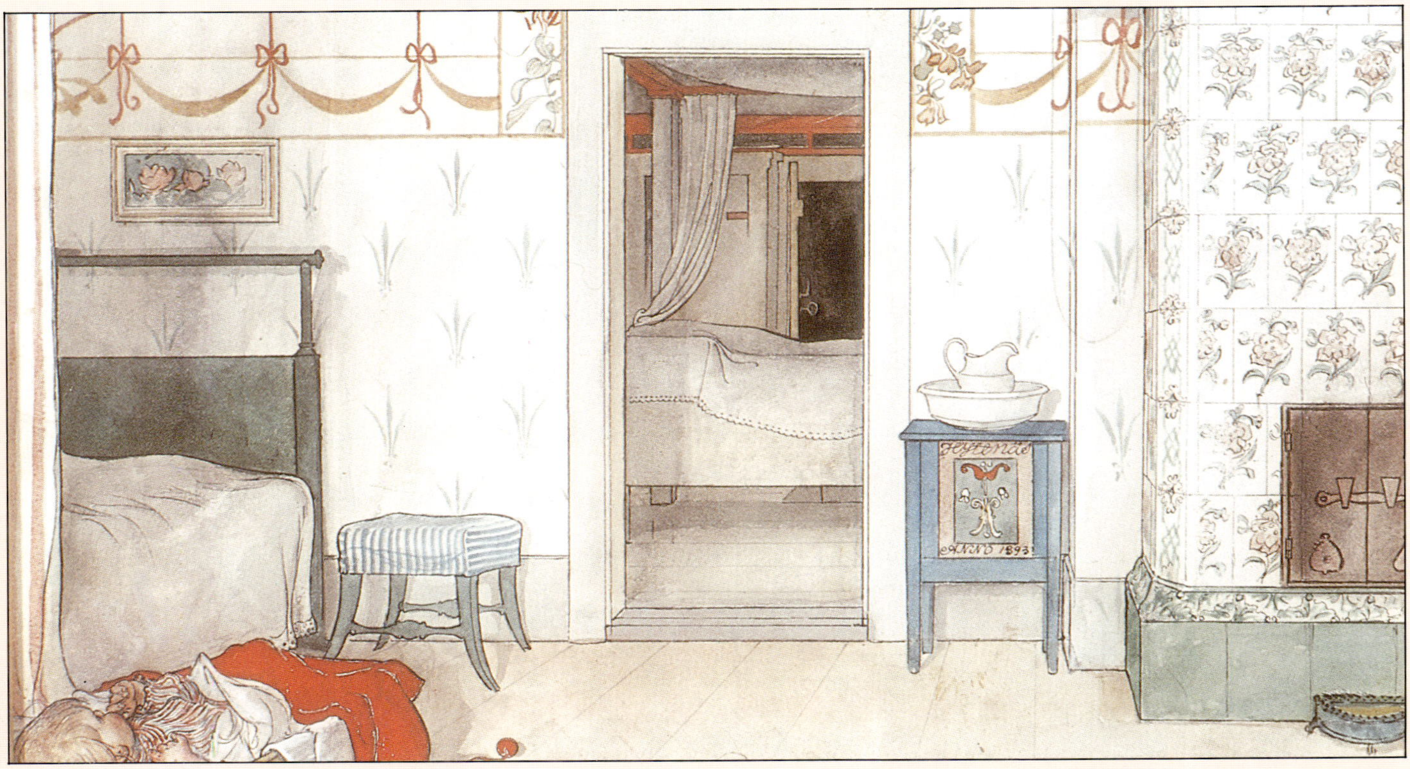

stove-makers' workshops rather than those of regular potters.

In Eastern Europe stove tiles and other wares were made by the Habaners, or New Christians, members of an anabaptist sect who had fled to Moravia, Slovakia, and Hungary to escape religious persecution in the 1520s. During the second half of the 16th century and throughout the 17th, despite intermittent persecution on the one hand and attacks by the Turks on the other, the Habaners lived in self-supporting communes regulated according to strict disciplines of work and prayer. Many of the Habaners were expert craftsmen, and their pottery in particular is outstanding for its quality and fineness compared with native wares of the same period. Their box-shaped stove tiles with relief moulding of scrolling leaves and shell patterns (their religion forbade them to depict humans or animals) were sometimes glazed plain white, or they were decorated with white, yellow and blue glazes. This sect preserved their exclusively independent way of life until the 18th century. Although by this time much of their craftsmanship continued to flourish, they became ethnically more relaxed, and began to merge with the local population. A new freedom of expression is evident in this Habaner-Slovak ware, combining both native and Habaner elements of decoration interpreted with an individualism which, like the figures, animals and birds that now appeared, would have been forbidden in earlier times.

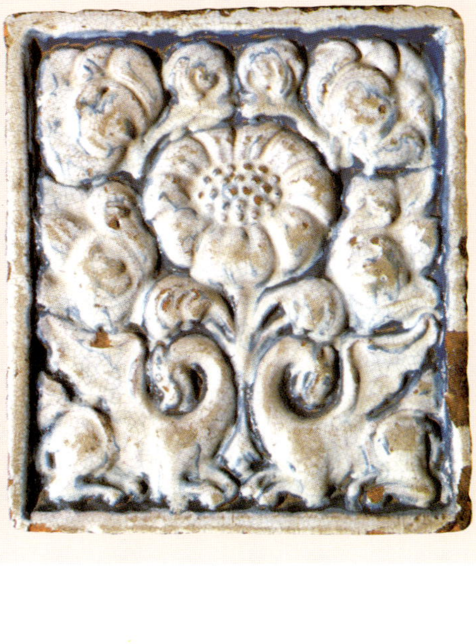

In Scandinavia the making of faïence began rather later than elsewhere in Europe (during the 1720s), but the tiled stove has become most evocative of the cosy and colourful interiors of these chilly northern climates. Tiled stoves were produced throughout the region and, in the case of Sweden particularly, many were made in small workshops. During the second half of the 18th century Stockholm had a number of these, producing tiles for the newly improved stoves made to the designs of the architect Carl Cronstedt.

The Copenhagen factory of Store Kongensgade enjoyed a monopoly on manufacturing faïence, or 'Delft Porcelain' as it was termed, from 1722 until 1762, during which time the importation of such wares was supposed to have been forbidden. Not surprisingly, tiles painted in blue, sometimes with a powdered manganese ground, formed a considerable proportion of the factory's output. Later in the 18th century, other factories, particularly that of Peter Hoffnagel at Østerbro, produced tiles of the same type. From 1738 to 1754, architectural ceramics, including tiles, were made at the Blaataarn (Blue Tower) factory set up by King Christian VI. Many of these tiles are decorated in relief, sometimes gilded. During most of the 18th century faïence stoves and stove tiles were made in several factories in Schleswig-Holstein, now part of northern Germany but then an area within the sphere of Danish political influence: Lubeck and Hamburg were notable centres of stove production.

In many parts of northern Europe tiled stoves were a continuing tradition throughout the 19th century, just as tiled fireplaces persisted in other areas, and tiled stoves are still produced today.

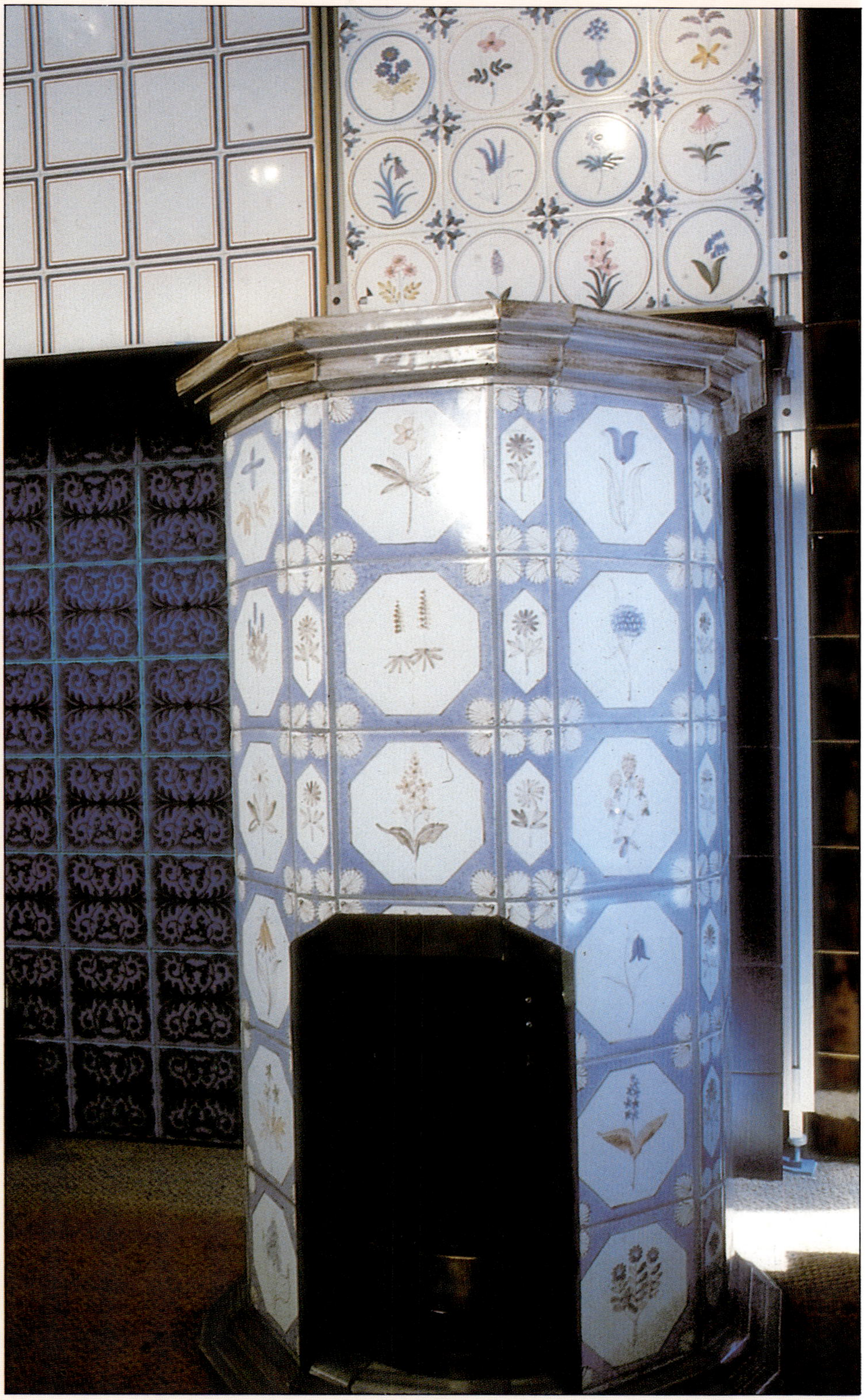

ABOVE LEFT Brita's Forty Winks, *watercolour by Carl Larsson (1853-1919) illustrating a Swedish country-house interior with a highly decorated ceramic-tiled stove, early 20th century.*

LEFT *Early 17th-century Continental relief-moulded tile, once part of a large central stove, with a deep flange at the back for insulation.*

RIGHT *A tiled stove in traditional style by Tarquin Cole, 1978.*

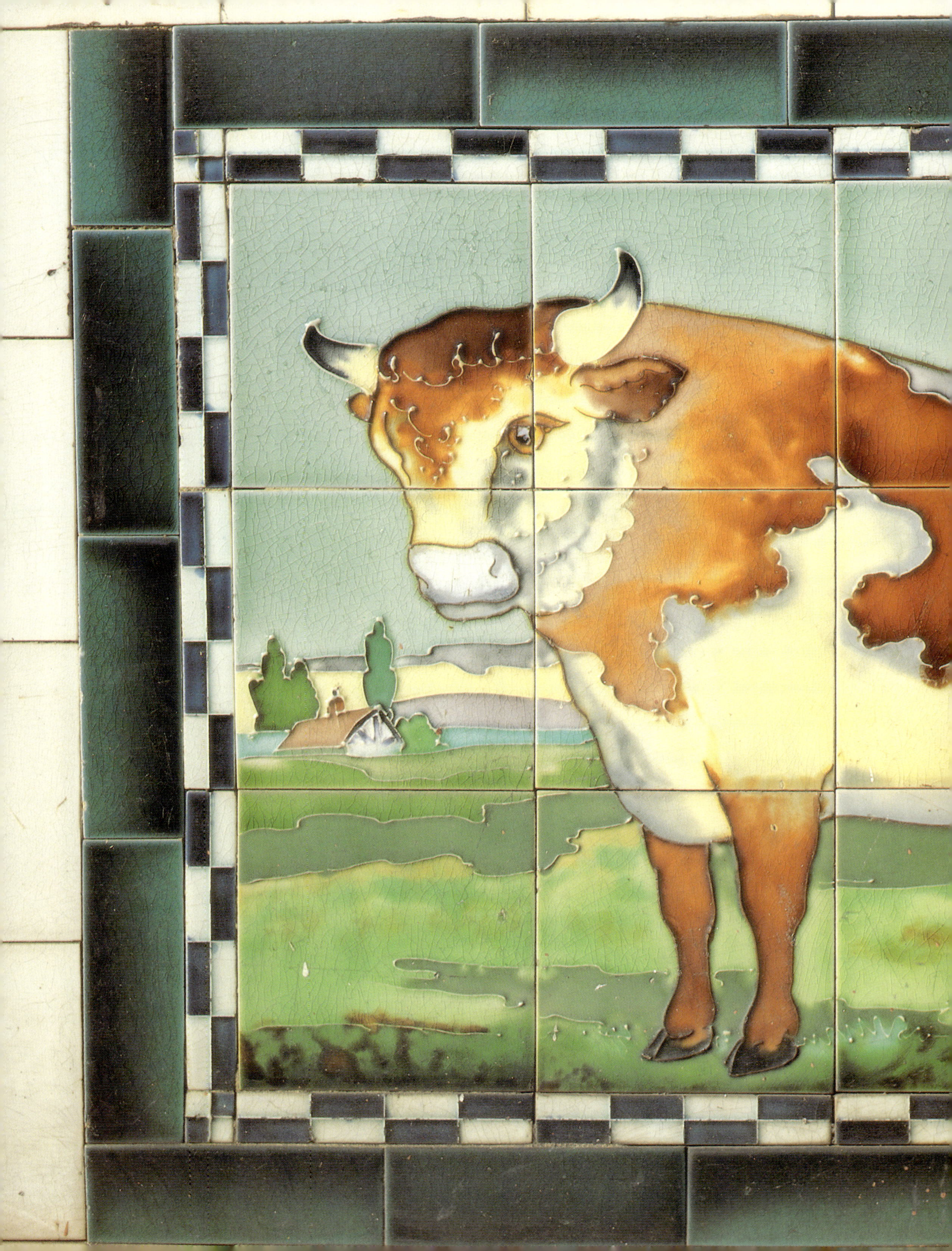

CHAPTER NINE

TILES OF THE VICTORIAN PERIOD

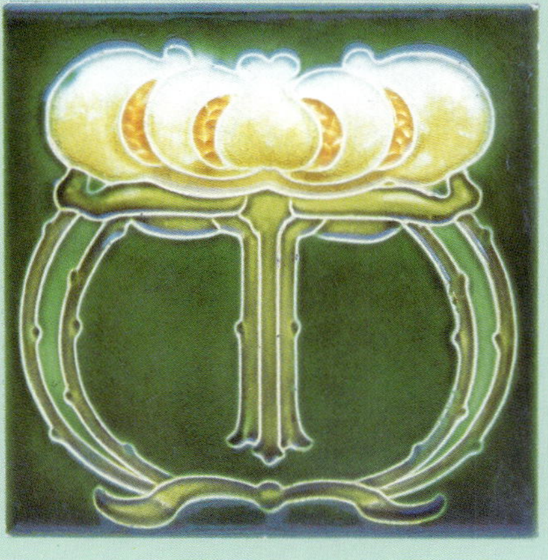

For virtually the first three decades of the 19th century, tile production in England was conspicuous for its absence. Apart from the traditional Dutch manufacture that continued, however sparsely and sporadically, the story was similar in the rest of the former tile-making centres of Europe. It was the 19th-century Gothic Revival that led to renewed interest in tile-making, at first occupying an obscure corner of the ceramics industry but later growing into one of the most successful manufacturing enterprises the world has ever seen.

OVERLEAF (BACKGROUND) *A tube-lined picture of a cow on the outside of a butcher's shop in St Ives, Cambridgeshire.*

OVERLEAF (INSET) *A tube-lined tile,* c. *1905, with an elegant floral design typical of the Art Nouveau period.*

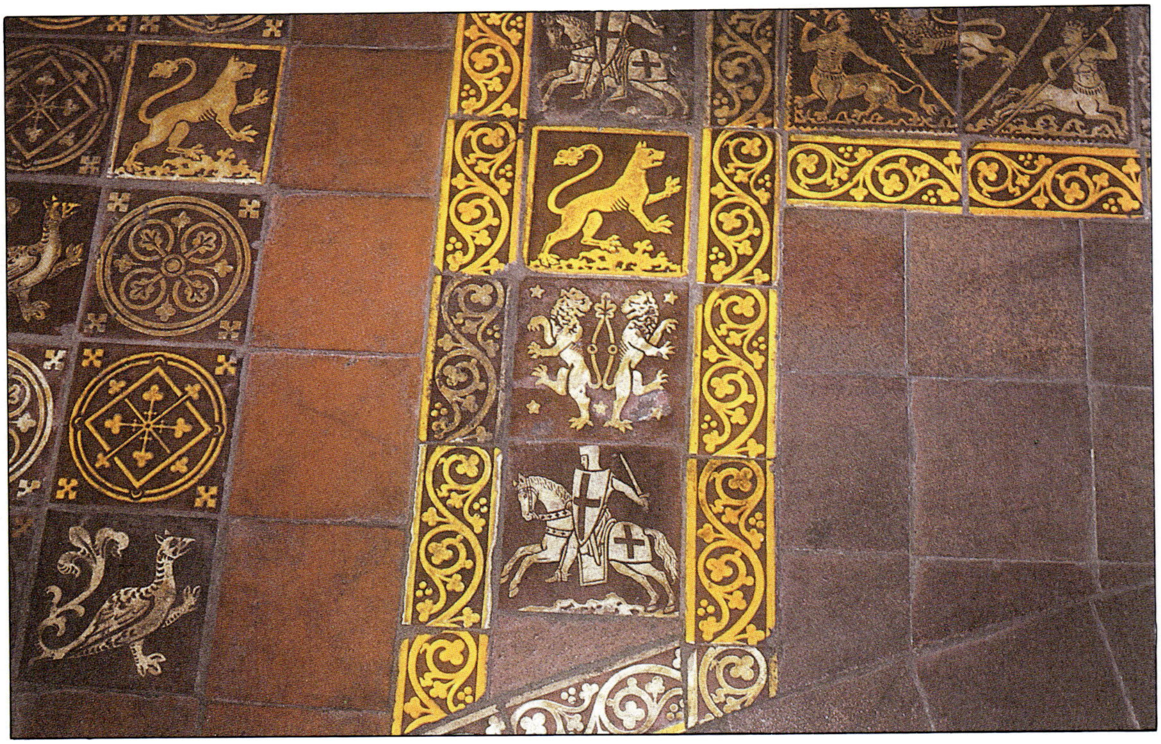

RIGHT *Encaustic tiles in the Temple Church, London, made by Minton,* c. *1842. During World War II, the church was badly damaged; afterwards, the tiles were taken out and the undamaged ones relaid in the gallery of the rotunda of the church, where they can still be seen. The tiles that have not been walked on retain the strong yellow enamel that was painted over the inlaid design.*

THE RETURNING fashion for Gothic decoration in the early 19th century prompted a demand for inlaid tiles of the medieval type, but as the art of making these had virtually died with the dissolution of the monasteries, a great deal of practical experiment was necessary before regular production could begin. Herbert Minton, son of Thomas Minton who had founded the firm of Minton's in 1793, began to study the problem and attempt to make inlaid tiles from about 1828; in 1830 he discovered that another potter with similar intentions, Samuel Wright of Shelton, had taken out a patent for the mechanical production of what now became known as encaustic tiles. Minton bought a share in Wright's patent and continued to develop the technique, which at this stage was far from perfected. The main difficulty lay in matching the contraction rates of the different clays used: if, on firing, the inlay contracted more than the body of the tile itself, it tended to fall out. There were also problems with tiles cracking, or becoming stained by the chemical action of impurities. A less patient and determined individual than Herbert Minton might well have abandoned the project, but his perseverence was rewarded and in 1835 he produced his first pattern book of encaustic tiles, containing 62 designs based on medieval originals.

Very soon Minton was receiving commissions for encaustic-tile pavements in mansions in various parts of Britain, and in 1841 he paved the Temple Church in London with tiles copied from the medieval examples in the Chapter House at Westminster Abbey. Minton's success seemed assured in 1844 when he made a pavement for Queen Victoria at Osborne House on the Isle of Wight: where Queen Victoria led, princes and potentates from all over the world soon followed, and Minton's encaustic tiles were in demand everywhere. The fashion for encaustic tiles was given its strongest impetus by the Gothic Revival architect Augustus Pugin, a personal friend and champion of Herbert Minton, who recommended them not only for church building and restoration but for all kinds of secular purposes, as part of his mission to 'improve' public taste. Pugin and Minton together laid the foundations for a mass market for encaustic tiles, although in the early days they were hardly a commercial proposition.

Encaustic tiles were made with 'plastic'

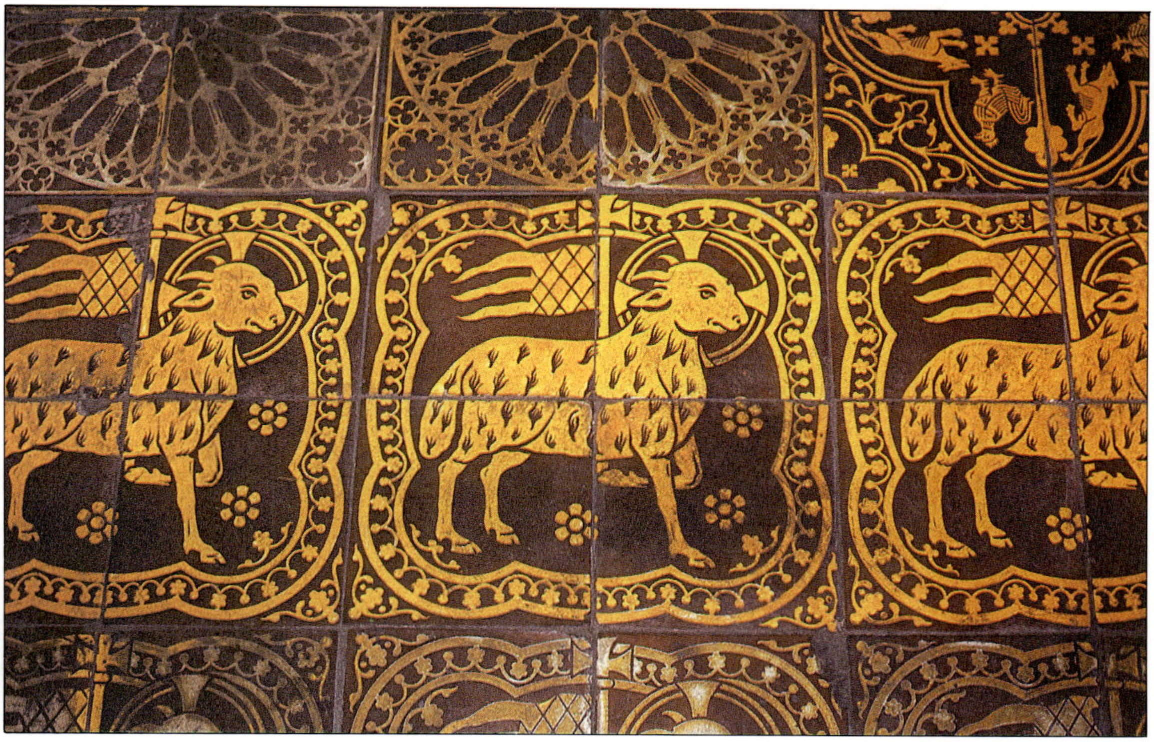

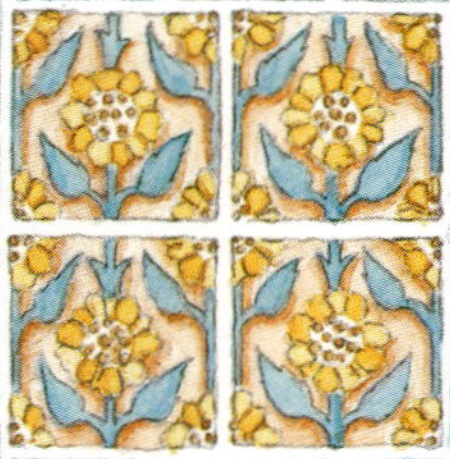

CHAPTER NINE

•

LEFT *Encaustic tiles in the Temple Church, London, made by Minton, c. 1842, depicting the Holy Lamb and the devices of the Inns of Court.*

or wet, clay inlaid with liquid slip, and much of their manufacture had to be carried out by hand rather than mechanical processes, which meant that they were very expensive. Most often they were made of a red clay body with white inlays, but black with buff tiles were also produced at this time. In 1840 Minton had bought a share in the patent of one Richard Prosser, who had developed a method of making ceramic buttons by compressing dry clay between metal dies. Minton saw this as a potential means of producing tiles at a much faster rate than before. Almost immediately he was proved right, and by 1842 he had 62 presses turning out wall tiles. The demand for white-glazed tiles like those produced by this new dust-pressing method was enormous: Minton could hardly keep up with it, but these mass-produced serviceable tiles must have subsidized the less profitable encaustic side of the business.

Dust-pressing became the usual method of making tiles for the rest of the century: by making tile production much speedier and more consistent, it enabled the tile boom of the later 19th century to gather its great momentum. In its early days, however, the dust-pressing method was found to be unsuited to encaustic tiles and it was not until much later, in 1863 and after Herbert Minton's death, that another firm, Boulton & Worthington, succeeded in making encaustic tiles with 'dry' clay.

Various methods for speeding up the production of plastic encaustic tiles by mechanical means were developed during the late 1840s and 1850s, and although they were still expensive their use had become widespread in all kinds of settings: they were laid in the new Houses of Parliament at Westminster (completed in 1852) and in the House of Representatives in the new Capitol in Washington, DC (1855). They were to be placed in palaces, mansions, schools, civic and domestic buildings and, above all, churches for the next half-century.

A growing number of firms followed Minton's lead in making encaustic tiles. Among the earliest were Copeland & Garrett of Stoke-on-Trent and the Worcester firm of Chamberlain, both of whom were making encaustic tiles in the late 1830s. In 1840 Chamberlain amalgamated with another Worcester firm, Fleming St John, G Barr and Co, and in 1844, when Wright's

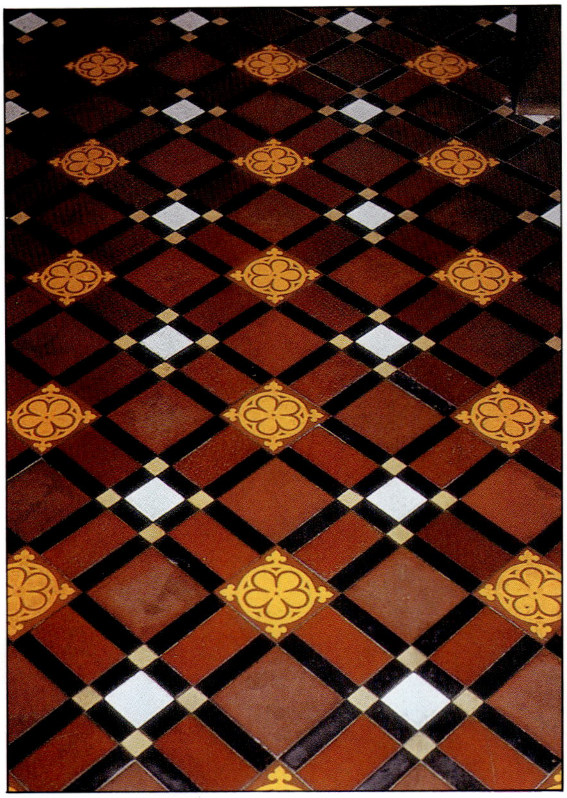

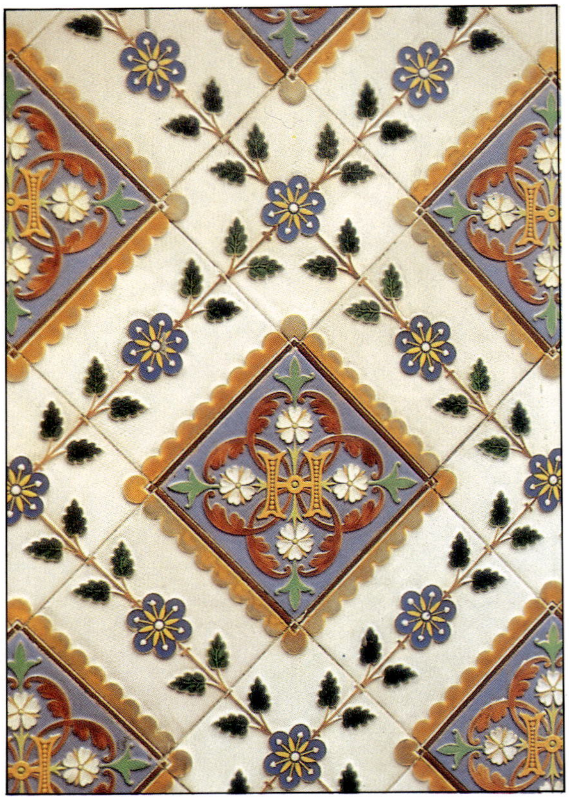

RIGHT *Geometric tiling on the floor of St Leonard's Church, Scarborough, made by Minton, 1857-59. The patterned encaustic tiles have yellow enamel painted over the inlaid clay.*

FAR RIGHT *Relief tiles with opaque maiolica glazes on the walls of the office staircase of the Minton, Hollins & Co factory, Stoke-on-Trent. The monogram 'H' on the tiles is the initial of M D Hollins, who owned the factory.*

patent was renewed, it was bought in equal shares by this Worcester company and Minton.

The local clays of Worcestershire were not suitable for encaustic tiles, and the fact that these had to be brought from further afield — with the consequent expense — led to a running-down of the Worcester business and its eventual purchase by Maw & Co in 1850. This firm committed itself to all types of tile manufacture and in 1852 moved to the Benthall Works at Broseley in Shropshire. During the 1850s Maw's large-scale production of encaustic tiles made it a rival to Minton and, like Minton, it was at the same time developing other aspects and techniques of tile-making. By the 1880s Maw was among the most wide-ranging and prolific of all the tile-producing firms.

Similar to encaustic tiles, and often used with them in small spaces like the halls and corridors of terraced houses, were geometric paving tiles. These were single-colour shaped segments of the usual 6-in (15-cm) square tile, which were laid in patterns in the same manner as the early medieval mosaic tiles. Because each tile was made of only one type of clay, these geometric tiles were suitable for the dust-pressing process from an early stage.

Once dust-pressing had been developed successfully to make encaustic tiles, they not only became cheaper, but they began to be produced in a greater range of colours and with more complex patterns. As well as the red-and-white and brown-and-buff tiles of the 1840s and 1850s, blue tiles with yellow or buff patterns were made in the 1860s and soon reds and greys, and greens and pinks were added. Unlike medieval tiles, which were made of natural-coloured clays, Victorian encaustic tiles were made of clays tinted with metallic oxides. As a general rule of thumb, the most complicated designs using the greatest range of colours belong to the latest (post-1880) period, while the peak of both technique and design was probably reached around the 1870s. Glazed encaustic tiles are also an indication of a late date.

Herbert Minton died in 1858, but the future of the business was already assured: in 1845 his wife's nephew, Michael Daintry Hollins, had become a partner. In 1846

Samuel Barlow Wright (son of Samuel Wright, the original patentee of encaustic tile-making), and in 1849 Colin Minton Campbell, another nephew, were also made partners. By this time the firm had split into two parts: the china side of the business was run as Minton & Co (under Campbell after Herbert Minton's death), while the tiles were produced under the name Minton Hollins & Co, with Hollins in charge. In 1863 Robert Minton Taylor became a partner in Minton Hollins, but in 1858 he left and set up his own business; in the same year Campbell and Hollins split their partnership to form two distinct companies.

In effect, by the early 1870s three independent firms called Minton were making tiles, and the confusion this caused then as well as now is compounded by the facts that Minton Hollins floor tiles were marked Minton & Co, and that Minton's China Works included decorative wall tiles in their output. It is an indication of the boom in tiles in the last quarter of the 19th century that in spite of lawsuits to clarify the position regarding the use of the name Minton, and in spite of the rivalry between them, all three firms prospered for a number of years, as indeed did a number of others.

Among those operating during the 1850s and 1860s were The Architectural Pottery Company of Poole in Dorset, the firm of Godwin in Hereford, Malkin Edge & Co and T & R Boote, who were the first to make encaustic tiles using the dust-pressing method patented by Boulton & Worthington in 1863. It was a period of experiment and development and apart from the huge success of encaustic tiles, new or revived techniques for decorating tiles were constantly being sought. 'Maiolica' glazes were developed by Leon Arnoux, Minton's art director, and were first shown in the Great Exhibition of 1851. They were particularly successful on embossed tiles and became one of the most widely used of surface finishes. As well as the shadows and relief effects that resulted from the 'pooling' of the glaze during firing, contrasting colours applied to the same tile could give especially bright results.

The greatest period of all for 19th-century

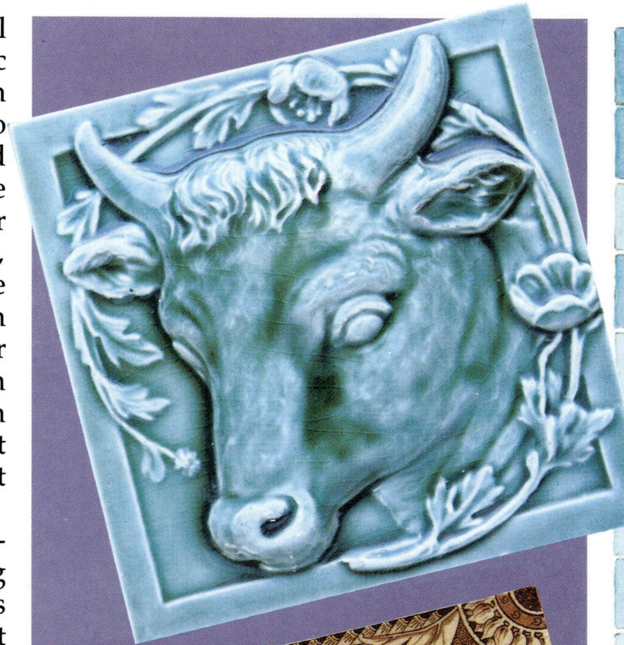

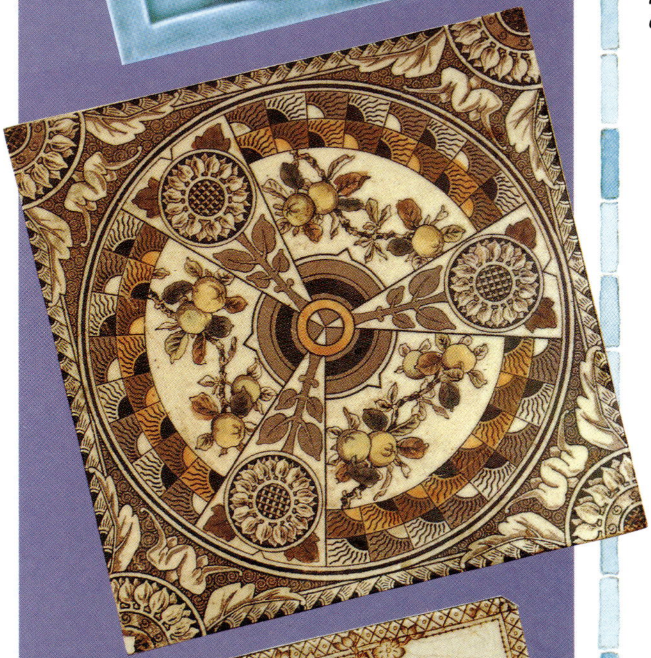

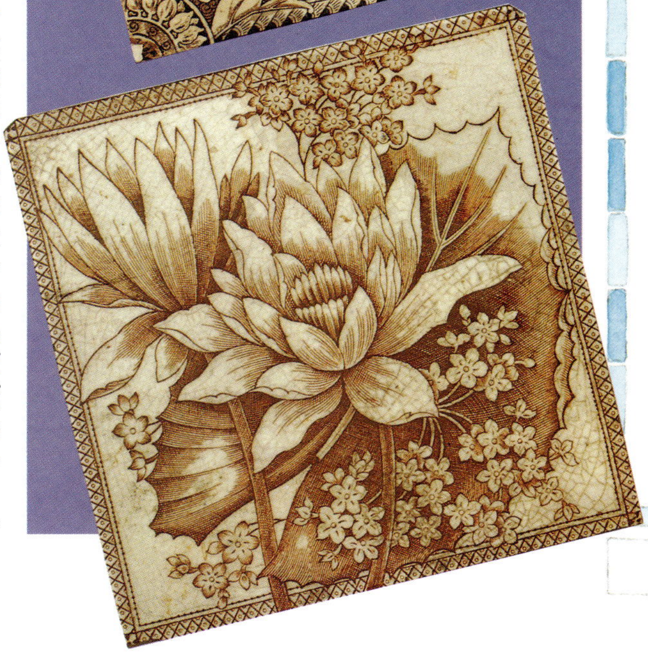

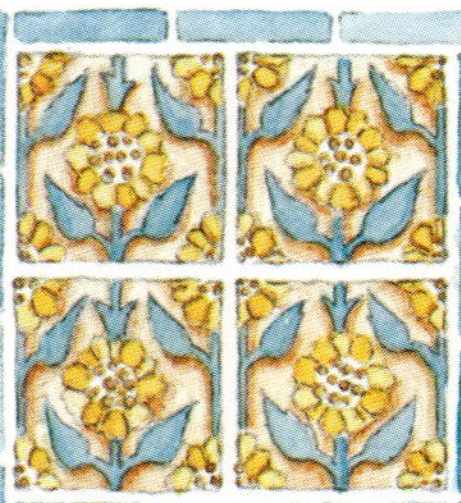

LEFT *Maiolica-glazed tile with the head of a cow pressed in relief, c. 1890.*

BELOW LEFT *Two flower-decorated, transfer-printed tiles, one with added hand-colouring.*

RIGHT *The public bar of the Philharmonic public house in Liverpool by Walter Thomas, 1898-1900.*

BELOW RIGHT *Tiled tableau of Britannia on the façade of Longbone & Sons, Berwick-upon-Tweed, build during the early 1900s as a fish shop and completely tiled by J Duncan Ltd of Glasgow. The shop now sells tartans.*

decorative tiling was from about 1870 to 1910, when more than 100 firms operated up and down the country, the vast majority in the six towns of the potteries in Staffordshire. New building was going on at an unprecedented rate, and tiles were welcomed as a hygienic, hard-wearing and attractive form of flooring and wall decoration in buildings. Their popularity among the masses was stimulated by the many 'top people', from Queen Victoria downward, who ordered tiles on a grand scale, while designers found in tiles a suitable vehicle for the new artistic styles of the time. Further stimulus came from the many national and international exhibitions of the period, when medals were awarded for inventing new techniques and perfecting old ones, giving publicity and prestige to the firms who won them.

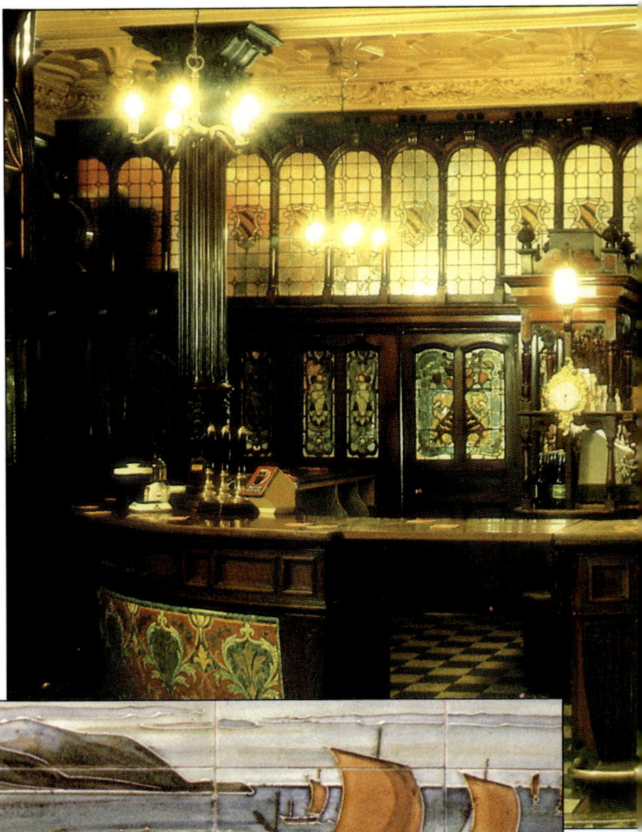

The range of decorative methods used by

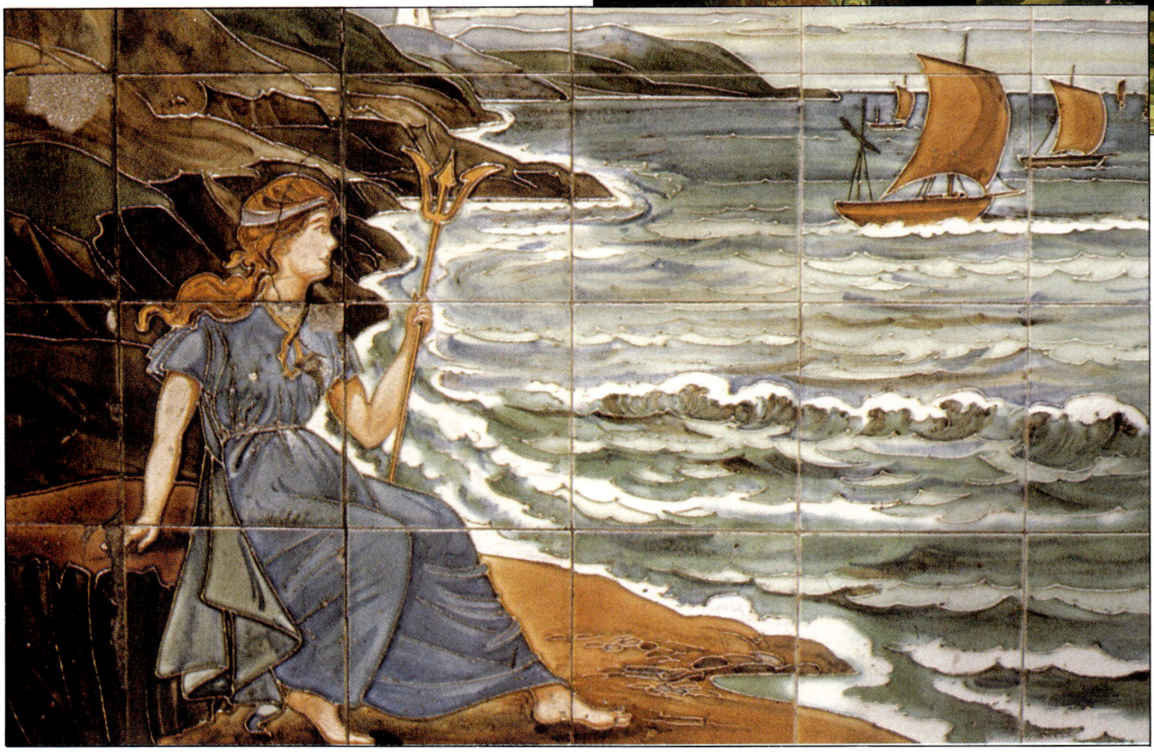

the Victorian tile-makers encompassed most of the traditional skills, as well as new developments. Transfer-printing was by far the most widely used technique, and took various forms; many transfer-printed tiles have hand-painted colour added either over or under the glaze. Again, Minton was at the forefront of new developments and as early as 1848 was using a block-printing process to apply colour to tiles. Later in the century direct colour printing on tiles was made easier by developments in lithography, while screen printing was a still later technical advance.

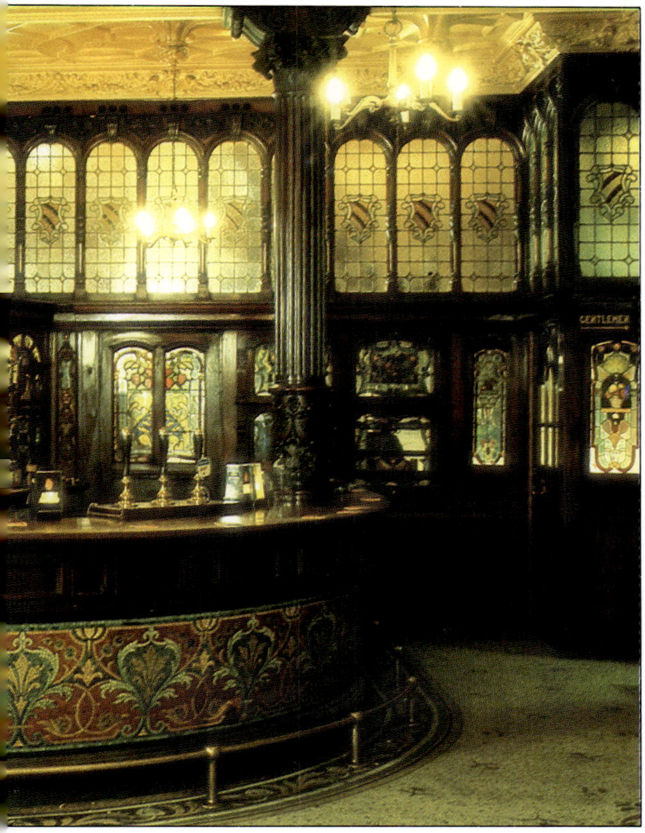

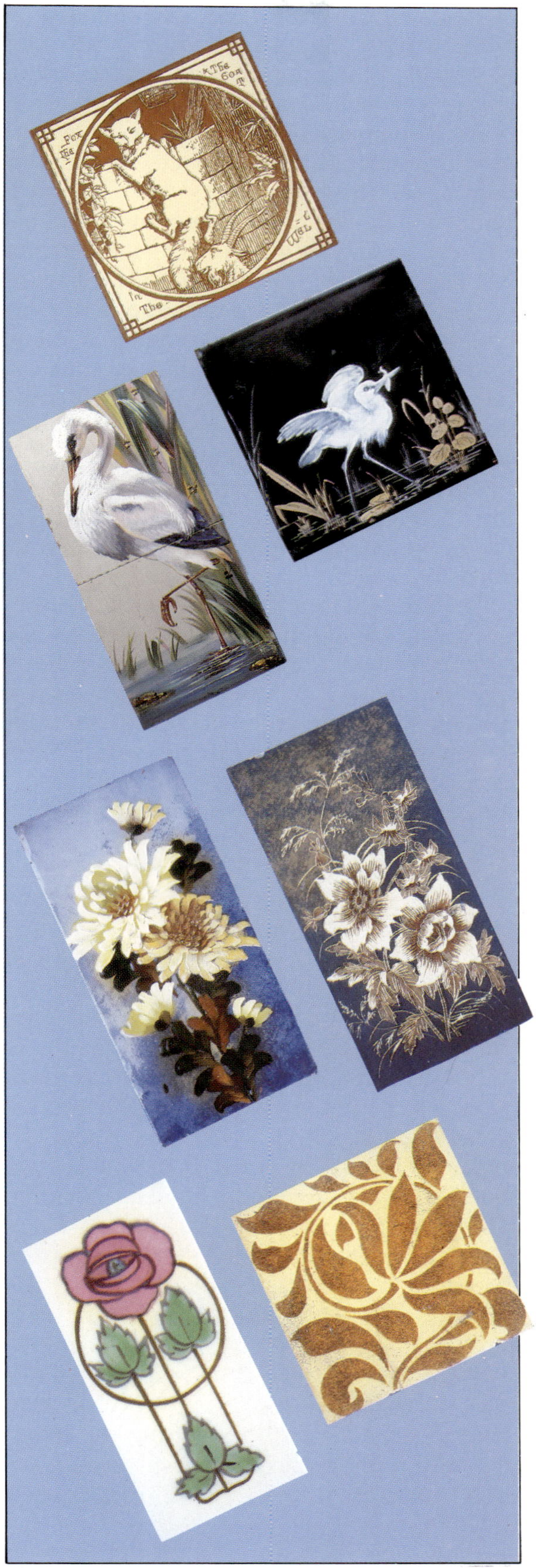

CHAPTER NINE

•

LEFT (FROM TOP TO BOTTOM)

Block-printed tile atttributed to Thomas Allen, Minton's China Works, c. 1875.

Pâte-sur-pâte tile with on-glaze painting in gold, Minton's China Works, c. 1885.

Two tiles depicting a stork, hand-painted by W Dixon for Minton, Hollins & Co, c. 1880.

Barbotine flower tile, made by Burmantofts of Leeds, c. 1885.

Sgraffito flower tile, c. 1890.

A tube-lined, Art Nouveau tile.

Tile decorated by aerography, Doulton, c. 1885.

Hand-painting was particularly favoured by the producers of tile pictures; many of the period's most accomplished artists painted on tiles, and while some pictures were effectively unique works of art, others could be repeated using the same method of pouncing as that of the Dutch. *Barbotine*, or slip painting, was a form of hand-painting using coloured slips instead of paint; a mechanical form of *barbotine* decoration was carried out at the Wedgwood factory in the 1880s.

Sgraffito was another ancient form revived by the Victorians: the body of the tile was coated with slip and the design was scratched onto and through this to reveal the dark tile body underneath. One of this technique's most successful exponents was Hannah Barlow, who made animal designs on tiles and other wares for Doulton.

Pâte-sur-pâte was a technique used for decorative plaques. First developed in France, it was perfected and used at Minton by the French artist Marc-Louis Solon from 1870 until the early 1900s. The process involved the building up of layers and layers of white slip to form relief decoration on a tinted Parian porcelain body. The design was formed by different thicknesses of slip, which gave subtle variations of tone.

Tube-lining was a Victorian development of the *cuerda seca* and *cuenca* techniques, both of which were also used on late 19th-century tiles. The design on a tube-lined tile was piped onto the surface in the form of clay slip that kept the coloured glazes apart. It was an expensive technique and was imitated for the mass market by a metal stamping method that produced similarly raised outlines on the tile surface. Tube-lining was much used during the Arts and Crafts and Art Nouveau periods.

Aerography was a form of spray-decorating through a stencil. It produced a very finely speckled effect but was only rarely used for tiles.

Toward the end of the 19th century photographic tiles appeared. They were the culmination of many years of experiment, first to fix a photographic image onto a ceramic surface, then to adapt the technique to commercial production. Several different processes were used. One, the 'dusting-on' method, was mainly adopted by photographers using mass-produced tile blanks that were later fired by specialist ceramic firms. Another, known as the Autotype process, was a lithographic method and was used at Wedgwood. It was developed most fully by the photographer George Grundy, who produced tiles printed with photographic views at his factory, the Photo Decorated Tile Co, near Derby. A third type, which was not a photographic process at all, but resulted in a near photo-like image, consisted of portraits of well-known personalities such as Queen Victoria, Abraham Lincoln and Gladstone. These portraits were modelled in relief from photographs and then covered in a thick glaze that ran off the raised areas and pooled in the deeper parts. The technique was known as *émail ombrant* and tiles of this type were produced by Wedgwood and Minton, among other firms, from the 1860s, and about 30 years later by George Cartlidge for Sherwin & Cotton and J H Barratt & Co.

Tiles were occasionally produced with

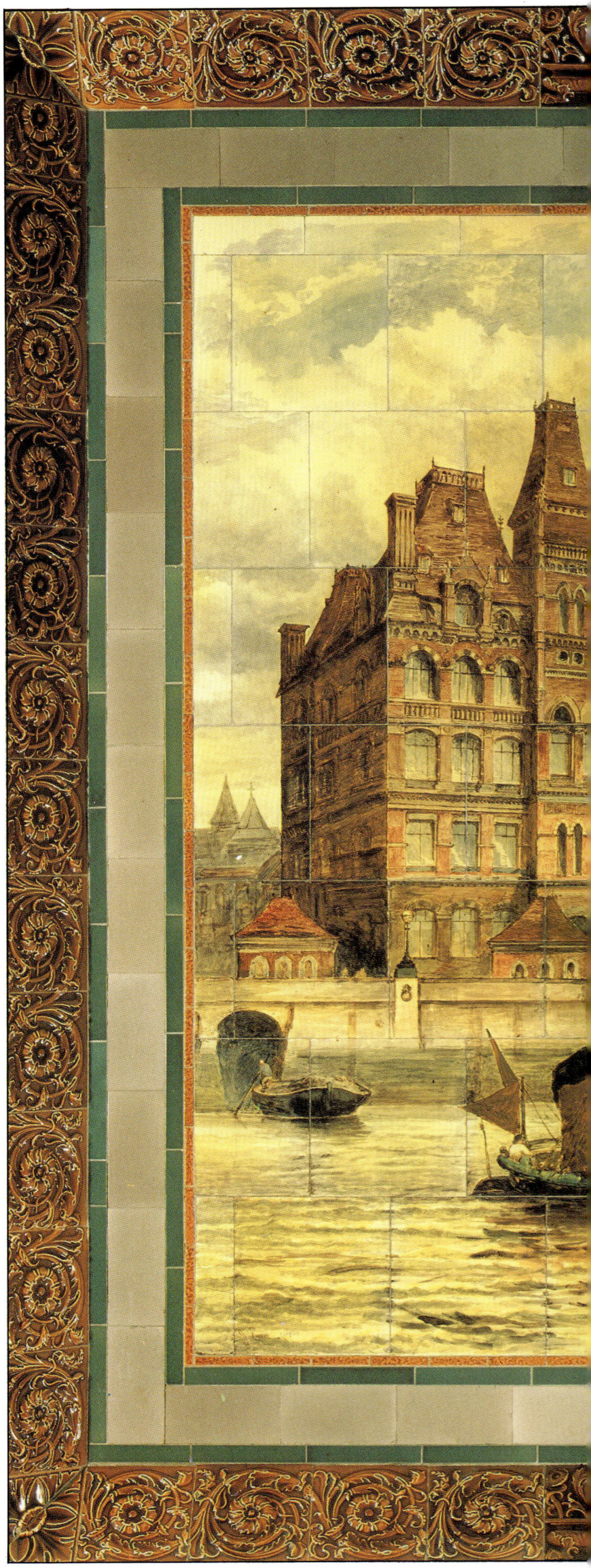

RIGHT *A tile picture of the Doulton factory in Lambeth, from across the Thames; designed by J Eyre and painted by Esther Lewis, 1885.*

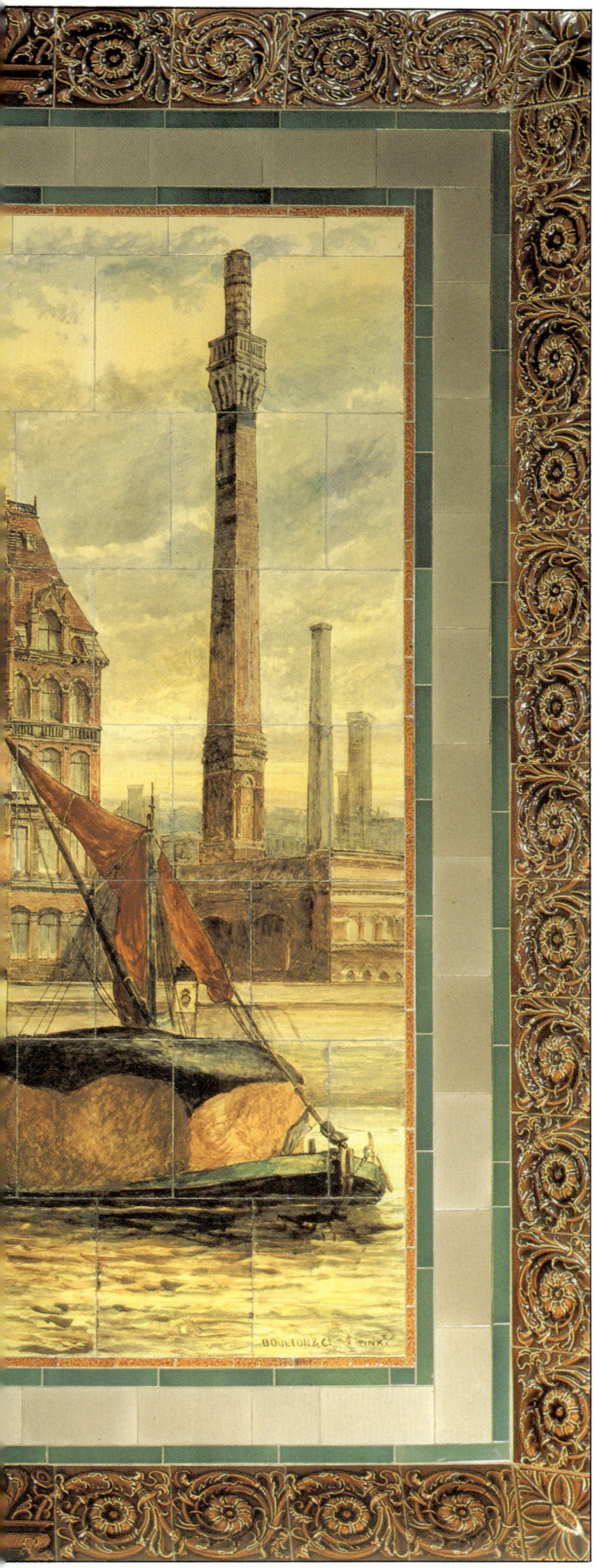

underglaze metallic decoration: these were expensive and only made for special commissions. On-glaze gilding was a more usual form of embellishment, notably used by Copeland. The metallic effects of lustre were also exploited during the 1880s and 1890s, largely through the efforts of William De Morgan.

Major tile-makers of the 1870-1910 period included, besides those already well-established such as Minton, Maw, Copeland and Boote, a number whose products were just as significant. Craven Dunnill, the main rivals of Maw in the Ironbridge Gorge, survived from 1871 until 1951, producing encaustic floor tiles and printed, enamelled and maiolica-glazed relief tiles for walls. Wedgwood opened a specialized tile department around 1870, making encaustic tiles by both the plastic and dust-pressing methods, and maiolica and transfer-printed wall tiles. Later, transfer-printing became the main method of decoration on Wedgwood tiles, and many of their tableware designs were reproduced on tiles.

The Pilkington Tile and Pottery Co was not founded until the 1890s, but unlike many others it has survived to this day. Pilkington employed some of the most eminent designers of the late 19th and early 20th centuries, including Walter Crane, C F A Voysey, Lewis Day and Gordon Forsyth and this, coupled with good management and unrivalled technical excellence, was surely the key to its success in the early days. Pilkington produced encaustic and plain-coloured tiles in a wide range of techniques — embossed, incised, block-printed, hand-coloured, tube-lined, lustred and maiolica-glazed.

In Poole, Dorset, The Architectural Pottery became an important producer of hand-painted tile murals in the 1880s, and later developed other techniques such as maiolica, lustre-decoration and tube-lining, processes which were vital in ensuring the firm's continued survival. The firm was bought out by Carter & Co in 1895. Tile manufacture also continued on a considerable scale in Hereford, where the two Godwin brothers, William and Henry, ran separate enterprises after 1878.

WILLIAM DE MORGAN

Although he must be regarded as a figure apart from tile mass-production, William De Morgan was a major influence on and force in tile design. Through his association with William Morris he was at the forefront of the progressive movement of the 1880s, particularly with regard to ceramic decoration, and his tiles are among the finest produced in any age. As a student at the Royal Academy Schools in the 1860s, De Morgan found himself sympathetic to the ideals of the Pre-Raphaelite Brotherhood and in 1863 he became associated with William Morris and his circle. Morris had been designing tiles since 1862 and De Morgan soon began to make designs for his firm, Morris, Marshall, Faulkner & Co. These included tiles and painted furniture, although stained glass was his chief preoccupation when he first decided to give up painting as a career. It was his work in stained glass and his discovery of the iridescence caused by silver in the paint used for it that led him to pursue the possibilities of lustre decoration on ceramic tiles.

From the early 1870s onward, in his Cheyne Row premises in Chelsea, De Morgan concentrated on the decoration of tiles, employing at first a single male assistant and half a dozen women painters. To begin with, they worked on tile blanks from other firms, including The Architectural Pottery and Carter, of Poole, Craven Dunnill, Wedgwood and some from the Netherlands, but later he began to make his own, by hand, from plastic clay containing a high proportion of 'grog' or coarse, strengthening material.

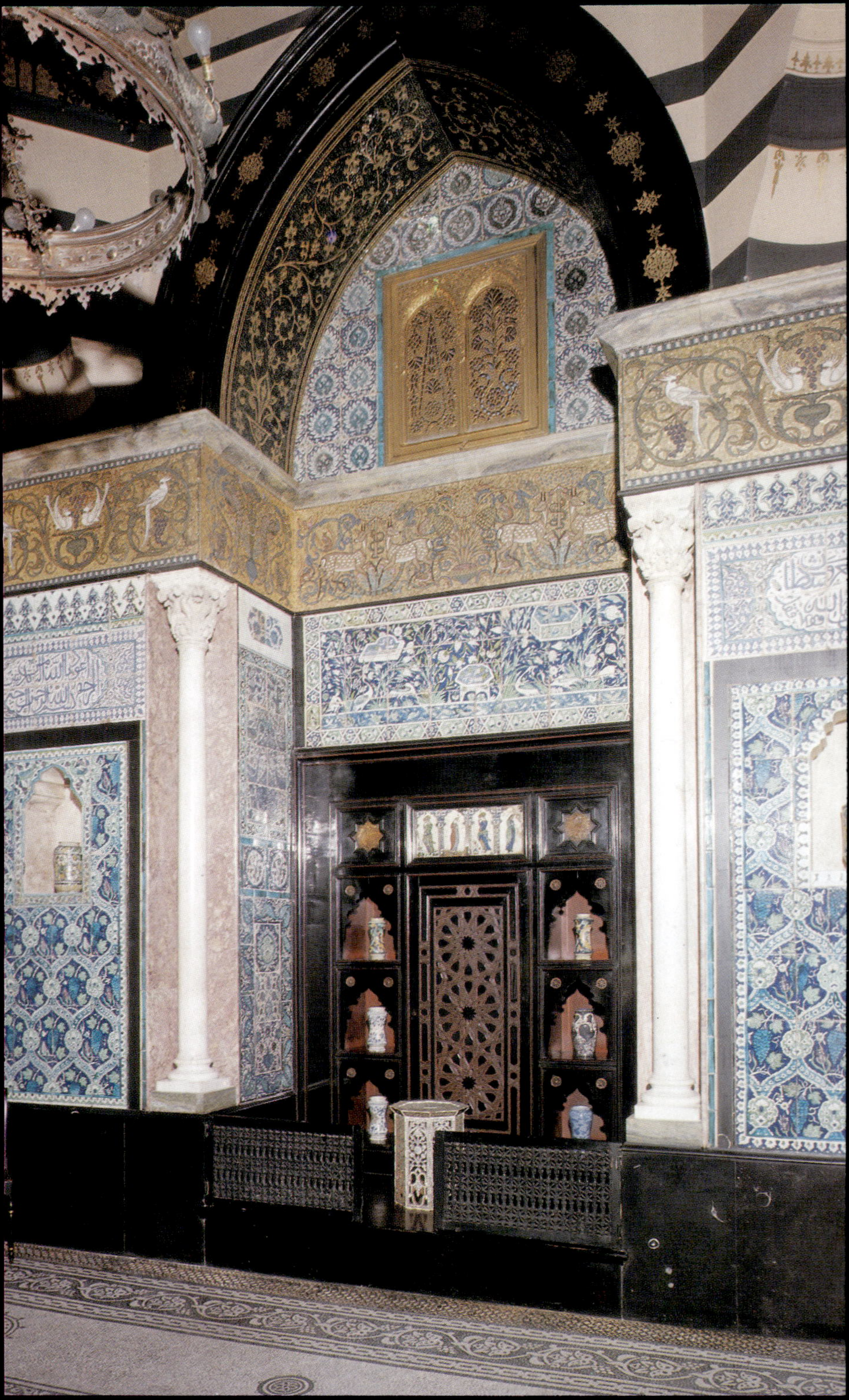

He produced as many as 300 designs during this 'Chelsea period' and also devised his own method for transferring the design onto the tile: the outline, on transparent paper, was pasted onto a sheet of glass and traced onto tissue from the other side. The colour pigments were filled in on this tissue paper, which was then fixed to the tile itself, which had been prepared with a coating of white slip for extra whiteness and brilliance. The tile, with its paper pattern attached, was covered in powdered glaze and fired, during which time the paper was burnt away, leaving the colour fixed to the tile body under the glaze.

Obviously De Morgan's methods, while producing tiles of exceptional quality and strength, were uncommercial compared to those produced in other factories by the dust-pressing method, and only the rich could afford them. Among his most famous commissions was a set of 'Islamic' tiles for the Arab Hall in Lord Leighton's house in Holland Park Road, London (1879). He also made many designs in imitation of 15th- and 16th-century Iznik wares. Flowers, birds, fishes, sailing ships and heraldic beasts were his favourite subjects, and whether executed in his well-known polychrome palette — with blues and greens predominating — or in red lustre, they are among the most distinguished and sought-after tiles of all.

In 1882 De Morgan moved to Merton Abbey in Surrey, where William Morris had already established a workshop. Here tiles began to take second place to the production of other types of pottery and in 1888 he moved to the Sands End Pottery in Fulham, entering into a partnership with the architect and tile enthusiast Halsey Ricardo. This was dissolved 10 years later and a new partnership formed with his long-time artists Charles and Fred Passenger, and Frank Iles, his original assistant. The firm continued to supply tiles for major commissions — including P & O liners — but De Morgan's failing health took him increasingly away from the business and the firm was clearly on a downward path by the late 1890s. Although it continued under the Passengers for two years after De Morgan's retirement in 1905, few new tile designs were produced.

Many of De Morgan's designs and techniques were copied by the industrial tile-makers, but his influence was also felt in a general way, as part of the Aesthetic Movement of the 1880s. Because so many of the period's most progressive artists made designs for mass-produced tiles, the new artistic ideas were widely disseminated and rapidly became popular.

Something of a bridge between De Morgan's hand-crafted approach and the mass-production methods of the tile factories was provided by Minton's Art Pottery Studio in Kensington Gore, which between 1871 and 1875 provided a great many one-of-a-kind tiles and panels and other decorative wares, and at the same time made mass-producible designs for its Stoke-on-Trent factory.

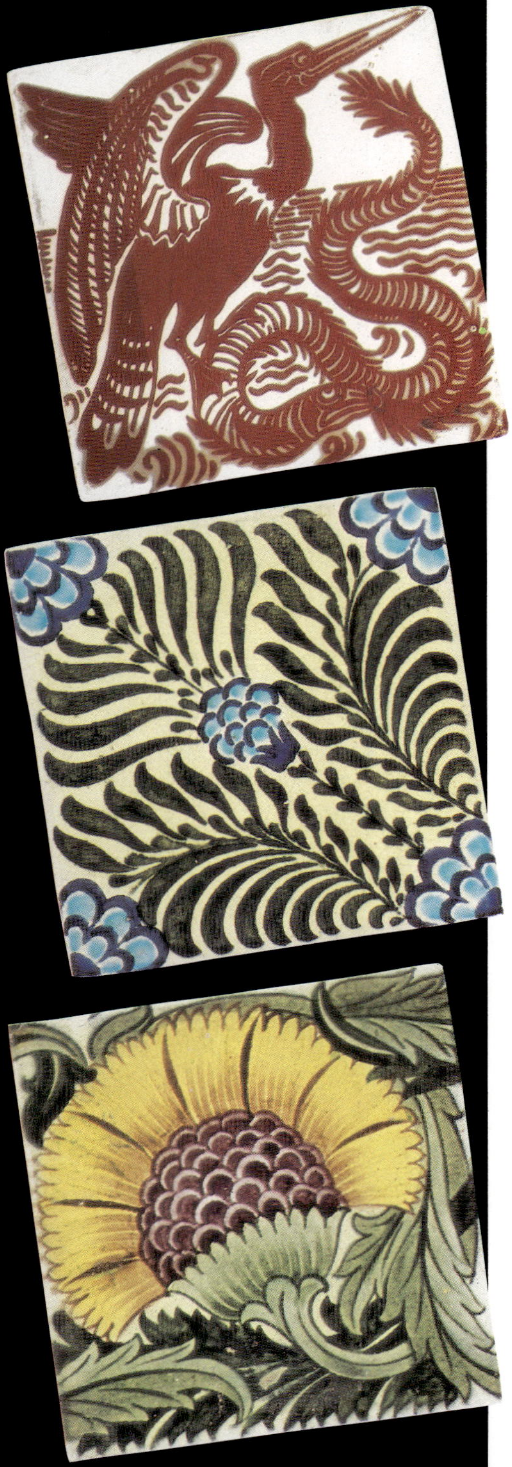

LEFT *The Arab Hall, Leighton House, London.*

RIGHT *Three underglaze-painted tiles by William De Morgan. Tiles like these were designed to form composite patterns on walls and at the sides of fireplaces.*

RIGHT *'The Sleeping Beauty', one of a series of panels designed by William Rowe and Margaret Thompson and made by Doulton for the children's ward at St Thomas's Hospital, London.*

Doulton of Lambeth specialized in tiles for the outside cladding of buildings. To meet the need for weather-resistance, it developed a highly vitrified salt-glazed stoneware called Doultonware in the 1870s; this was followed by the less shiny and reflective Carraraware in the 1880s. As well as architectural tiling, Doulton produced quantities of panels hand-painted by eminent artists.

An existing pottery, W & E Corn, of Longport, Staffordshire, began to produce glazed wall tiles in 1891. Renamed Corn Brothers, it became a major producer of transfer-printed and maiolica tiles in the Arts and Crafts and Art Nouveau styles.

Among other firms notable either for the high quality of their products or their enterprise in developing technical processes were the Crystal Porcelain Co of Cobridge, which made porcelain tiles; W B Simpson & Sons, producers of hand-painted 'art' tiles (from other firms' blanks), and Sherwin & Cotton of Hanley, makers of 'photographic' portraits, 'niello', and flower-decorated *barbotine* tiles. J C Edwards, George Wooliscroft and Henry Abraham Ollivant are also names to be remembered.

Minton was at the forefront in its employment of well-respected artists. Its tiles include designs by Augustus Pugin in the early period, and William Steven Coleman, Christopher Dresser, Walter Crane, H W Foster, Henry Stacey Marks, Sir Edward Poynter, John Moyr Smith and William Wise later in the century. Some, like the many sets by Moyr Smith, are instantly recognizable as classics of their time. They include Occupations, Idylls of the King, Nursery Rhymes, Children's Stories, Early English History, Shakespeare and the Waverley Novels. Thomas Allen worked both for Minton and for Wedgwood, where he was art director from 1880 to 1900. His designs include several series for Wedgwood, including Hats, Ivanhoe, Courses of a Meal and A Midsummer Night's Dream. Other Wedgwood picture tiles were made to designs by Walter Crane.

Maw was one of the leaders of tile production in quality as well as quantity, and the firm's designers included G E Street, Sir Matthew Digby Wyatt, Lewis Day, George

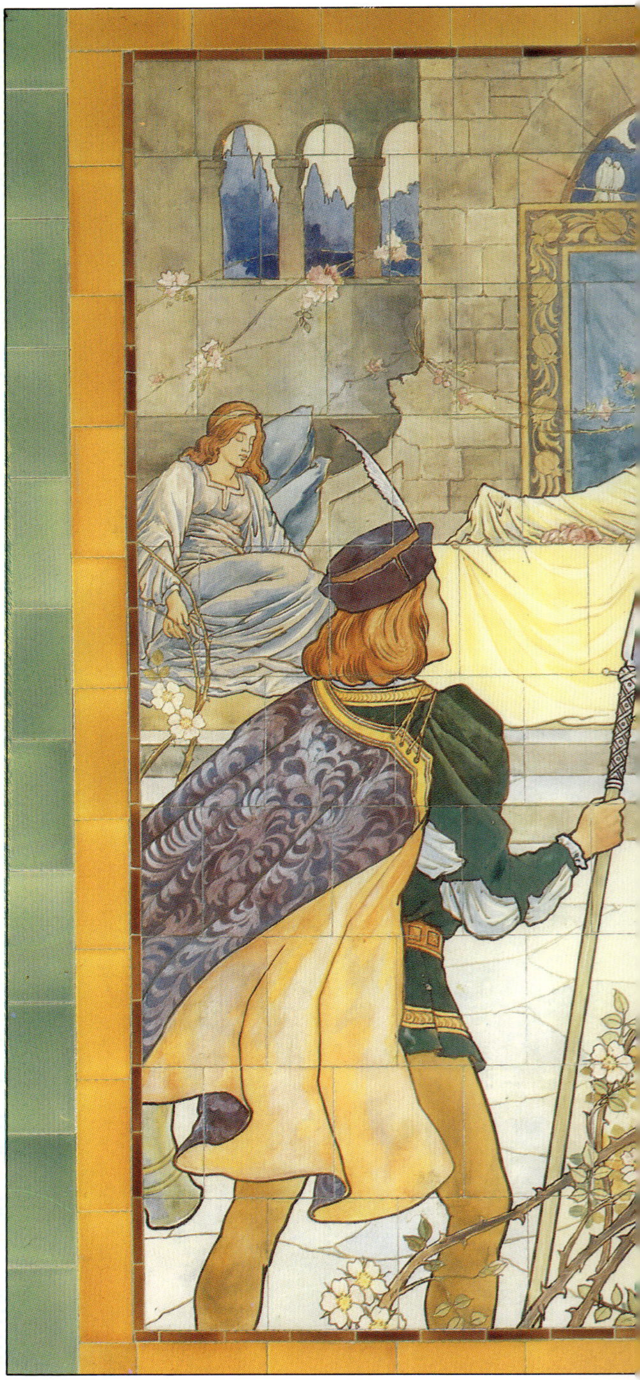

Goldie, Owen Jones, Charles Temple and the ubiquitous Walter Crane. Some were freelance artists whose work was used by several tile companies. Walter Crane was typical: his designs were used by Minton, Wedgwood and Pilkington, as well as Maw. Lewis Day also made designs for Pilkington and J C Edwards; George Goldie for Craven Dunnill, and Owen Jones for Minton. Kate

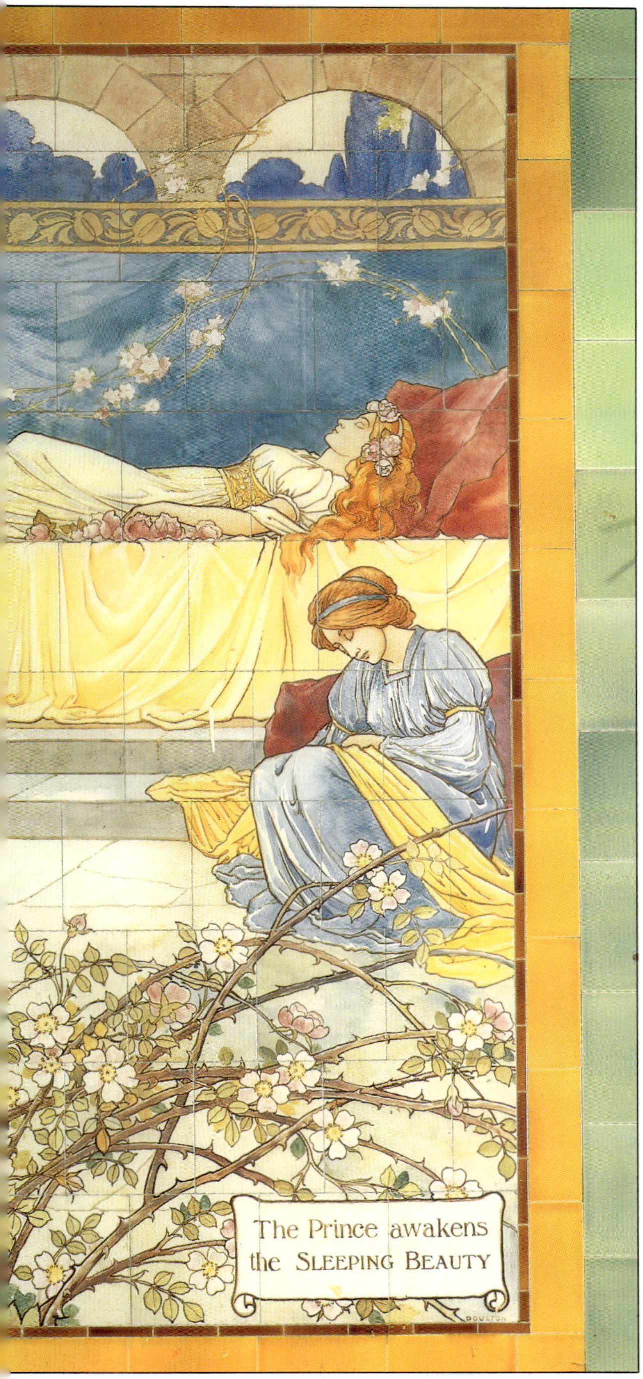

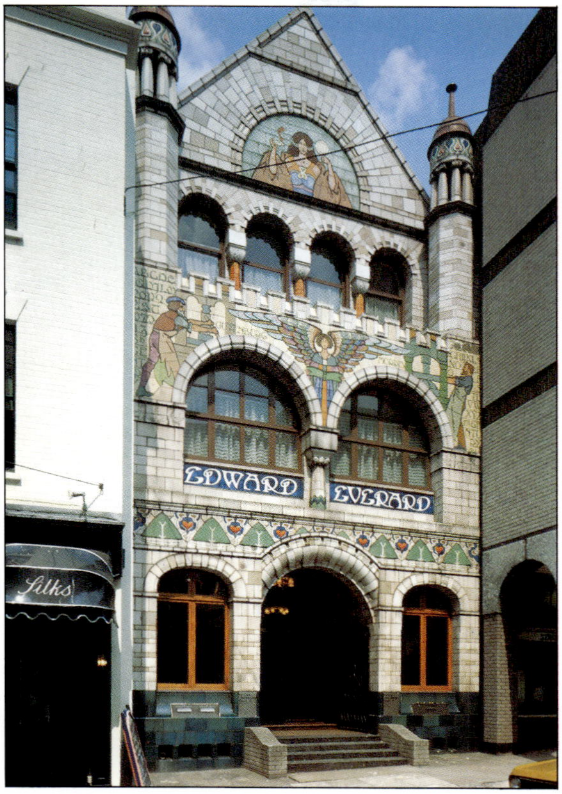

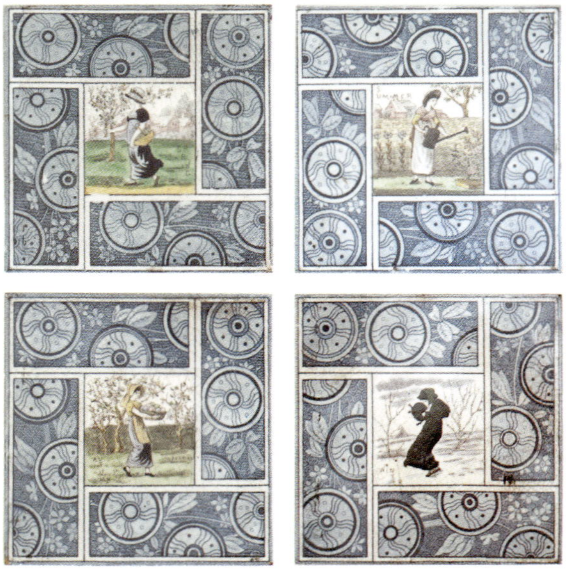

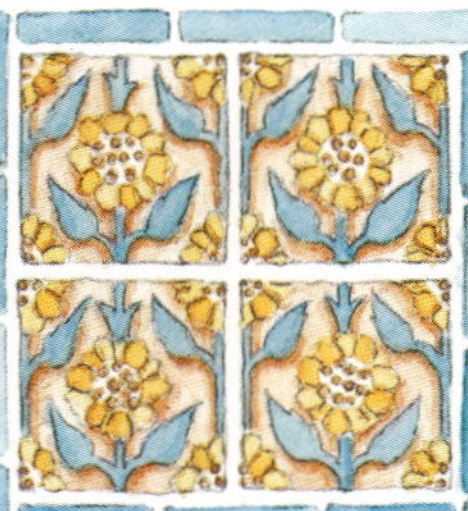

CHAPTER NINE

•

LEFT *W J Neatby's tiled façade for the Bristol printer Edward Everard, made by Doulton, 1901.*

BELOW LEFT *A set of Four Seasons tiles, transfer-printed and hand-coloured by T & R Boote from designs attributed to Kate Greenaway, 1881.*

Greenaway designs appear on tiles by T & R Boote.

Doulton's most celebrated designers were Hannah Barlow, W J Neatby, J H McLennan and Margaret Thompson, while among Copeland's distinguished were Robert Frederic Abraham and his son Robert John Abraham, George and John Eyre (who later worked at Doulton), and Lucien Besche (previously with Minton).

English tiles were exported all over the world, and most of the major companies had agents in many countries. Eventually some of these set up their own companies. Among them were Germany, France, Australia and, above all, the United States, where a number of English designers took up employment.

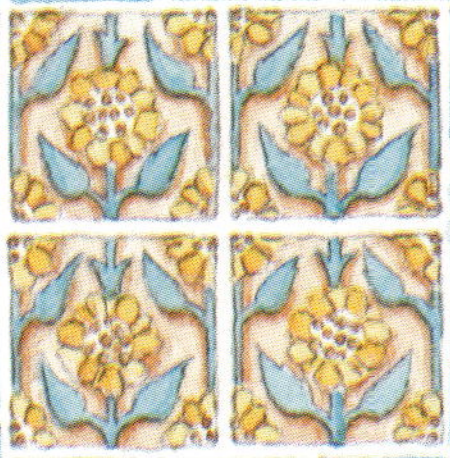

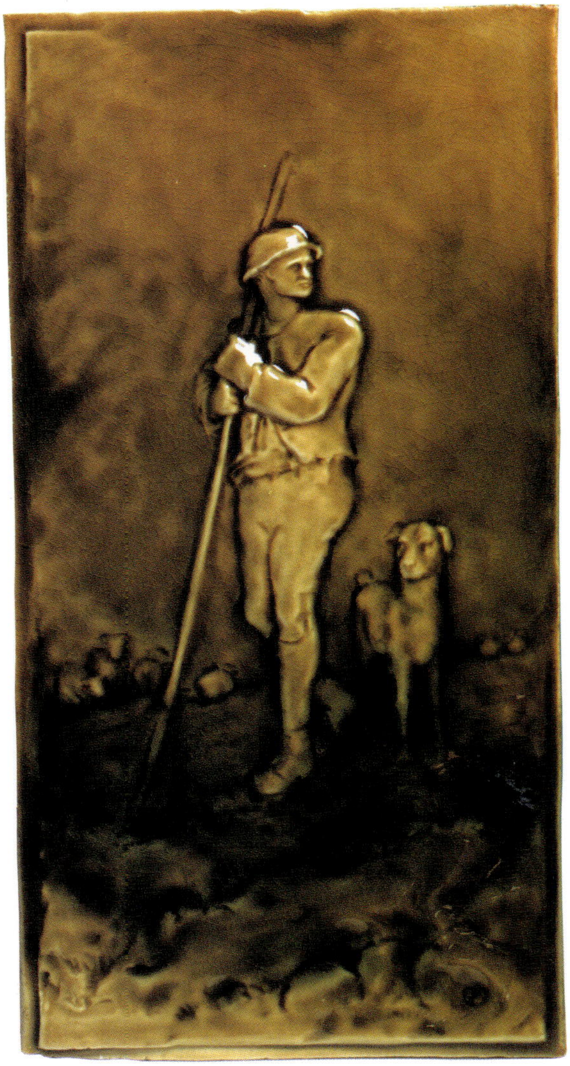

RIGHT *J & J G Low tile of a shepherd and his dog and flock, signed by Arthur Osborne, c. 1880. Such landscape and genre scenes by Osborne, Low's chief modeller, were typical of the massive output of this Massachusetts pottery, as was the clouded, or pooled, glaze effect, which can be clearly seen on the mottled sky area. The tile is quite large, measuring 15 × 8 in (38 × 20 cm).*

FAR RIGHT *Galleon tile by Grueby Faience Co of Boston, c. 1905. Grueby created the market for the fired matt glaze, and the firm produced lovely hand-decorated tiles in the sturdy Arts and Crafts mode. This vintage ship has sails in a creamy matt colour, and is set on a deep blue sky-and-sea background.*

In the United States, the hey-day of tile production was roughly the period from 1870 to 1930. Hand in hand with so-called 'art pottery', art tiles — as opposed to tiles with transfer-printed designs — were being produced all over the country. These were sometimes much more sophisticated in style and technique than their European antecedents and counterparts, although of course greatly indebted to them. Some American factories were rapidly successful, but others failed in a matter of years, or were soon incorporated into or taken over by other firms. The story of the various American potteries was often a volatile one, with only a handful lasting more than a decade or, at most, two.

One of the first American tile companies was the Pittsburgh Encaustic Tile Co, established in 1876, which later became the Star Encaustic Tiling Co. There were other major producers of encaustic floor tiles, such as the United States Encaustic Tile Works in Indianapolis, but it was in the field of decorative wall tiling rather than encaustic floor tiles that the Americans were most successful, responsive as they were to the ideals of Aestheticism and the Arts and Crafts Movement.

Art-tile producers were spread out across the vast United States, with factories as far east as Massachusetts and west as California. In the middle of the country, potteries thrived in Ohio, Indiana and Michigan, no less because of the excellent qualities of the local clays than the impressive talents of local craftsmen and women.

The Boston area produced several notable tile firms, including two in the town of Chelsea. The Chelsea Keramic Arts Works was established by Alexander W Robertson in 1872, and in 1878 John Gardner Low, who had worked at Robertson's pottery, founded Art Tile Works, trading first as J & J G Low and from 1883 as J G & J F Low. Both companies produced an amazing variety of tiles in the late 19th century, Chelsea Keramic's output including reproductions of Greek tiles as well as tiles with Oriental glazes and designs. The firm failed in 1888 and a new one, Chelsea Pottery, was formed in 1891 by Alexander Robertson's brother, Hugh; Chelsea Pottery is best known for its crackle glazes. Five years later, however, a move caused the company to trade as Dedham Pottery, which also became renowned for its glazes — sometimes iridescent and brightly hued, sometimes rough and bubbly.

Low's tiles were even more admired in their time — and today — than those of Chelsea Keramic. Decorated with relief designs in florid or geometric patterns, these tiles were also highlighted with coloured glazes that collected, or 'clouded' or 'pooled', in a square's crevices. Although many of Low's tiles were for architectural and furnishing uses, for example, fireplace surrounds and clock cases, they were also produced as artistic entities, and as such sold in ornate metal frames. A 'natural process' of embellishing tiles was developed by Low, whereby tiles were moulded from impressions of leaves or grasses. One such tile, with a greenish-yellow glaze, was lightly embossed with a fan shape, a patterned circle and grasses, directly reproducing natural objects. It seems amazingly abstract and modern, although it represents a true impression of nature (the plant forms were gently pressed into the clay and then carefully lifted away). Other Low pieces depicted portraits, landscapes and genre scenes (included among the latter was an amusing tile showing five hogs feeding at a trough). Arthur Osborne, the firm's chief modeller, was responsible for many of these tiles, including a series of American Presidential portraits.

An interesting Massachusetts firm was Marblehead Pottery, founded in 1905 by Dr Herbert J Hall as part of a group of crafts ventures for 'nervously worn out patients' in a sanitorium. Before 1912, matt glazes were commonplace at Marblehead (some with Japoniste designs, such as ornamental fish swimming amid seaweed), but later bright, tin-enamel glazes were the order of the day. Tile decorations also included Massachusetts flora and fauna, as well as local sailing ships.

Two Boston potteries producing tiles were the Paul Revere Pottery, founded in the early 20th century to train girls from indigent, immigrant families (the firm was also known as the Saturday Evening Girls' Club, and their wares often signed 'SEG'), and Grueby Faience Co, best known for creating the market for the popular fired matt glaze. Although Grueby is mostly thought of in terms of its vases — which today command the highest prices among discerning collectors of American art pottery — the firm also produced lovely tiles in the sturdy Arts and Crafts mode, hand-decorated examples with floral patterns, animals, medieval knights and assorted landscapes. Matt glazes in yellow, brown, blue and most especially a rich, dark, forest green are distinctive to Grueby, which was formed in 1894 by William H Grueby, who trained with the Lows of Art Tile Works.

In New York, an interesting phenomenon was The Tile Club, a group of artists who, between 1877 and 1887, regularly and quite uncommercially met to decorate tiles. The great Louis Comfort Tiffany, best known for his stained-glass windows, ornate lamps and Favrile-glass vases, also included tiles in his prolific output. From *c.* 1905, his firm produced vases, tiles and other pottery with glazes most often in shades of mossy green, harvest gold and creamy ivory, their decoration taken from nature.

Other New York and New Jersey firms included the International Tile and Trim Co in Brooklyn, the Maywood Tile Co in New Jersey, and the Trent Tile Co and Providential Tile Co, both in Trenton, New Jersey. Also in Trenton, a major East Coast

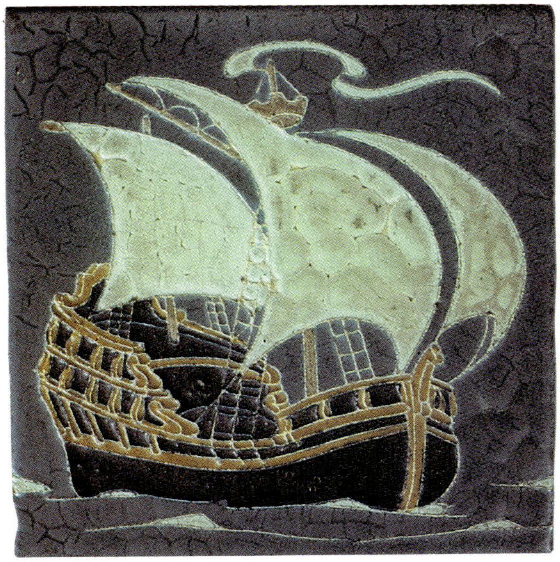

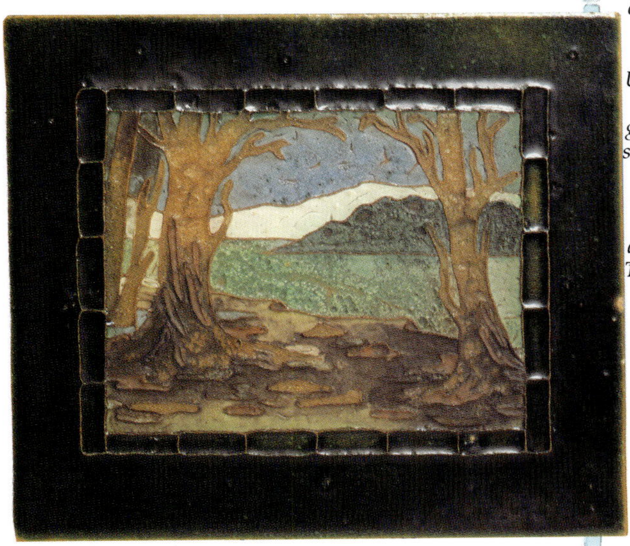

BELOW LEFT
Landscape tile by Atlantic Tile Manufacturing Co of New Jersey, c. 1910. This rectangular tile comprises a colourful landscape within a handsome 'frame'. Unlike other tiles that were often part of a group – for a fireplace surround, for example – this work is a singular entity, and was most likely displayed on its own. The Atlantic Tile firm was taken over by Ohio's American Encaustic Tiling in 1912.

RIGHT *Portrait tile by F H Robertson, 1914. George Beede Robertson, the boy whose profile is shown, was the son of the tile's maker, who later founded the Claycraft company in Los Angeles in 1921. The initials 'ESP' are those of the tile's decorator, Emily Sterns Perry.*

BELOW RIGHT *Fox tile by the Paul Revere Pottery, c. 1910. The Pottery, also known as the Saturday Evening Girls' Club (or 'SEG', as the tiles were often signed), was founded in Boston in the early 1900s for the purpose of training needy girls from immigrant families.*

pottery centre, was Mueller Mosaic, opened in 1908 by Herman Carl Mueller, who came to the United States from Germany as a fledgling sculptor in 1878. He established a cement business in Ohio in 1879, turning to ceramics as a medium in the 1880s. Before starting Mueller Mosaic, he designed and produced pottery and tiles for a number of firms — including the American Encaustic Tiling Co in Zanesville, Ohio, where he became known for his relief panels of plump children or female figures in landscapes and as parts of genre scenes. Mueller's 50-year-long career also included ceramic designing on a large scale — huge tiled panels for both interior and exterior settings, such as the mural of Columbus landing in the New World, completed in 1899 for St Nicholas Catholic Church in Zanesville, and the 15-panel history of the domestication of the cow, finished in 1930 for the Walker-Gordon Dairy in Plainsboro, New Jersey (glazed tile was used throughout the dairy, since it conformed best to the strictest sanitary conditions). Mueller Mosaic remained open until the 1940s, and it also created many of the tile designs for the New York City subway system, some of which are still extant.

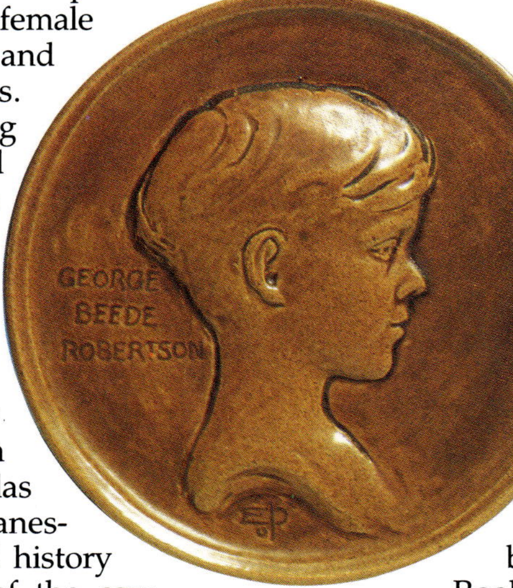

In the nearby state of Pennsylvania, Henry Chapman Mercer's Moravian Pottery and Tile Works in Doylestown flourished in the early decades of the 20th century. Mercer's home, Fonthill, was decorated with assorted tiles, many reflecting his archaeological and antiquarian interests. Pennsylvania-Dutch designs, as well as classical and medieval subjects such as dragons, lions and armoured knights, adorn his tiles, which have a rough, hand-hewn appearance. (Interestingly enough, Mercer and Herman Carl Mueller shared the same initials, and experts have speculated that Mueller had a hand in designing some of Fonthill's tiles.)

The American Encaustic Tiling Co of Zanesville, Ohio, was established in 1875, one of several major potteries in that Mid-western state. American Encaustic produced both floor and wall tiles and, besides employing Herman Carl Mueller, also used the talents of the brothers Paul and Léon V Solon, the latter of whom was the chief designer at the Minton factory in Britain from 1900 to 1909. One of Léon Solon's tiles for American Encaustic, this of the late 1920s, is an Art Deco masterpiece, with its zigzag and floral design in metallic silver, red and black.

The Rookwood Pottery of Cincinnati, Ohio, was also in some way a response to the period's enthusiasm for decorating tiles, although its major output consisted of vases (its signature piece, however, was a tile of a rook perched on a branch). Founded in 1880 by Maria Longworth Nichols, Rookwood's wares were at first much influenced by Japanese motifs, these eventually giving way to more naturalistic depictions of flora and fauna. Matt glazes were introduced around 1904, concomitant with relief plaques and tiles, some of these tin-glazed, many made for fireplaces and walls and depicting animals, plants and fruits. (In fact, the pottery's premises were enlarged to accommodate its burgeoning arm of tile manufacture.) An especially charming Rookwood tile of 1911 shows a pair of stylized rabbits surrounding a tulip tree. The symmetry and stylization of such a tile are indebted to both the Art Nouveau style and the Arts and Crafts Movement, yet the piece — like most of the company's outstanding wares — is distinctively Rookwood.

There were several other tile-making potteries begun and mostly staffed by women in the American Mid-West. The Pewabic Pottery in Detroit, Michigan, was founded by Mary Chase Perry around 1903 (the firm survived until 1961); it was best known for its rich blue, gold and iridescent glazes, often layered and many adorning tiles. The Overbeck Pottery in Indiana was begun by the four Overbeck sisters.

On the West Coast, several California firms produced tiles, including the Western Art Tile Co and Berkeley's California Faience. The latter's tiles were distinctive for their unique brick-red relief contour lines and vivid glazes of rich earth-and-sky tones — brown, ochre, cactus green, azure. Local desert landscapes were depicted, as well as lovely floral portraits.

Ernest A Batchelder (1875–1957) was one of the strongest design personalities in American art-tile production. Born in New Hampshire and educated in Massachusetts, he also trained at the Birmingham School of Arts and Crafts in Britain. He became associated with various American crafts schools, eventually setting up his own school of arts and crafts in Pasadena, California, in 1909. Although he was a writer and potter, he is best known as a tile designer, one very much influenced by the Gothic Revival and the English Arts and Crafts Movement. Among his distinctive cast-ceramic tiles were images of medievalized lions, Art Nouveau peacocks, leaping hares and deer, and Japoniste trees and landscapes. Although very much akin in spirit and subject matter to the painted tiles of William De Morgan, the relief tiles of Batchelder are very much American, with their strong, moulded-relief designs.

By 1930, the fashion for the art tile in the United States had diminished to the point where such tiles were regarded as merely utilitarian objects. The Depression forced many commercial firms to close, with art potters turning to university teaching to ensure their financial survival. Indeed, some American tile-producing potteries are still open — and studio potters still create lovely tiles — but there is nothing like the popular demand and consequent mass-production that existed in the six decades encompassing 1870 and 1930.

However, the significance of American tiles in the history of tile-making has been recognized and interest in them has grown considerably in the last decade, as several museum exhibitions and commercial publications have shown.

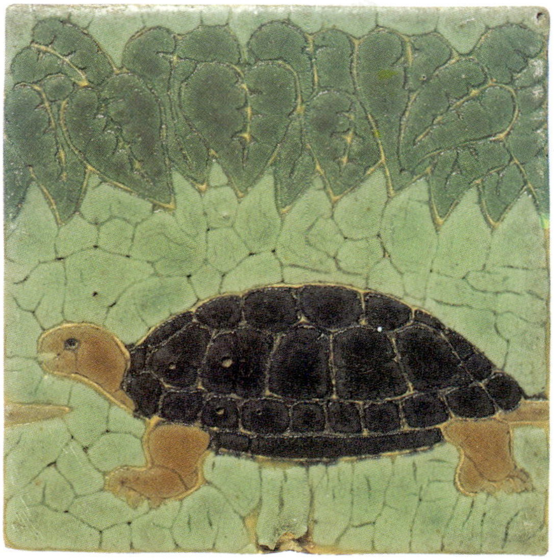

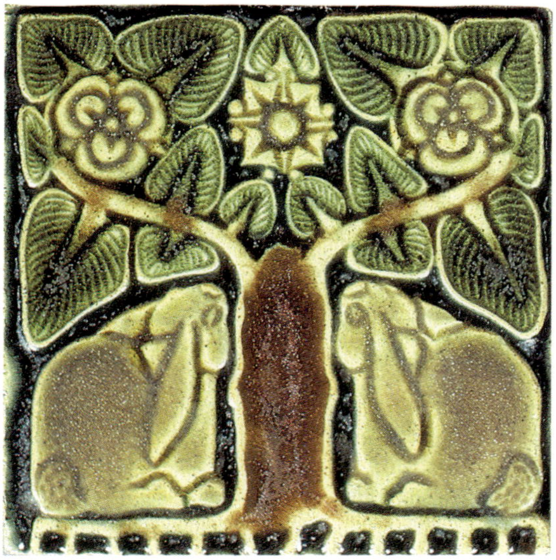

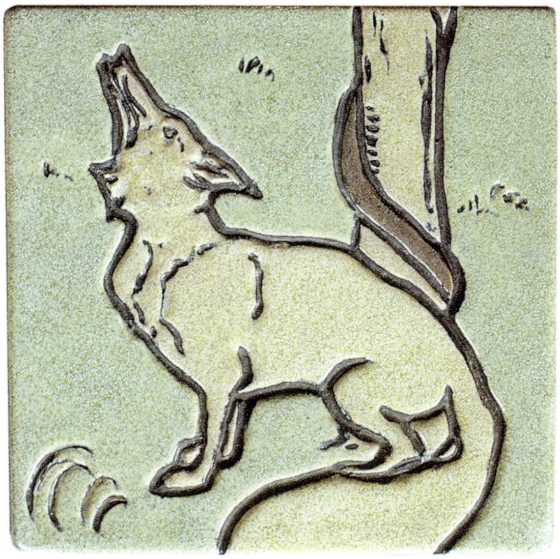

LEFT *Turtle tile by Grueby Faience of Boston,* c. *1905. This charming tile has the blue, green and yellow matt glazes distinctive of this New England firm. The mottled effect on the light-green background seems to echo the natural pattern on the turtle's shell; the gold outline on the crevices of the spade-shaped leaves and the turtle's body is quite unusual.*

BELOW LEFT *Rookwood relief tile depicting a pair of rabbits round a tulip tree, 1911. The symmetry and stylization of this lovely animal tile are indebted to both Art Nouveau design and the Arts and Crafts Movement. The way the image fills the square so fully is a typical characteristic of many American tiles, as are the matt glazes in earth tones.*

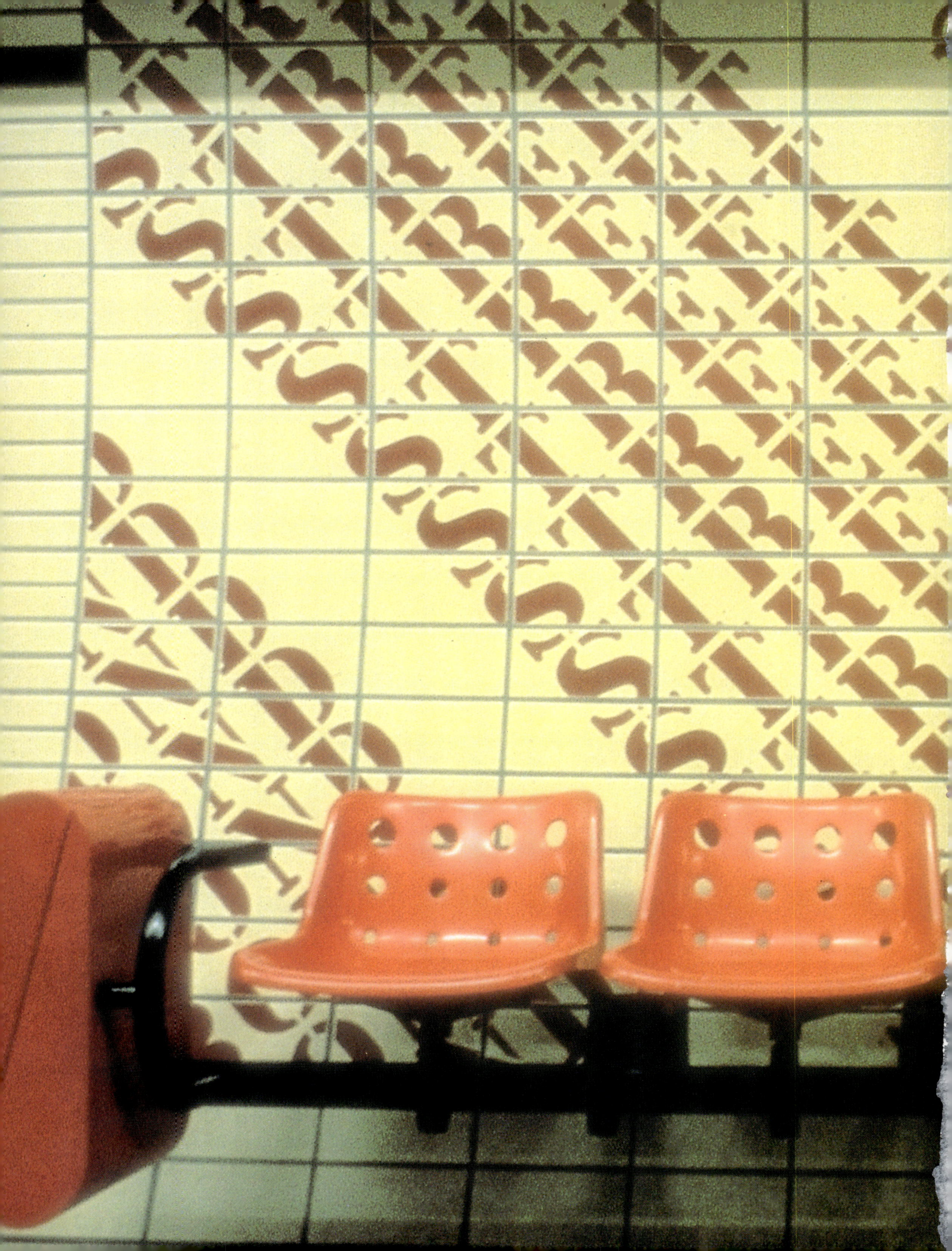

CHAPTER TEN

TILES OF THE 20TH CENTURY

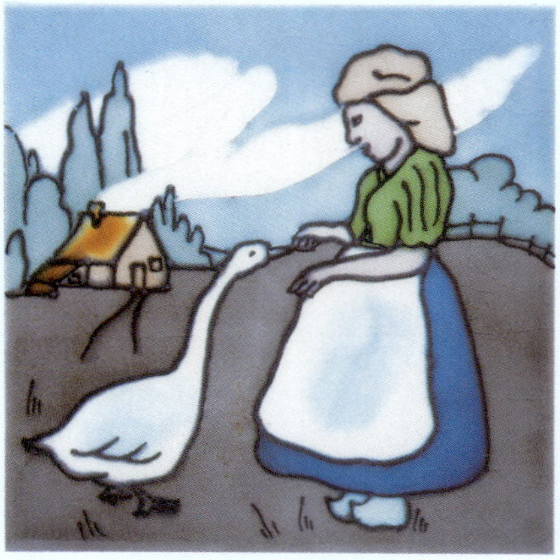

THE ART Nouveau style was the last real flowering of the great Victorian tile boom, both in England and on the Continent. By the beginning of the First World War many of the factories that proliferated in England during the last three decades of the 19th century and in the United States a little later were forced to close; others contracted or amalgamated in order to survive. While tiles in the Art Deco style of the 1920s and 1930s were produced and used for various purposes, a slump in the tile industry had already set in. Fashions had moved away from the Victorians' all-pervasive use of tiles, and public demand was reduced to a trickle.

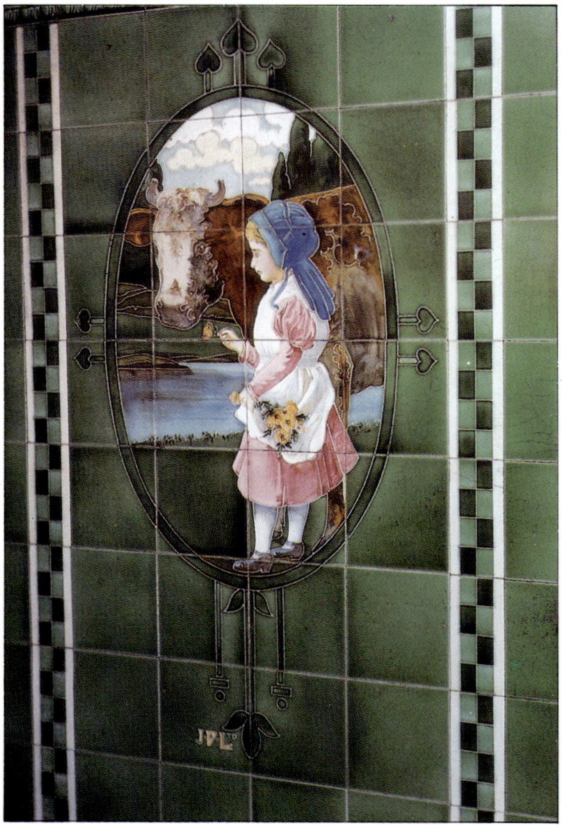

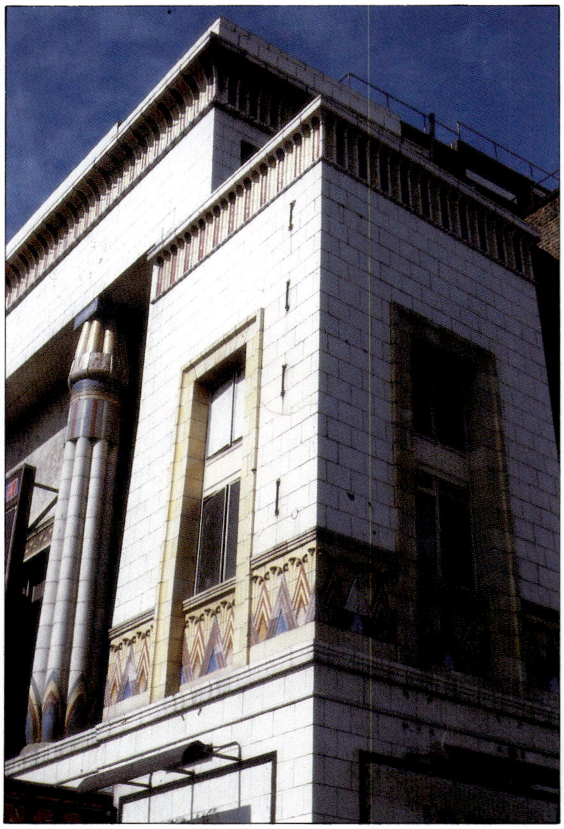

OVERLEAF (INSET) *Tube-lined tile showing a country girl with a goose, made by Richards Tile Co, c. 1930.*

ABOVE RIGHT *Slip-trailed panel at the entrance of the Buttercup Dairy Co in Cowdenbeath, Scotland, c. 1925. The panel was made by the Glasgow tile decorator, J Duncan Ltd and depicts a small girl feeding buttercups to a cow.*

ABOVE FAR RIGHT *Side view of the Carlton Cinema, Essex Road, London, designed by George Coles, 1930.*

BELOW RIGHT *Hand-painted tile with a flying seagull, made by H & R Johnson, c. 1925.*

AMONG THE British tile-making firms that survived through the 1920s and 1930s were Minton Hollins, Maw, Craven Dunnill, the Campbell Tile Co, Pilkington, Carter of Poole, Godwin of Hereford (which had become Godwin & Thynne in 1909 and H&G Thynne in 1925), Doulton, Henry Richards, J C Edwards, T & R Boote, George Wooliscroft and Malkin Edge. In recent years many of these have been absorbed into the two remaining giants on the tile-manufacturing scene — H & R Johnson and Pilkington.

Doulton, with their range of architectural ceramics, continued to be innovative, and were encouraged by some of the leading architects of the day, and by the sculptor Gilbert Bayes. Their Carraraware tiles in plain colours provided an appropriate finish to the stark outlines of the new architecture. In 1922 a Doulton artist, A E Pearce, won a colour-in-building competition organized by the Royal Institute of British Architects, with his design for a bank clad in green, blue and white tiles arranged in bands and geometric patterns. Such colourful ceramic facings were well suited to the new cinema buildings that were a feature of the 1920s and 1930s, and some of these still survive.

In spite of the reduction in output during the Art Deco period, a good deal of interesting internal tiling was produced, especially by Maw & Co and Craven Dunnill, who not

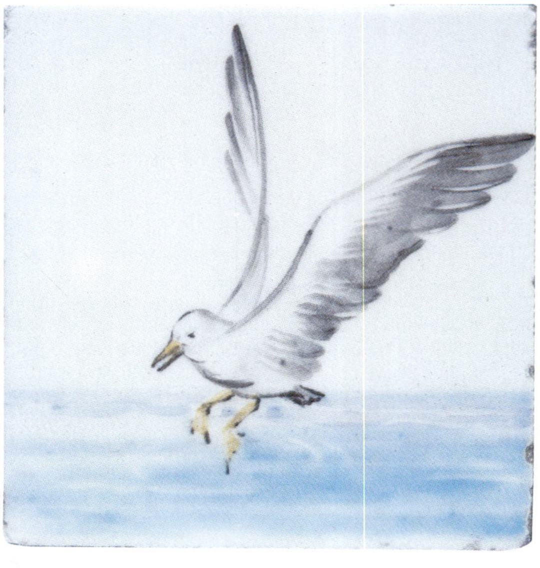

only explored the elegant and colourful geometry of the Art Deco style but continued to develop new glaze effects. However, the vast majority of industrially made tiles were undecorated, in keeping with the swing away from the cluttered Victorian interior toward an almost clinical plainness. Fireplaces and bathrooms were clad in rows of pastel-coloured tiles with only a few decorated tiles interspersed for relief, or geometrically patterned tiles were arranged into stark but stylish repeating schemes.

In a slender way, the art-tile tradition continued. During the 1920s and 1930s Britain's Bernard Leach was making tiles whose inspiration came as much from medieval English tradition as from Japan, and he was influential on several of the prewar generation's craftsmen, notably Dora Billington, whose painted tile compositions are highly collectable evocations of their period. Tiles were decorated by several members of Roger Fry's Omega Workshops, including Vanessa Bell and Duncan Grant, but these, like the tile paintings of the French painters Fernand Léger and André Dérain, were hardly part of the major thrust of tile decoration during the interwar years. An art-pottery studio set up by Alfred and Louise Powell in association with Wedgwood began in 1909 and continued until the Second World War: tiles were among its products.

Probably the most important art-tile production was at Poole, where Carter, Stabler & Adams, a studio-pottery subsidiary of the original Carter company, had been formed in 1921. As well as carefully crafted and highly original wares with characteristic softly coloured in-glaze decoration, a range of tiles, some decorated by the artist Edward Bawden, met with considerable acclaim.

Tile-making probably reached its lowest ebb in the immediate postwar years: many manufacturers, particularly in the decorative field, ceased production, and those that continued tended to concentrate on emphatically serviceable tiles for institutional and domestic use. A mere handful of architectural schemes involved tiling for exterior finishes. However, this seeming vacuum was inevitably destined to be filled,

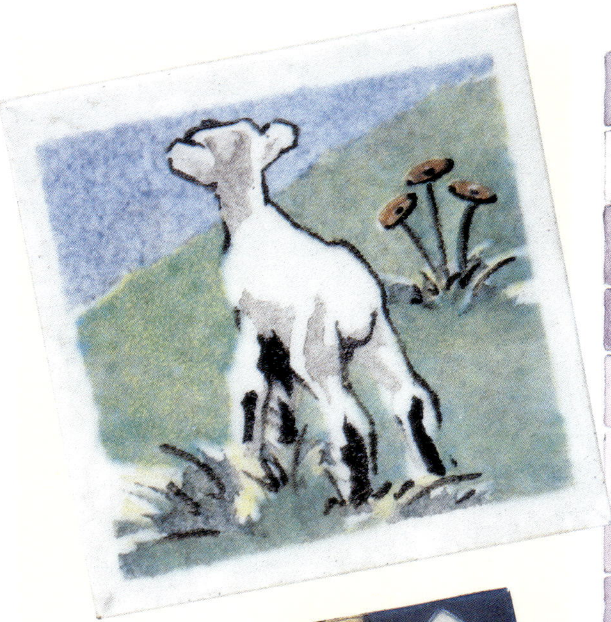

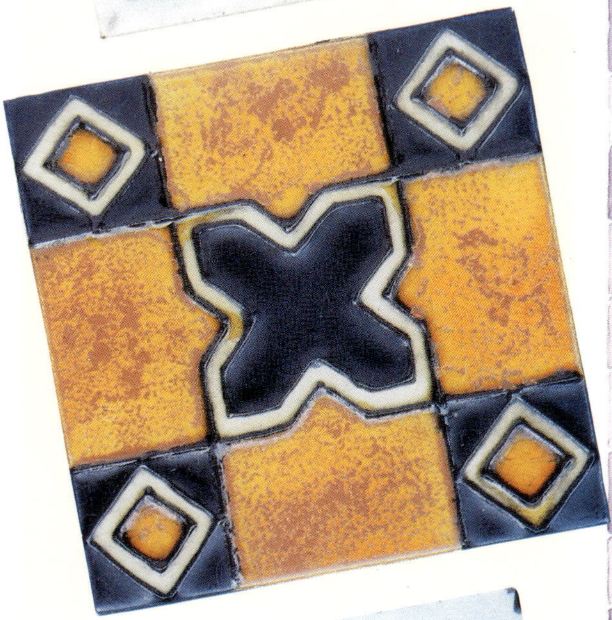

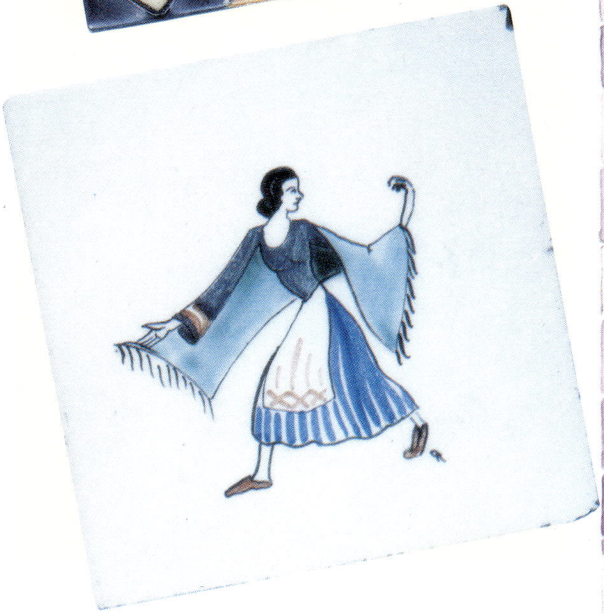

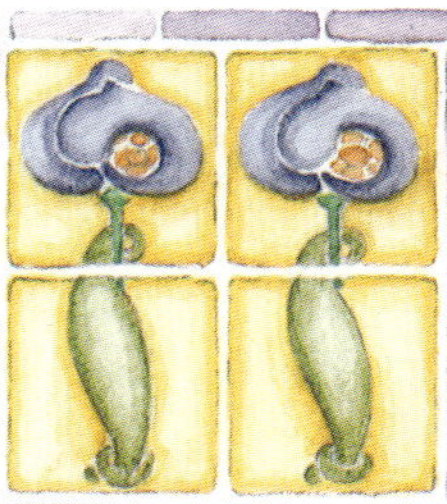

LEFT *Tile with stencilled design depicting a lamb in a meadow, made by Minton,* c. *1930.*

CENTRE LEFT *Tube-lined Art Deco tile with black and orange eggshell glazes, made by Pilkingtons,* c. *1925.*

BELOW LEFT *Hand-painted tile by Rosalind Ord, partner in the firm of Packard & Ord, Marlborough, Wiltshire,* c. *1935; signed RO.*

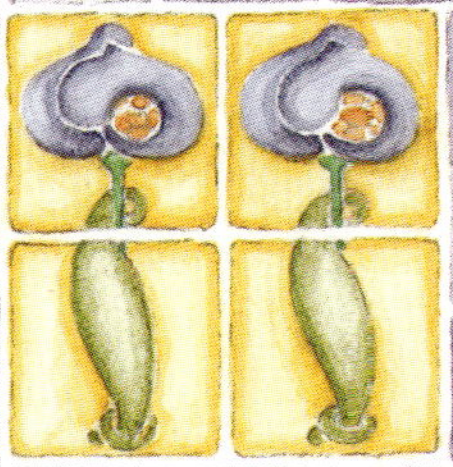

RIGHT *Tones, tiles in Pilkington's Whisper series.*

BELOW RIGHT *Paul Portelli's Ebbtide range.*

and during the past 15 years or so there has been a tremendous increase in tile interest. This has been due in part to the enthusiasm for Victoriana, which has both stimulated collectors to seek out Victorian tiles and restorers to make good some of the losses in architectural schemes that resulted from more than 50 years of disregard for the art of the Victorian period. More refreshingly, the fashion for new tiles has been stimulated by architects and interior designers and their clients, all of whom have awakened to the practical and decorative possibilities of tiling, particularly in present-day kitchens.

Traditional tile industries have been revived throughout the world to supply an eager market: those of Brazil, France, Portugal, Spain and Italy are among the most successful, while factories large and small are producing tiles to suit all tastes and pockets.

The traditional hand-made tiles of Normandy, Provence, Mexico and Portugal are thicker and heavier — and correspondingly higher in price — than most of the factory-produced ranges, which are thin and relatively lightweight but considerably cheaper. About 58% of the industrially made tiles to be found in home-decorating shops throughout Britain are imports from foreign countries.

The charm of hand-crafted tiles can rarely be matched by that of industrially made examples, with their perfect regularity of shape and patterning, yet many designers are showing a new enterprise in their approach, giving us relatively inexpensive tiles of great variety. Among these, John Lauthton's and Wendy Dickinson's Whisper series for Pikington, Paul Portelli's designs for World's End Tiles & Flooring, the hand-screenprinted plant patterns of Eleanor Greeves, the 'system murals' of Sally Anderson, the lustred effects of Margery Clinton, and the usefully varied shapes and design permutations of Kenneth & Anne Clark should be mentioned. The firm of Maw & Co, under the H & R Johnson umbrella, has been revived as a producer of art tiles: their tile pictures and other composite schemes use both painting and slip-trailing in their decoration.

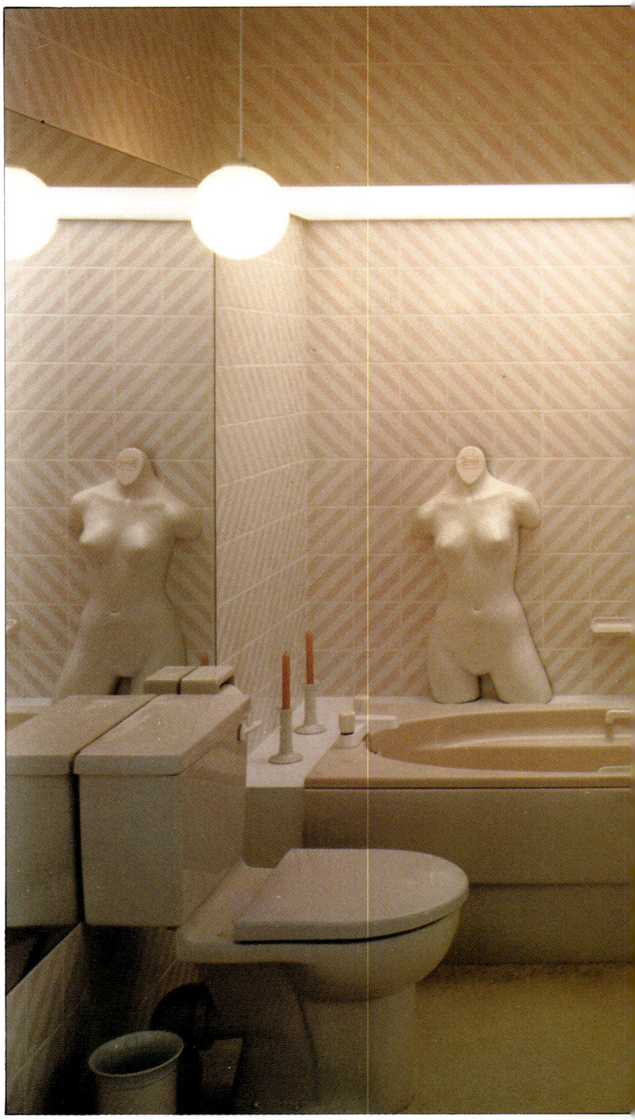

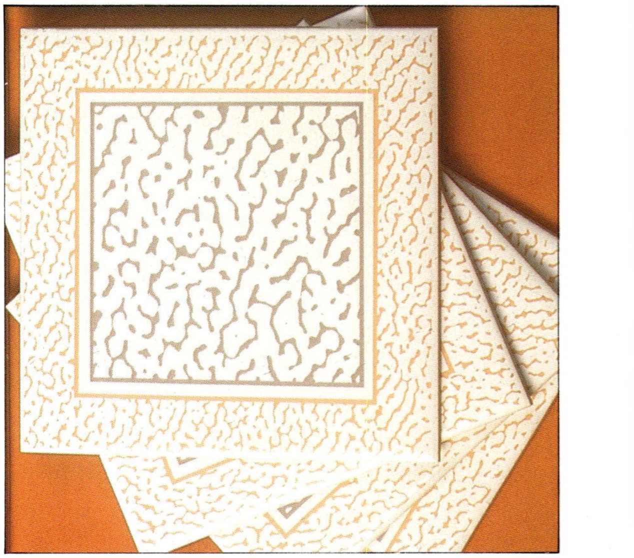

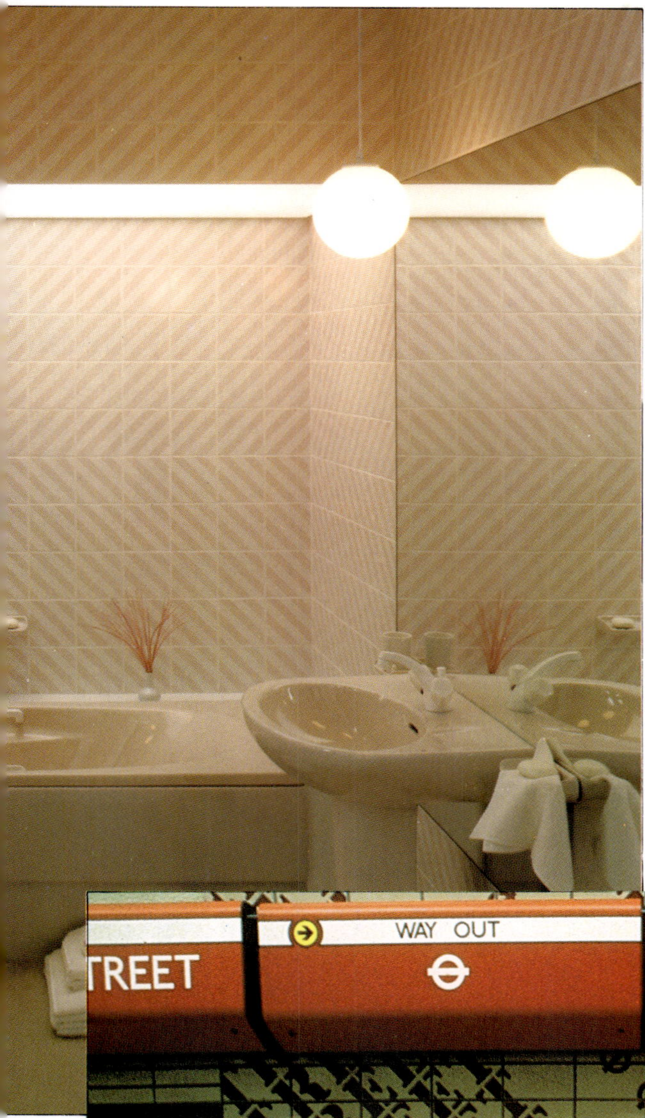

As well as these industrially oriented tile designers a healthy number still work in the individual craft tradition, making repetitive tile designs as well as executing one-of-a-kind mural commissions. Outstanding are Alan Caiger-Smith, well known for his painted and lustred tin-glazed earthenwares, Tarquin Cole, Liam Curtis & Wendy Jones, Alison Britton and Sarah Walton. Kenneth & Anne Clark also design individual tile murals. Artist-craftsmen on the Continent have shown special interest in sculptured relief effects in which the full extent of tiles as an art form is explored.

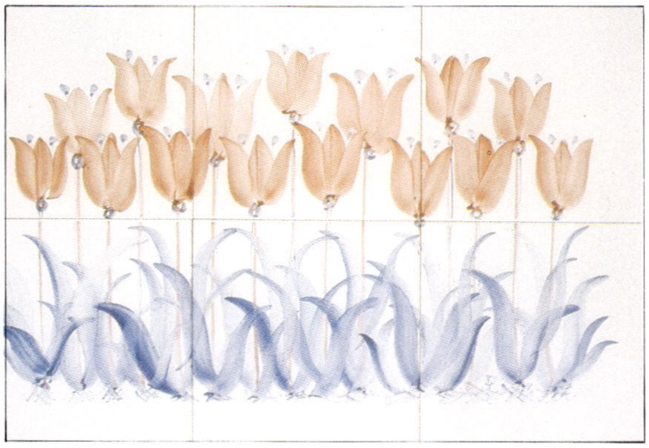

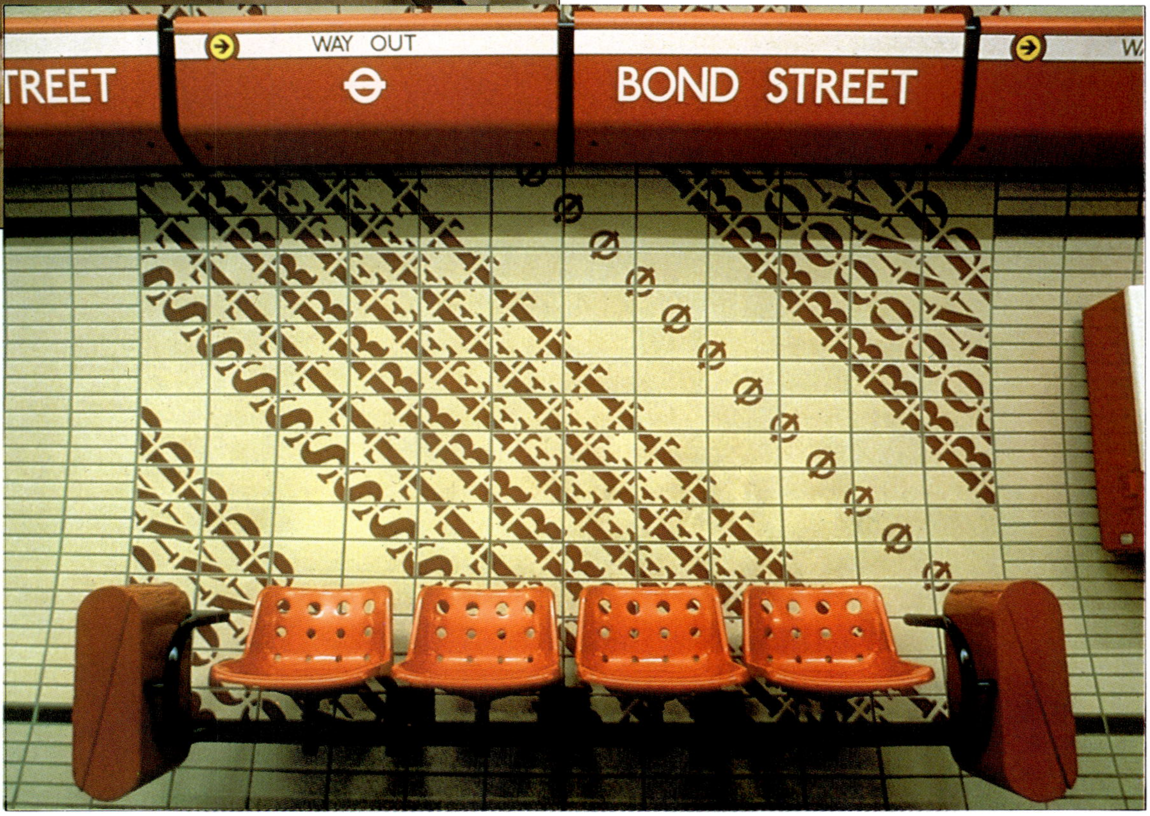

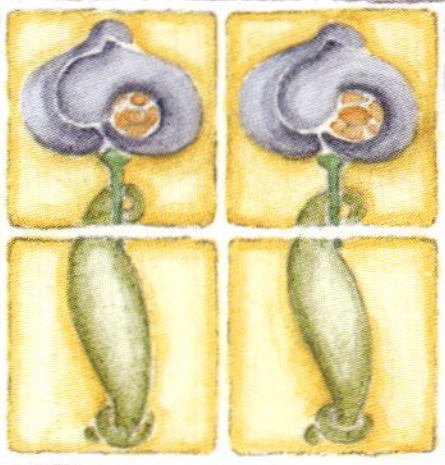

•

LEFT *Tulip pattern by Tarquin Cole, 1983.*

BELOW LEFT *The tiled walls of Bond Street Underground station, London, recently redecorated.*

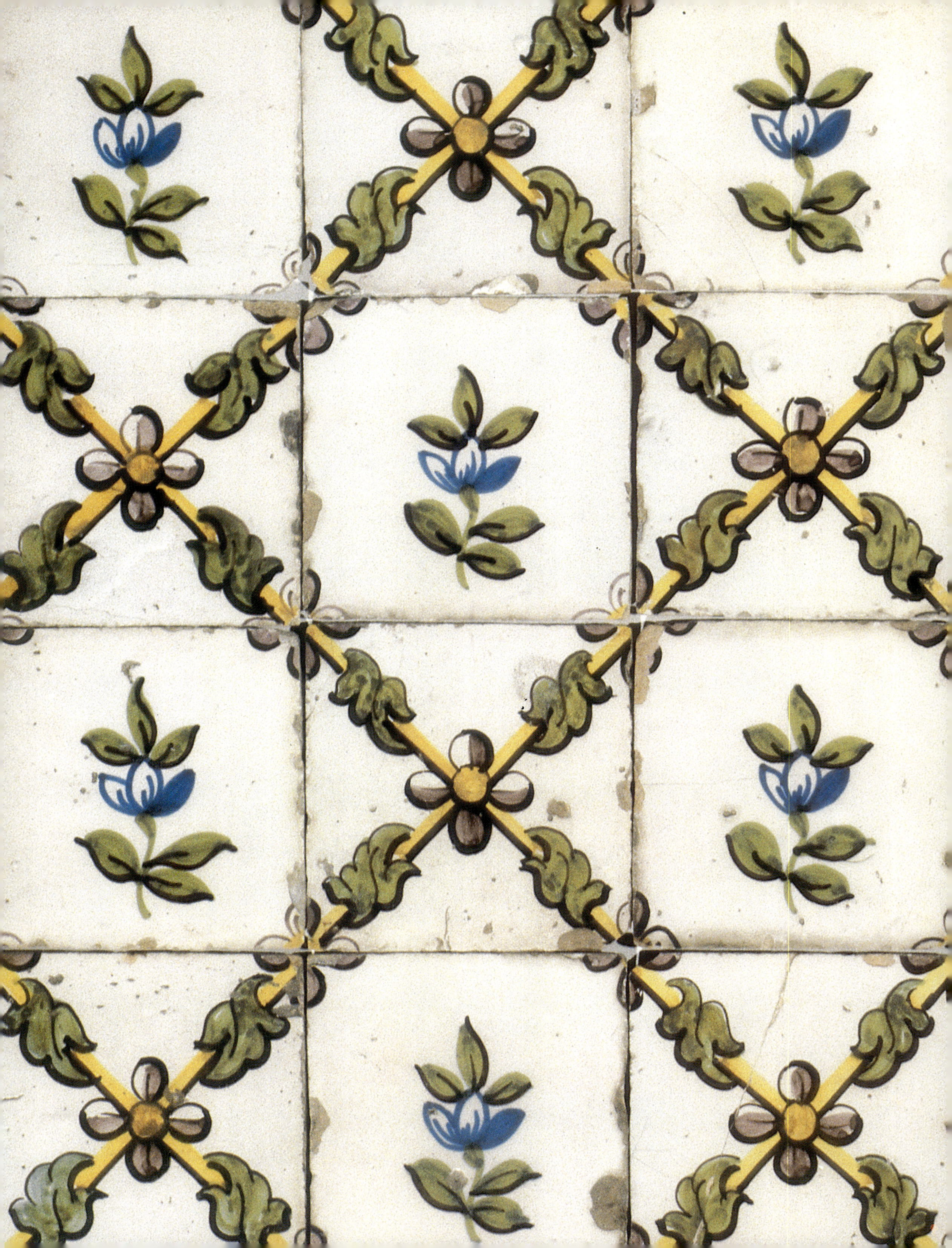

CHAPTER ELEVEN

COLLECTING TILES

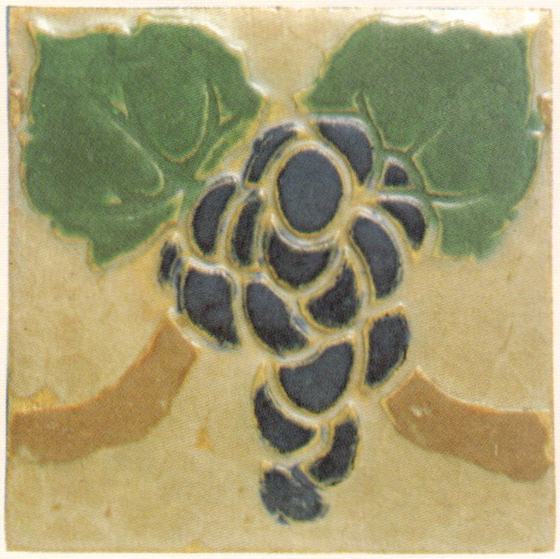

TILES OFFER an intriguing field for collectors of assorted tastes and means; whether £3 ($5) or £3,000 ($5000), is spent on a single tile, there is quarry to be hunted and found, and the interest of the chase is likely to be as great as the joy of discovery.

TILE ART

•

OVERLEAF (BACKGROUND) *Portuguese tile of Pombaline-style pattern, c. 1760-80.*

OVERLEAF (INSET) *Tile depicting grapes by Grueby Faience Co, Boston, c. 1905.*

RIGHT *Tile collecting can be undertaken thematically: here the theme is birds, but in a variety of decorative techniques.*

FAR RIGHT *Page of Minton's first printed tile catalogue, entitled* Examples of Old English Tiles, *1842. The designs for inlaid tiles shown here are copies from the medieval tiles in the Chapter House, Westminster Abbey.*

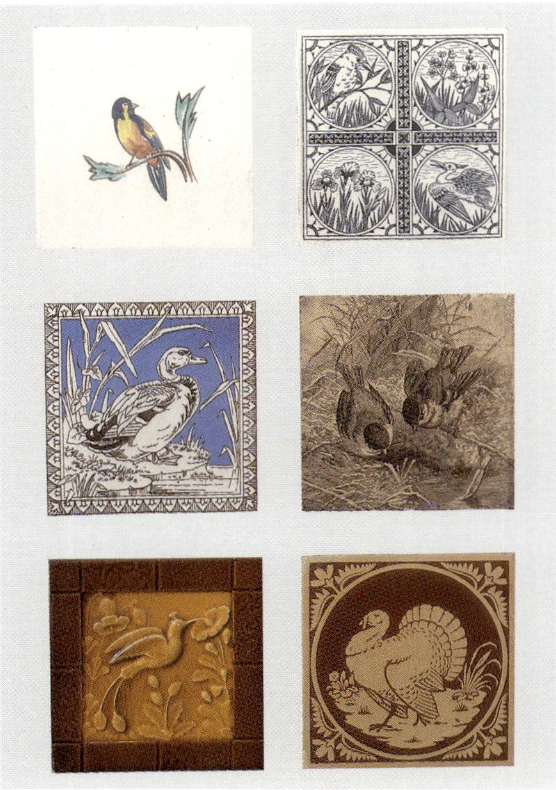

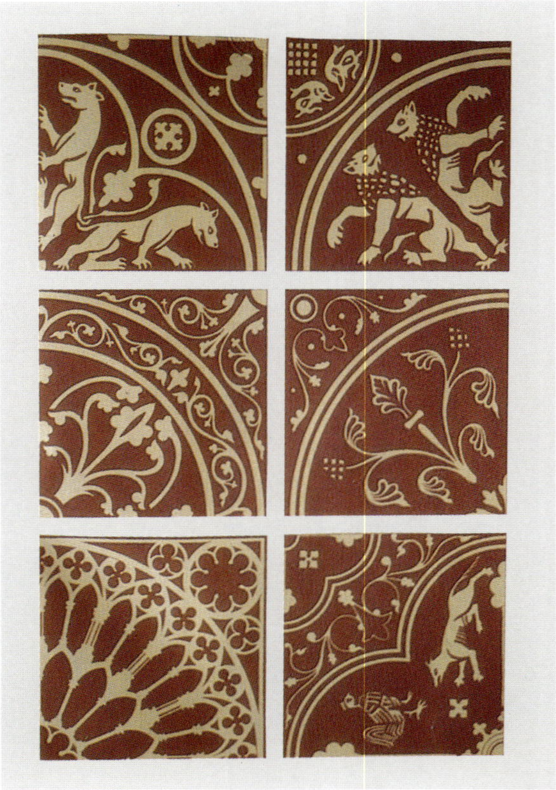

WITH SUCH a wide-ranging subject it is unlikely that many collectors will encompass the whole field, nor should they try. Specializing, at least to some degree, is likely to be far more satisfactory, mainly because it will lead to a greater depth of knowledge. This in itself brings satisfaction, but knowledge, as is well known, is the main ingredient of successful collecting. The more that is known about a subject, albeit a narrow one, the more likely a discovery can be made — or a bargain spotted. Perhaps more usefully, a collector can learn to recognize the genuine from the spurious or misattributed, and can know whether he is being overcharged.

Such broad areas as Islamic, medieval, Dutch, 18th-century English, and Victorian tiles are obvious possibilities for specialization, and in learning about them a collector will assimilate a good deal of experience in various ceramic disciplines — glaze techniques, recognition of clay bodies, decorative processes and so on — to say nothing of social, technological and even political history.

Perhaps a speciality that cuts across historical periods or national boundaries is more appealing. For example, tin-glazed earthenware tiles would encompass some Islamic as well as maiolica, delftware and faïence tiles made in all parts of Europe over several centuries. Stove tiles, flower- or bird-decorated tiles, lustred tiles, and blue-and-white tiles are other possibilities. Even within certain types or classes there is scope for detailed exploration: among those that spring to mind are medieval inlaid tiles; Dutch soldier tiles; the *bianco sopra bianco* borders of Bristol, or the Sadler and Green prints of Liverpool. Individual Victorian factories like Maw or Minton, smaller enterprises like J C Edwards or W B Simpson, or the designs of particular artists like Walter Crane, Lewis Day or Hannah Barlow could also be collected.

Clearly the later the period of choice, the greater the research possibilities. Many of the 19th-century tile manufacturers' records survive and these can be a fascinating resource for the collector who is prepared to put in some spadework. Such documents as artists' designs, factory pattern books and

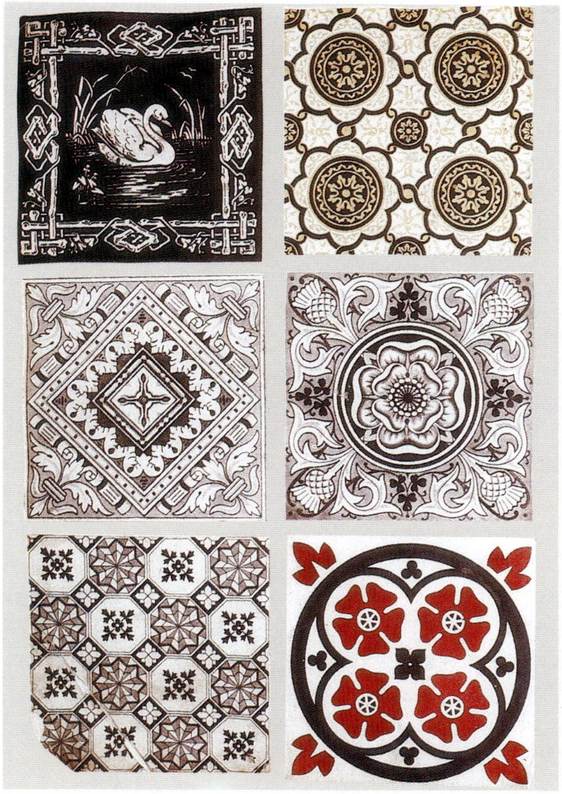

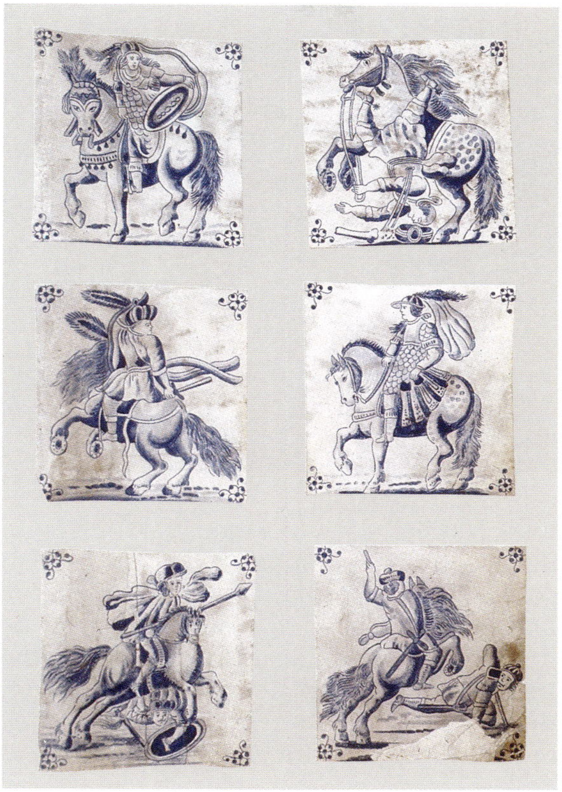

FAR LEFT *Pattern book of Minton, Hollins & Co showing page with six different tile designs, c. 1880. These pattern books were kept at the factory and provided a stock of master designs.*

LEFT *Page from the pattern book of Minton, Hollins & Co, c. 1875, showing engraved designs of warriors on horseback copied from 17th-century Dutch tiles.*

manufacturers' catalogues are not only aids to identifying individual tiles but also can reveal the purposes for which they were made, their prices and the length of time a particular design was produced. The extensive Minton archives are in the safekeeping of Royal Doulton Tableware at Stoke-on-Trent and are available for study by special arrangement, while Copeland's pattern books and tile designs are kept by the present firm of Spode. The Wedgwood Museum, Barlaston, houses material relating to Wedgwood's tile production, and records of Maw & Co can be found in the District Library and Clive House Museum in Shrewsbury, as well as at the Ironbridge Gorge Museum Trust Library at Ironbridge. Other tile-makers' records are at the City of Stoke-on-Trent Reference Library and in the Victoria & Albert Museum.

While documentary records are an invaluable tool for the serious collector, there is no substitute for looking at and, whenever possible, handling tiles. Museum collections all over the world are rich in decorative tiles from many sources and periods, and no chance to study them should be lost. Often they are the best examples of a particular type and provide a yardstick against which others can be judged. The Gladstone Pottery Museum at Longton, Stoke-on-Trent, has a particularly fine display of Victorian tiles, for example. Rarely, however, can museum tiles be handled, and the less restricted opportunities available in the major auction houses and in dealers' showrooms should be welcomed. The back of a tile, after all, can be as informative as the front: the value of printed and impressed marks, for example on Victorian tiles, is obvious, but such guides to attribution as the colour and texture of the clay body can often be studied only from the back.

Finding a good dealer for a particular speciality is well worth the time and trouble. He or she will not simply become a source of tiles to add to the collection, but by sharing knowledge and experience will increase a collector's expertise and enjoyment. One area where a dealer can be especially helpful is on the question of fakes and reproductions. Although until recently individual tiles were not of sufficient value

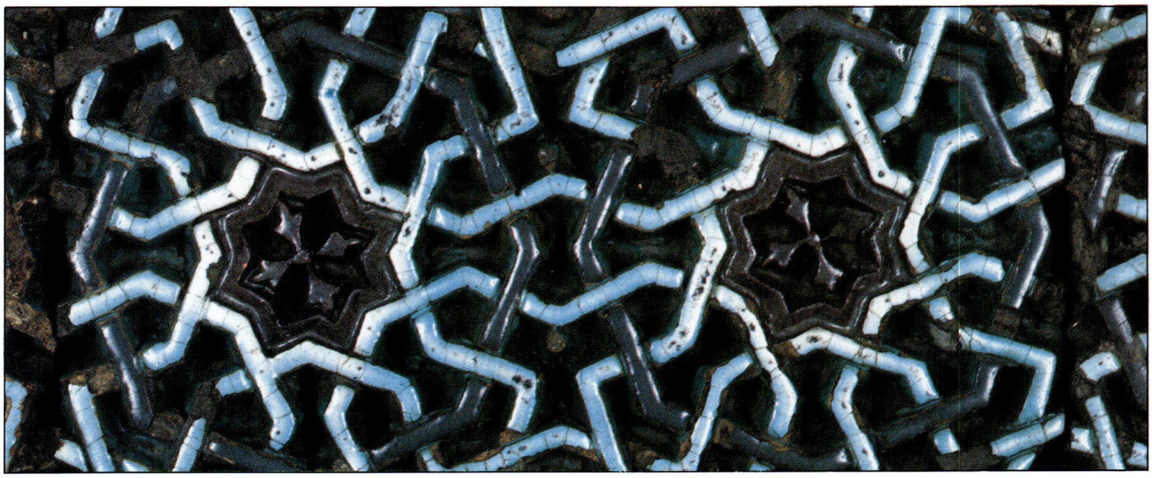

RIGHT *A Central Asian carved pottery tile frieze from the tomb of Buyan Kuli Chan (d. 1358). This rarity, which has probably been in the West for a century or more, fetched £3,800 ($6,270) at Sotheby's in 1986.*

BELOW RIGHT *A late 19th-century Dutch tile showing a Saracen knight on horseback, with fleur-de-lis corner motifs.*

BELOW FAR RIGHT *A 19th-century Dutch tile made in Friesland, showing a flower and a butterfly. Tiles such as these, made by traditional methods and decorated with traditional designs, can be hard to distinguish from genuine early examples.*

to attract the skills of serious fakers, reproductions have abounded since the 19th century. For example 100-year-old copies of Dutch 17th- and 18th-century tiles can be deceptive, and while they were made by the traditional methods and may be attractive, their prices should reflect the fact that they are later copies of a highly desirable type.

The 'right' price to pay for a tile is a vexed question and one that can be answered only with the knowledge that comes from experience. Having established that a particular tile is what it purports to be, a collector is prepared to pay more or less according to how badly he wants it for his collection, bearing in mind that buying the best example one can afford is good policy. The tile with the lowest price tag may not, in the long run, prove to be the cheapest.

Rare early tiles are going to be the most expensive, and collectors expect to pay between £1,000 and £3,000 ($1,500–$5,000) for certain types of 12th- and 13th-century Islamic tiles. Inscriptions usually enhance values. The lustred-star and hexagon-shaped tiles of 14th-century Kashan are likely to be between £300 and £500 ($500–$800) each. The rarity of medieval English tiles is reflected in their prices: while £250 (or about $400) might secure an inlaid tile with a simple geometric pattern, the collector will have to pay at least £1000 (or $1500-plus) for one with a desirable figurative design such as a knight on horseback.

European tin-glazed tiles cover a wide range, not just of historical period and

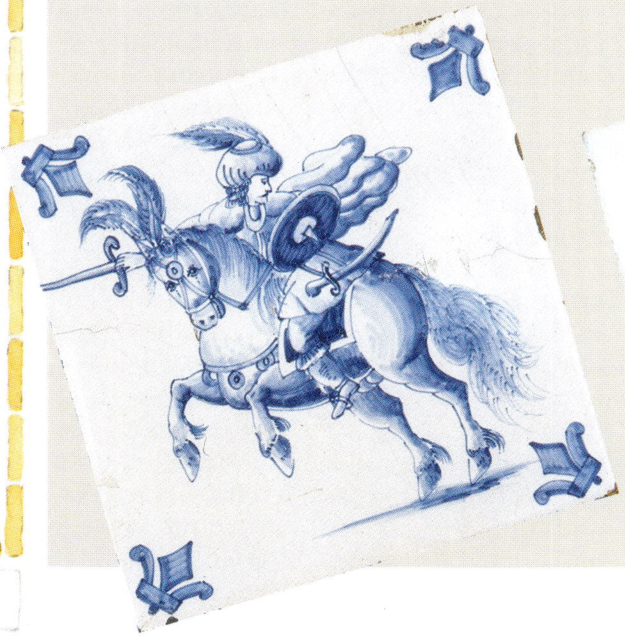

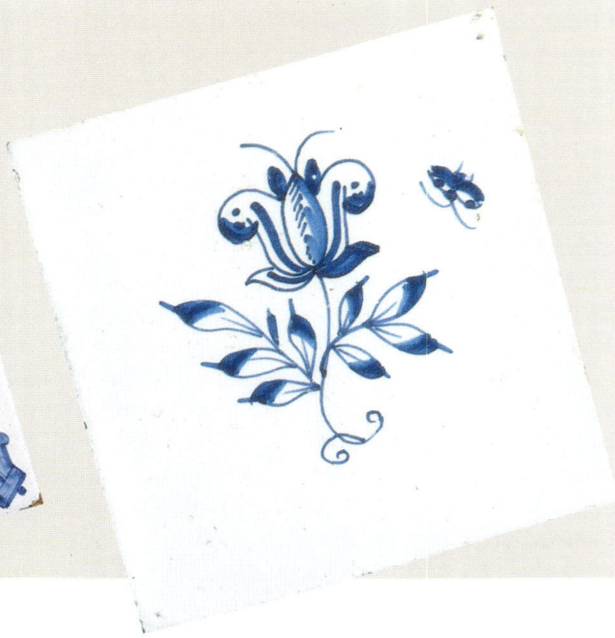

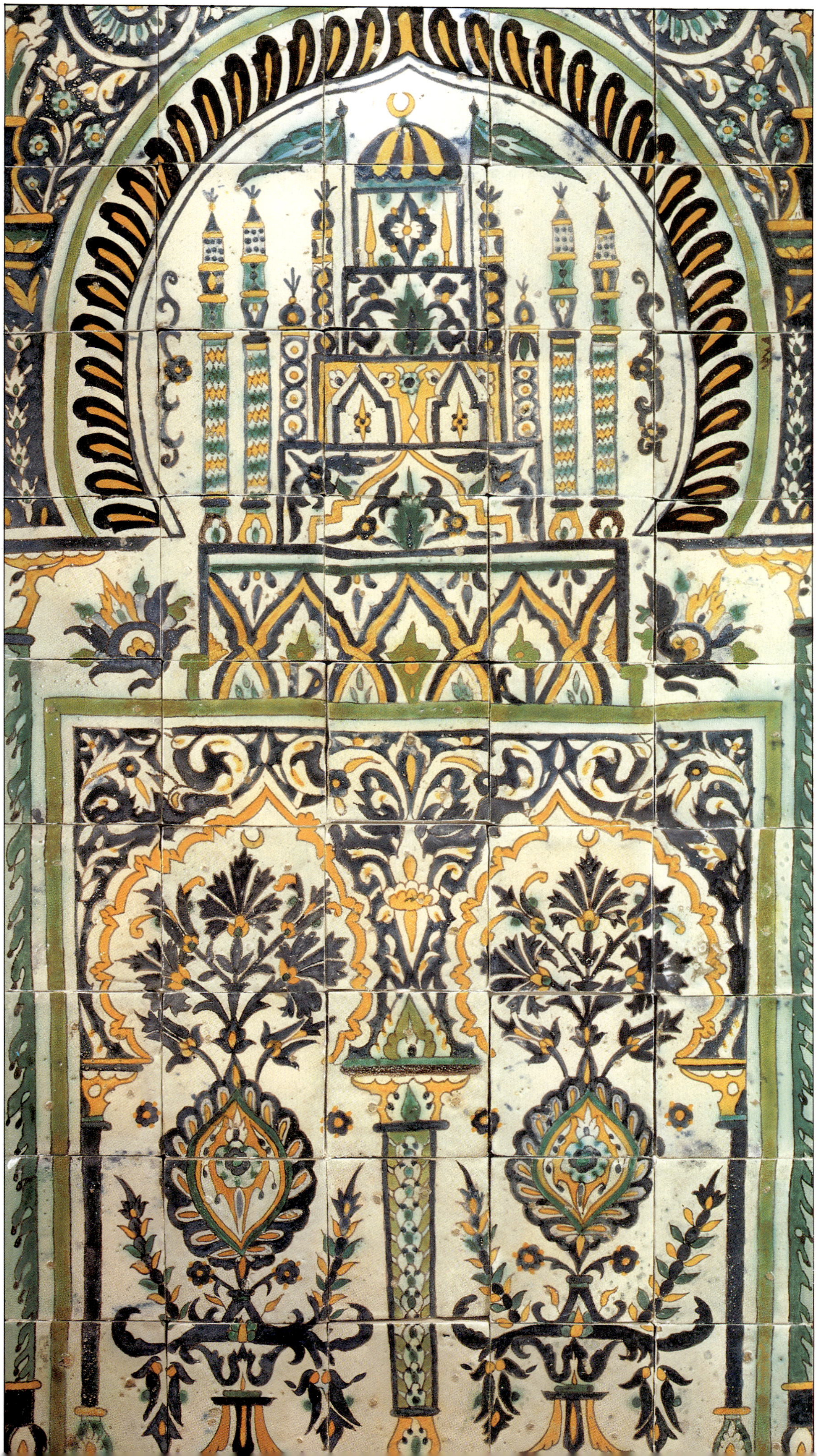

CHAPTER ELEVEN

•

LEFT *A large tile panel from Tunisia, 18th century. It fetched £2,600 ($3,300) in a sale at Sotheby's in 1987.*

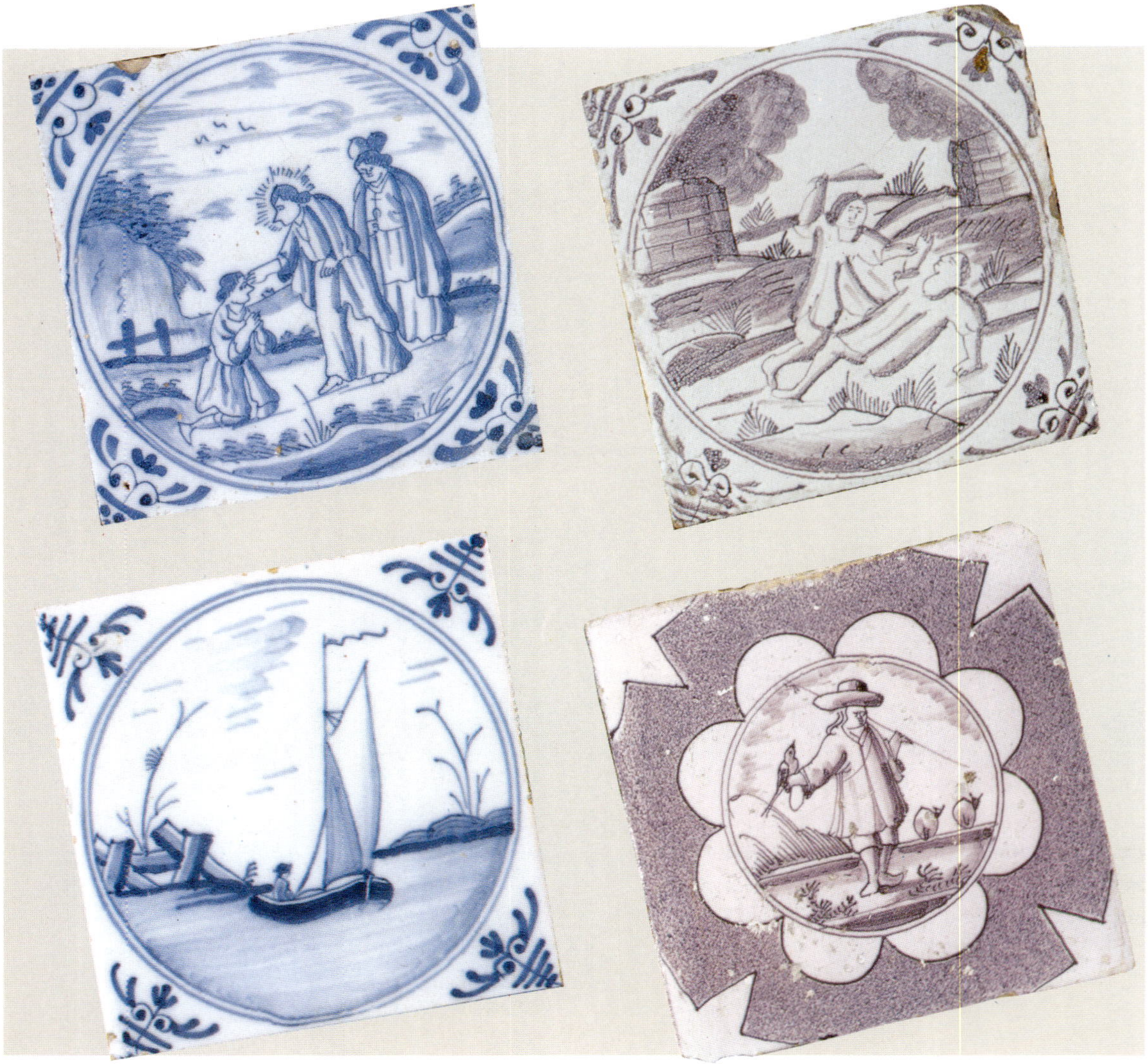

RIGHT *Four English and Dutch 18th-century Delftware tiles in the under £40 ($60) price range.*

style, but of desirability and scarcity. The most numerous types are the Dutch, and these are, generally speaking, cheaper than English equivalents, but will vary greatly according to subject matter. Polychrome examples, whether Dutch or English, are invariably more highly priced than blue and white.

Whereas biblical tiles were among the most expensive at the time they were made, now they are only a little more pricey than landscapes, which are often the most reasonably procured, at around £20 ($30) each. A single English polychrome flower or bird tile can cost £150 ($250), and animals tend to be even more. Sadler and Green printed tiles range in price from about £80 ($125) to as much as £300 ($500) each.

Victorian tiles obviously offer the greatest variety of techniques, styles, artists and subject matter, and price bands are similarly wide. The early lustred tiles of William De Morgan, at between £200 and £400 ($300–$650) each, are probably the most expensive, but his flowery Iznik designs can be had for about £50 to £60 ($80–$100) each. Series of tiles designed by artists such as Moyr Smith, Walter Crane, Kate Greenaway or Thomas Allen may also run into the low three figures: tiles in complete sets are always priced higher pro rata than isolated examples. At the other end of the scale, about £6 ($10) will purchase many of the attractive Victorian designs that were originally destined for composite patterns, but can stand on their own quite successfully. Transfer prints of the 1870s and 1880s, and relief decoration of the Art Nouveau period, are enormously varied — and still relatively easy to find. Perhaps the least

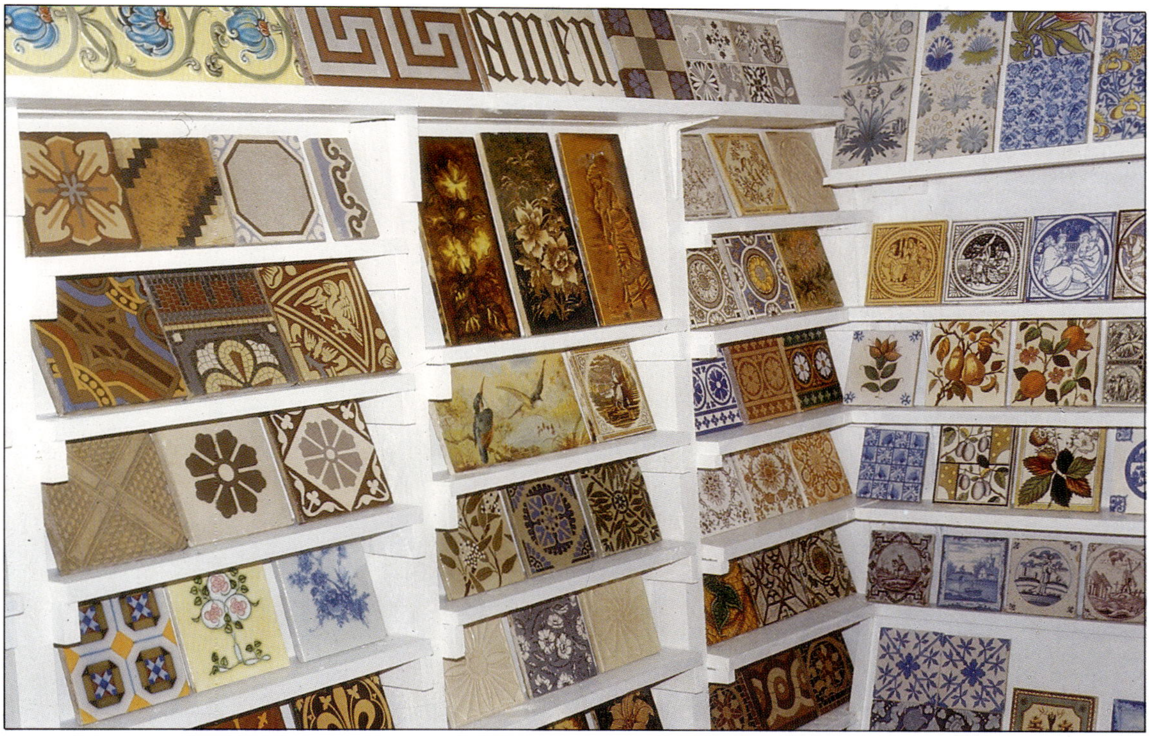

LEFT *Corner of an extensive collection of English and other European tiles displayed on special stands.*

exploited area — and one of the most interesting — is the period between the two world wars, when some fine, and in many instances documented, tiles were produced: rich pickings undoubtedly await the persistent and discerning.

Condition must always be a consideration in collecting: whereas damaged tiles should by no means be ignored — kiln damage in particular can provide interesting insights into the problems of manufacture and many a desirable tile may have imperfections — any damage should be reflected in the price charged. Many tiles are mutilated when removed from their original sites: it is almost impossible successfully to rescue tiles embedded in concrete for example. As well as chips and cracks evident on the front surface, the backs may also be spoiled. With Victorian tiles, many of which have useful identification marks and keying patterns on the backs, such loss of information may make a tile almost valueless. Hand-painted, tin-glazed tiles, however, tell a different story. The chips to which these tiles are especially prone may be acceptable as long as they do not deface the image unduly. At the same time damage is bound to affect the value, and such imperfect tiles should be a good deal cheaper than mint examples.

Restoration should also be given due regard. Experience will help to develop an ability to recognize repaired damage, and this may be quite legitimate as long as it is not intended to deceive. However, such practices as overpainting, to which some Islamic tiles have been subjected, have no place in honourable restoration, and constitute forgery.

Displaying a collection of tiles should be a pleasant and rewarding task. They can be arranged on grooved shelves, placed on window sills, or framed and hung on walls. Tiles can be set into furniture or fireplaces, laid around kitchens and bathrooms, or used as table mats or teapot stands. In the best of all possible worlds, they remain where they originally belonged — around the porch of the Victorian terraced house, set into the wall of a shop or hospital ward, or arranged as a splash back on a Victorian washstand.

Obviously this is impossible with all but a few examples — and those mostly 19th-century tiles — but whatever the origin of these most collectable treasures, they can always be found an appropriate setting and enjoyed to the fullest.

BIBLIOGRAPHY

ANSCOMBE, Isabelle and GERE, Charlotte, *Arts & Crafts in Britain and America*, Rizzoli International Publications Inc, New York, 1978.

AUSTWICK, J & B, *The Decorated Tile*, Pitman Publishing Ltd, London, 1980.

BARNARD, Julian, *Victorian Ceramic Tiles*, Studio Vista/Christies, London, 1972.

BERENDSEN, Anne, *Tiles: A General History*, Faber & Faber Ltd, London, 1967.

BRUHN, Thomas P, *American Decorative Tiles 1870-1930*, The William Benton Museum of Art (University of Connecticut), Storrs, Connecticut, 1979.

CAIGER-SMITH, Alan, *Tin-Glaze Pottery*, Faber & Faber Ltd, London, 1973.

CATLEUGH, John, *William De Morgan: Tiles*, Trefoil Books Ltd, London, 1983.

CHARLESTON, Robert J, *World Ceramics*, Hamlyn Publishing Group Ltd, London, 1968.

CLARK, Garth and HUGHTO, Margie, *A Century of Ceramics in the United States 1878-1978*, Dutton, New York, 1979.

CLARK, Robert Judson (ed.), *The Arts and Crafts Movement in America 1876-1916*, Princeton University Press, Princeton, NJ, 1972.

EAMES, Elizabeth S, *Medieval Tiles*, British Museum Publications, London, 1968.

HAMILTON, David, *Architectural Ceramics*, Thames & Hudson Ltd, London, 1978.

DE JONGE, C H, *Dutch Tiles*, Pall Mall Press, London, 1971.

KEEN, Kirsten, *American Art Pottery, 1875-1930*, Delaware Art Museum, Wilmington, Delaware, 1978.

KELLY, Alison, *Decorative Wedgwood in Architecture and Furniture*, Country Life Books, London, 1965.

KORF, Dingeman, *Dutch Tiles*, Merlin Press Ltd, London, 1963.

VAN LEMMEN, Hans, *Tiles, A Collector's Guide*, Souvenir Press Ltd, London, 1979.

VAN LEMMEN, Hans, *Victorian Tiles*, Shire Publications Ltd, Aylesbury, Bucks, 1981

LOCKETT, Terry, *Collecting Victorian Tiles*, Antique Collector's Club, Woodbridge, Suffolk, 1979.

Metropolitan Museum of Art, *In Pursuit of Beauty: Americans and the Aesthetic Movement*, Metropolitan Museum of Art, New York, 1987.

RAY, Anthony, *English Delftware Tiles*, Faber & Faber Ltd, London, 1973.

SOUTHWELL, B C, *Making and Decorating Pottery Tiles*, Faber & Faber Ltd, London, 1972.

TRAPP, Kenneth R, *Ode to Nature: Flowers and Landscapes of the Rookwood Pottery, 1890-1940*, Jordan-Volpe Gallery, New York, 1980.

WIGHT, Jane A, *Medieval Floor Tiles*, John Baker Publishers Ltd, London, 1975.

INDEX

Page numbers in *italic* refer to illustrations

A

B

C

D

E

F

G

H

I

J